Agile Enterprise Risk Management

Security, Audit and Leadership Series
Series Editor: Dan Swanson, Dan Swanson and Associates, Ltd., Winnipeg, Manitoba, Canada.

The ***Security, Audit and Leadership Series*** publishes leading-edge books on critical subjects facing security and audit executives as well as business leaders. Key topics addressed include Leadership, Cybersecurity, Security Leadership, Privacy, Strategic Risk Management, Auditing IT, Audit Management, and Leadership.

Rising from the Mailroom to the Boardroom: Unique Insights for Governance, Risk, Compliance and Audit Leaders
Mark Tarallo

Modern Management and Leadership: Best Practice Essentials with CISO/CSO Applications
Mark Tarallo

Agile Enterprise Risk Management: Risk-Based Thinking, Multi-Disciplinary Management and Digital Transformation
Howard M. Wiener

Operational Auditing: Principles and Techniques for a Changing World (Second Edition)
Hernan Murdock

CyRM^{SM}: Mastering the Management of Cybersecurity
David X Martin

The Complete Guide for CISA Examination Preparation
Richard E. Cascarino

Blockchain for Cybersecurity and Privacy: Architectures, Challenges, and Applications
Yassine Maleh, Mohammad Shojafar, Mamoun Alazab, Imed Romdhani

The Cybersecurity Body of Knowledge: The ACM/IEEE/AIS/IFIP Recommendations for a Complete Curriculum in Cybersecurity
Daniel Shoemaker, Anne Kohnke, Ken Sigler

Corporate Governance: A Pragmatic Guide for Auditors, Directors, Investors, and Accountants
Vasant Raval

The Audit Value Factor
Daniel Samson

Managing IoT Systems for Institutions and Cities
Chuck Benson

Fraud Auditing Using CAATT: A Manual for Auditors and Forensic Accountants to Detect Organizational Fraud
Shaun Aghili

How to Build a Cyber-Resilient Organization
Dan Shoemaker, Anne Kohnke, Ken Sigler

Agile Enterprise Risk Management

Risk-Based Thinking, Multi-Disciplinary Management and Digital Transformation

Howard M. Wiener, MSIA, CERM, PMP

CRC Press
Taylor & Francis Group
Boca Raton London New York

CRC Press is an imprint of the
Taylor & Francis Group, an **informa** business

Cover image: Howard M. Wiener

First edition published 2022
by CRC Press
6000 Broken Sound Parkway NW, Suite 300, Boca Raton, FL 33487-2742

and by CRC Press
4 Park Square, Milton Park, Abingdon, Oxon, OX14 4RN

CRC Press is an imprint of Taylor & Francis Group, LLC

ISBN: 978-1-032-03703-5 (hbk)
ISBN: 978-1-032-03704-2 (pbk)
ISBN: 978-1-003-18860-5 (ebk)

DOI: 10.1201/9781003188605

Typeset in Sabon
by SPi Technologies India Pvt Ltd (Straive)

Content

List of Illustrations xv
Acknowledgments xvii
About this book xix

Introduction 1

What's driving the change we're experiencing? 2
Technology and technology-driven business models and the shift from capex to opex 2
Process automation can displace people, even high-level people 3
Cloud infrastructures level the playing field between startups and established companies 3
Your company's valuation depends on your keeping up with these trends 3
Societal changes 4
How can you prepare to compete? 5
Implementing Agile ERM 6
Agile ERM Artifacts 6
Agile ERM operational processes 6
Where do we go from here? 7

1 Context—COVID, BLM and upheaval 9

Covered in this chapter 9
VUCA: our current state 11
Agile vs. agility 12
Business agility, the one thing you need to survive 13
The challenges you're facing 13
The pressure to execute a digital transformation 14
Managing your business and risks as you transform 15
Traditional approaches to strategy are losing validity 15
Forces driving the need for new strategic approaches 17
Traditional business management practices that no longer work 21
Traditional risk management practices are seriously flawed 22

All management is risk management 23
You already manage risks—you intuitively know how to do this 24
But are we actually any good at it? 25
Why you need multi-disciplinary, integrated risk management 25
Why multi-disciplinary? 26
Why integrated? 26
Any transformation has risks 28
Controlled transformation is key to managing transformation risks 29
The disciplines you will need to execute your controlled transformation 30
Chapter summary 33

2 Enterprise risk management today 35

Covered in this chapter 35
Introduction 36
The emergence and evolution of risk management 38
RM vs. TRM vs. ERM vs. AERM 39
Current state of RM 42
The ERM process 43
Set context in which ERM will operate 43
Establish risk appetite and tolerance 44
What is risk? 44
Inventory risk sources 48
Identify, map and prioritize where general operating risks occur 49
Identify external drivers or forces that create risks and opportunities 50
Identify recurring and ad hoc decision processes 51
Perform a risk assessment: inventory and analyze risks and develop management strategies 52
Identify risks 53
Analyze risks 53
The traditional way 53
A better way: quantitative analysis, incorporating uncertainty and variance 55
Evaluate strategies and alternative treatments for each risk 63
Select treatment for each risk 64
Document your plan 65
Establish integrated RM controls, policies and processes 65
Implement, execute and monitor ERM performance 66
Risk audit and risk assurance 67
Evolve and improve your ERM 70
Causes of substandard risk management 71
Your goals for improving your risk management 72

Why won't traditional approaches to managing risk work going forward? 73
Chapter summary 75

3 **Digital transformation, business agility and risk** 77

Covered in this chapter 77
Invention and innovation 78
Invention and innovation cycles drive markets 78
Various models illustrate cycles' impact 79
The BCG Growth-Share Matrix 79
The Invincible Company: a portfolio of businesses 80
Parallels among the models 80
Implications for your business 81
Digital's strategic impact is forcing enterprises to rethink execution 83
A strategy that reflects today's digital realities demands revised operational capabilities 85
Traditional enterprise structural and management models that will have to change 86
The goals and challenges of transformation 86
How and why risk management needs to change 89
Chapter summary 89

4 **The company you need to be** 91

Covered in this chapter 91
Forces driving the target model of a business architected for the future 92
Why do I need a digital transformation? 93
The anatomy of your company—enterprise and business architecture 94
A definition of enterprise 94
Enterprise architecture 94
Business architecture 100
The anatomy of a digital business 100
Operational infrastructure and API services 101
Operational infrastructure 101
API services 102
Digital products and services factory 103
Business intelligence and analytics 104
Partner development platform 105
Distributed governance model 105
Digital transformation means transforming your enterprise architecture 108
A preview of the transformation journey 110

As-is EA and BA models 110
To-be EA and BA models 112
Gap analysis and implementation initiatives 112
Execution competency and capability gaps 113
Roadmap and execution plan 113
Risk management and the controlled transformation journey 114
Haven't I already done some of this? 115
AERM and the digital enterprise 116
Chapter summary 118
A bi-level model for early-stage and established businesses 119
The case: a street cart 119
Pre-MVP risk management—experimental and developmental phases 121
Experimentation 121
Development 124
An enterprise and business architecture model of the business 124
Applying the EA model to manage risk: elementary AERM 125

5 Planning the transformation journey and managing its risks 129

Covered in this chapter 129
Change vs. transformation 131
Risk management and the transformational digital enterprise 132
Three layers of risk 132
Managing risks in conjunction with transformation 134
Scoping and planning the transformation journey 138
Establish who's governing during the transformation and after 139
Articulate your strategy 139
Establish your physical model infrastructure—EA/BA models, KM repository, pattern library 141
Establish the logical designs of your metadata repositories 142
Your EA/BA models 142
Your Taxonomy 142
Your Pattern Library 145
Initiate and monitor the ongoing governance and management processes of your EA/AERM effort 145
Scope, plan and conduct your discovery effort 146
Prioritize and schedule your discovery tasks 147
Focus on business processes 148
Business process discovery and management decision mapping 148
Example: an order management process 150
Inventory and document management and governance processes 153
Execute discovery 154
Compile the as-is EA/BA model 156
Populate your as-is model 156

Map known risks to your as-is model 157
Establish your preliminary to-be model 158
Precepts underlying to-be design decisions 158
The to-be model framework 161
Operational Infrastructure (OI) 162
API services (API) 163
Digital Products and Services Factory (DPSF) 164
Business Intelligence and Analytics (BI/A) 164
Partner Development Platform (PDP) 165
Distributed governance model 165
Define to-be governance and management processes 166
Map as-is to to-be and conduct gap analysis 167
AERM's EA-driven approach to managing the risks of transformation 169
Distill transformation initiatives and populate portfolio 171
Analyze the portfolio and develop your transformation program 174
Establish concrete business goals 174
Establish priorities to sequence your transformation 175
Chapter summary 178
Company overview 178
HiCTools' strategic transformation goals 179
Transformation risk considerations 181
As-is model 181
Organization and governance 182
Product management and customer-facing elements 182
Operational Infrastructure, API services 184
Business intelligence/analytics 184
To-be model 184
Redesign of the organization, responsibility allocation and governance model 185
Product management and the digital products and services factory 186
Perform market research 187
Produce product design and prototype 188
Perform market test, exposing product to customers 189
Commercialize and roll product out 189
Operational Infrastructure, API services 191
Business intelligence/analytics 191
Partner development platform 192
Gap analysis 192
Organization and governance—people issues 192
Operational Infrastructure 193
API management 194
Product management 194
Business intelligence and analytics 194

Partnership enablement 195
Governance 195
Capabilities and enablers—technologies, processes and assets 197
Operational Infrastructure 197
API management 199
Product management, digital products and services factory 199
Business intelligence and analytics 201
Partner development platform 201
Portfolio formulation and program design 202
Guiding objectives 202
Foundation and initiation: priority 1 initiatives 204
Create plan to address cultural issues 204
Select transformation leadership 204
Stand up the change management team (transformation program management office) 205
Define transformation governance processes to be employed 205
Plan for organizational redesign 205
Compile training and upskilling requirements 206
Plan for transforming the product management function 206
Define architectural subject matter expert (SME) team requirements 207
Stand up the enterprise and business architecture team 207
Stand up the knowledge management team 207
Stand up the business process management team 208
Compile a work-in-progress inventory 208
Create a preliminary master program schedule 209
Program execution: priority 2 initiatives 209
Operationalize change management processes 210
Produce technical architecture deliverables 210
Deliver training 211
Perform EA/BA modeling 211
Knowledge management and taxonomy creation 211
Business process mining—process inventory creation 211
Digital Products and Services factory 211
Design API architecture and implement API management 211
Operational Infrastructure architecture and migration 212
Program execution: priority 3 initiatives 212
Produce technical architecture deliverables 212
Business intelligence/analytics migration and implementation planning 213
Developmental business lifecycle implementation 213
Partner development platform 213
How risks are reflected in the program 213
Case 2 summary 215

6 Integration—Executing your digital transformation and integrating Agile ERM 217

Covered in this chapter 217
Ab initio 218
Transformation and operational disciplines 219
Disciplines enabling digital transformation 219
Disciplines enabling Agile Enterprise Risk Management 220
Disciplines for managing transformation 220
Management and governance processes for transformation and ongoing operations 220
Monitoring and management processes for transformation execution 220
Transformation program outcome monitoring and management processes 222
Operational management and governance processes 225
Product development processes 226
Value-stream Product Management 226
Rapid product evolution and delivery 227
Site Reliability Engineering (SRE) 227
Developmental product portfolio management 227
Operational management and governance processes 227
Implementing Agile ERM 229
Precursors 229
AERM operational processes 230
Retrospective processes 230
Measuring your progress 230
Chapter summary 232
Overview 233
The lifecycle of an HPTCo bicycle 233
The competition line 234
The standard line 235
Opportunities and challenges: the children's division and digital transformation 237
Strategic level 238
Business model level 238
Operating model level 239
Operational architecture level 240
Risk considerations and management 241
Strategic risks 242
Operational risks 244
Transformational Risks 251
As-is EA/BA model 253
Existing standard division operations 253

Capabilities 253
Enablers 253
Existing HPTCo digital capabilities and enablers 254
Operational infrastructure 254
API management 254
Digital products and services factory 255
Business intelligence and analytics 255
Partner development platform 255
Distributed governance 255
To-be EA/BA model scenarios 256
Targeted to-be business and operating models 256
Operating Model and Operational Architecture Scenarios 257
Risk-based thinking, risk-based decision-making 261
Assumptions and concerns 261
Gap analysis, transformation portfolio construction 262
Transformation portfolio analysis and program construction 263
Dependencies 264
The combined transformation program 265
Program task breakdown by stage 265
Risk management as reflected in the program design 267
Case 3 summary 268

7 Book summary and the future of work **269**

Covered in this chapter 269
Summary 269
Context 270
Traditional ERM 271
Digital transformation, business agility and risk 273
Digital transformation and business agility 273
Traditional enterprise structural and management models that will have to change 276
Managing the risks around transformation 276
The company you need to be 277
A definition of enterprise 277
Goals and drivers 278
The anatomy of a company 278
The anatomy of a digital business 280
Digital transformation means transforming your enterprise architecture 281
Planning the transformation journey and managing its risks 282
Change vs. transformation 282
Risk management and the transformational digital enterprise 282
The transformation lifecycle 284

The to-be model framework 288
Map as-is to to-be and conduct gap analysis 289
The AERM EA-driven approach to managing the risks of transformation 289
Distill transformation initiatives and populate transformation portfolio 289
Executing your transformation 291
What you should have in place at this point 291
Transformation and operational disciplines 292
Management and governance processes: transformation, ongoing operations 292
Monitoring and management processes: transformation program outcomes 293
Management and governance processes: operations 293
Implementing AERM 294
AERM operational processes 294
The future of work 297
AERM, the future of work and your company 299
Conclusion 300
Glossary 301

Illustrations

FIGURES

1.1	GE historical weekly stock price.	17
1.2	Sears holdings historical weekly stock price.	17
2.1	Probability-weighted returns.	46
2.2	A typical risk heat map.	54
2.3	Outage probability distribution.	58
2.4	Two normal distributions with different standard deviations.	59
2.5	Bayes network diagram.	63
2.6	The three lines of defense model.	69
3.1	The Boston Consulting Group's Growth-Share model.	80
3.2	Typical cash flows across lifecycle stages.	81
3.3	Comparison of the BCG and Wardley lifecycle stages.	81
4.1	AERM EA/BA Architecture Model.	95
4.2	Graph representation of a generic company's EA.	98
4.3	Detail showing value streams, capabilities and enablers from the graph in Figure 4.2.	99
4.4	Anatomy of a digital company.	101
4.5	Operational infrastructure and API services.	101
4.6	Digital products and services factory.	103
4.7	Business intelligence and analytics.	104
4.8	Partner development platform.	105
CS1.1	EA graph of the cart business.	124
5.1	The three tiers of risk.	132
5.2	An order-to-cash process.	151
5.3	As-is mapping approach.	156
5.4	To-be mapping approach.	168
CS2.1	Capabilities in the develop product process stream.	187
CS2.2	Capabilities and enablers in the market research process stream.	188
CS2.3	The design product process stream.	188
CS2.4	Market test process stream.	189
CS2.5	Commercial process stream.	190

CS3.1 Simulated consolidated sales distribution year 1. 248
CS3.2 Simulated consolidated sales distribution year 2. 249
CS3.3 Simulated consolidated sales distribution year 3. 250
7.1 AERM Arch model. 279
7.2 Digital business anatomy. 280
7.3 Three-tier risk schematic. 283
7.4 Transformation journey. 284
7.5 Business process flow. 286
7.6 As-is mapping. 287
7.7 To-be mapping. 290

TABLES

2.1 Data for the probability example. 45
CS3.1 Summary of aggregate factory utilization statistics. 246

Acknowledgments

I have had help from many people in writing this book. I would like to recognize some of them for providing direction and guidance or input into its content.

A sincere **Thank You** to Greg Hutchins, Dan Swanson, Stephen Villaescusa, Allen Roberts, Clifford Berg, Darren Penner, Spencer Pickett, Jeff Brown, Freda Salatino, Bruce Turner, Ron Hoffer and John Fraser. If I have omitted anyone, my apologies.

About this book

THEN

I have been working in the business and IT world for longer than I would like to admit to—since just after the advent of minicomputers and before the age of desktop computers, local area networks and, certainly, the Internet. In my early career, people having a computer at their desk was, at first, impossible, later, a rarity, but now, ubiquitous. Then, paper proliferated.

While I was in business school, I roomed with a computer science grad student and we played online games from the university's computer center with people at other universities over the DARPA net[1], the Department of Defense-funded precursor to the Internet.

From the beginning, my interests have centered around employing automation to help companies do things better. At the time I started in IT, businesses focused their IT dollars on operations. Application systems were, for the most part, transactional. They accumulated lots of information about what had happened and almost nothing about what was going to happen.

Change, if it happened at all, happened slowly. Business Process Redesign hadn't emerged as a discipline yet. Reworking business processes around shared information and data was entirely outside the purview of us geeks. If we couldn't find a senior enough sponsor from 'the business,' it would never happen. Most of the senior people whose ear we could chew were operations folks, and few of them had any interest in upending their working life, potential benefits be damned. As Upton Sinclair said,

> It is difficult to get a man to understand something when his salary depends on his not understanding it.[2]

For someone itching to use technology to make change, it was a frustrating time.

---

1 https://en.wikipedia.org/wiki/DARPA

2 https://quoteinvestigator.com/2017/11/30/salary/

NOW

Fast forward a few decades and everything is different. Now, evolutionary technology is driving a lot of the business change we see. It is almost impossible to imagine a business of any size, even a local retail-level one, that does not have some reliance on technology. At a minimum, every mom-and-pop shop needs and can have a website and the ability to provide services through it that complement what they sell and that their customers expect and demand.

Operating a business successfully these days requires competences and integration across many disciplines, some of which have bloomed within only the past few years. While some large and technologically sophisticated businesses are remaking themselves to take maximal advantage of what is possible, most of the rest of the world is caught in a miasma of change. They are taking one step forward on technology and then another to re-engineer their company to make optimal use of it. Unfortunately, things are going too fast for that to be a sustainable strategy. Companies will have to learn to evolve along multiple dimensions in parallel if they are going to remain viable. *The* subjects of the moment are **Digital Transformation** and **the Future of Work**. Prestigious consultancies and universities, the business and technology press and pretty much anyone else with a voice are shouting non-stop about the need for you to undergo the former in order to survive the latter.

They're not wrong. You do have to undertake a Digital Transformation. You're probably doing some of it now, but you have to step back, look at the bigger picture and integrate your efforts across several areas to achieve what digital transformation promises. It's complicated, expensive, risky, big and scary.

Given this backdrop, one of the things that I have wondered about is how companies will govern themselves through the process of transformation. Governance processes are tied to either or both of *what* the company is doing and *how* it does it. I'm not in a position to opine on all governance disciplines, but I have concerns about Risk Management in these circumstances, given what I know about how it's practiced at many companies. Where it's operated on a periodic schedule, with perhaps some special ops teams deployed occasionally, how can it keep up with the rate of change that will become the new normal?

Governance processes must be tied to something, usually business and decision processes within the organization; so, more *how* than *what*. In many cases, *how* is prescribed. There are standardized business processes, defined steps and stages and conditional branches, some of it automated or semi-automated. Assumedly, risk-based thinking was applied in the design of these things but what happens when they need to change? What is it that triggers the process of reformulating the policies and controls that must take place when a process is modified? And what about the propagation of changes to whatever might be connected and the impact on existing risks that this that might create?

It occurred to me that keeping on top of transformation would require a central repository of metadata[3] about the structure and anatomy of a company that would trigger updates to all sorts of management and governance processes. Transactions in the repository would represent prospective or actual change events that the company should review and act upon. Enterprise and Business Architecture models, along with a few other artifacts, are the right tools for this job, *if* (and this is a pretty big *if*) the repositories are kept current. Enterprise Architecture, as it is often practiced, is way too granular and slow to fulfill this requirement. I assert that a reduced-scope EA model, one with only a handful of entities, is the backbone of what is needed and that's what I present in this book.

I call the version of Risk Management that I describe **Agile Enterprise Risk Management** (Agile ERM or AERM). It is designed and intended to be operated on a continuous basis, rather than the periodic basis that is in common use today, and it is driven by what should be common management disciplines and the information artifacts that are produced in the course of executing them.

So, what makes this ***agile***? It's simple, really. Changes that your company is contemplating should be screened against its current state, which is represented in the Enterprise Architecture (EA) repository, a model of its anatomy. When entities are added or changed, risks attached to them can propagate throughout your enterprise from dependencies or interrelationships, which can be missed by after-the-fact, intermittent governance processes. Transactions in the model, therefore, should trigger scrutiny by multiple groups—architecture groups, governance groups, operational teams and so on ***before*** the changes are implemented. This is the best moment to exert control over how your business evolves and it's the right time to apply risk management, risk-based thinking and risk-based decision-making to inform and guide your evolution. Given the rate of change required to maintain your sustainability in the environment in which you are operating, you'll need this to keep up.

Perhaps you don't have an Enterprise Architecture or Business Architecture team or formally employ any of the other disciplines that I believe should be management-as-usual for any business. Perhaps you have a skeptical view of EA and the 'boil-the-ocean' approach with which it's often executed. AERM is based on a minimum-viable version of EA, one that relies on a small palette of entities in its model framework, specifically to make it feasible for smaller or less sophisticated management teams to employ. While AERM relies upon several disciplines to implement, it requires only what is necessary from each to succeed.

[3] https://en.wikipedia.org/wiki/Metadata

So, you are facing one transformation that you cannot avoid—a Digital Transformation—and one that you should not avoid—an AERM adoption. My goal is to show you that AERM adoption can more than coexist with your digital transformation; it can facilitate your success in it.

WHO IS THIS BOOK FOR?

There is a fable written by Aesop[4] entitled *The Bat, Birds and The Beasts*. The moral of the fable is:

> **He that is neither one thing nor the other has no friends.**

and that is very much the way that I felt early in my postgraduate career. I wasn't part of 'the business' and I wasn't interested enough in technology for its own sake to make it the entire focus of my career. My real interest was in employing technology to make businesses work better and, as I've observed, it was something of an uphill climb.

Today, I believe that straddling the line between geekdom and 'being a user' has become the sweet spot to which I had aspired all along. Lean Startup, value-stream product management, machine learning and artificial intelligence-driven marketing, Agile/DevOps software development and all sorts of other technology-enabled practices are so vital to competitiveness now that it's nearly impossible to run a business of any size or complexity without a foot in both camps.

This book is intended to help business executives and functional managers to get their hands around what they need to know about technology—what to ask their technologists to implement, how their staff should integrate with them and what capabilities they should hope to enable. It is also intended to help technologists better understand how they should integrate with their business counterparts—what capabilities are targeted, how their work can enable a new style of product management and how important their work is to enable their organization to become more agile, competitive and sustainable.

It's also targeted toward executives and managers responsible for governance, most specifically risk managers. It provides guidance to help them to envision how they might retool their disciplines to adapt to the rate at which the environment in which companies operate is evolving and help achieve business agility while maintaining the level of scrutiny required to fulfill their mandates.

I cover the disciplines I address at the level of 'what is …?' not 'how do I …?' It's way outside the scope of the book to provide detailed advice on how to conduct a cloud migration or how to re-engineer business processes.

[4] https://fablesofaesop.com/the-bat-birds-and-the-beasts.html

I identify these as things that you need to do and provide some high-level examples so that, hopefully, you will be positioned to ask relevant and intelligent questions or at least seek additional information. You may think of the book as something of a syllabus.

Ultimately, the goal is for subject matter experts from all disciplines to understand how they can integrate with their colleagues to evolve their company for the better. The watchwords for all of this are *multidisciplinary* and *integrated*.

ORGANIZATION OF THE BOOK

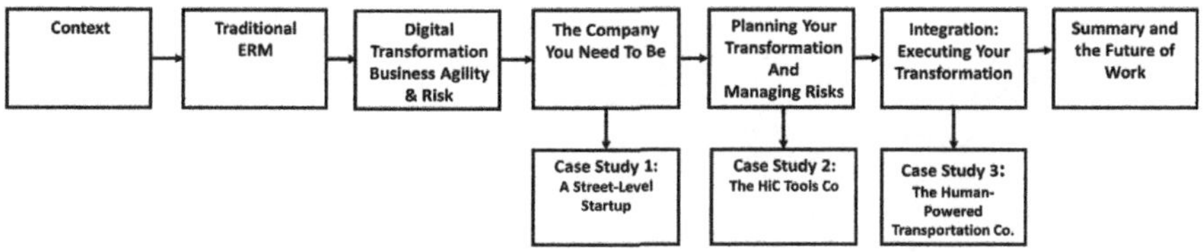

The contents of the book include:

- **Context**—what's driving the environment in which companies find themselves,
- **Traditional risk management**—how it's been done and why it can't persist the way it is,
- **Digital transformation, business agility and risk**—what it is, why you need to do it, what your goals should be for it and how risk management will fit in,
- **The company you need to be**—what your company needs to look like to succeed and sustain,
- **Planning for transformation**—what you need to do to prepare yourself to transform,
- **Executing transformation**—how to execute, monitor, manage your transformation and
- **The future of work**—how things will be going forward.

I've also included three case studies that illustrate various aspects of the program that you will need to execute.

Introduction

Risk and Risk Management have become driving concerns and COVID-19 has only increased the emphasis on them. Businesses, government agencies and all manner of other institutions have increased their focus on them. There are a number of authoritative entities, like the International Organization for Standardization[1] (ISO), the Committee of Sponsoring Organizations of the Treadway Commission[2] (COSO), and the National Institute of Standards and Technology[3] (NIST) that have promulgated approaches and processes relating to them and many enterprises and institutions practice them. However, the way that many companies do it appears not to be very effective at preventing avoidable negative outcomes and they aren't getting better, even with experience.

This is not to say that there is anything in the ISO, COSO or NIST prescriptions that is inherently wrong or inadequate. It is just that if they are not followed conscientiously, they won't work. If you don't take medication you are prescribed, as it was prescribed, then it won't cure whatever is ailing you.

Some common major weaknesses in risk management as it is often practiced are:

- Failure to keep pace with changes in the enterprise as it evolves to meet new business challenges,
- Incomplete identification of risks, too much focus on what's obvious or on specific areas of risk and not enough on the holistic enterprise and the environment in which it operates,
- Poor understanding of dependencies and interconnectedness of elements of the business that contribute to creating or reinforcing risks,
- Poor understanding of linkage between risks and their impact on the company's strategic goals and the Critical Success Factors (CSFs) and Key Performance Indicators (KPIs) employed to monitor or measure them and

1 https://www.iso.org/home.html
2 https://www.coso.org/Pages/default.aspx
3 https://www.nist.gov/

DOI: 10.1201/9781003188605-1

- Not enough introspection and quantitative analysis of risk management performance and its application to continuous improvement.

WHAT'S DRIVING THE CHANGE WE'RE EXPERIENCING?

A variety of forces are creating change and amplifying volatility in all areas of our personal and professional lives. Companies are being affected in profound ways and how they're managed must change for them to survive, if not thrive. Some of these forces include:

Technology and technology-driven business models and the shift from capex to opex

The acts of manipulating and making physical 'things,' employing workers and large asset bases can be strategic liabilities to a business that sells products and services to consumers and end-users. Connections to customer across multiple channels are prized assets. For a number of reasons, companies are likely to contract out as much of what goes into producing and delivering what is sold as possible. Creativity, design, intellectual property and content are major drivers of business value now. Business models are explicitly designed to avoid unnecessary dependence on depreciating assets or business relationships that may ultimately weigh on the enterprise when new models come along.

The business models of Uber,[4] Lyft[5] and Airbnb[6] are prime examples of this. Each of these companies provides services predicated on physical assets, either cars or homes, which they do not own. Their value add is in facilitating transactions and providing some level of customer service. These companies own next to nothing and are worth $78 billion, $24 billion and $75 billion, respectively, as of the time of this writing.

This is not to say that your business shouldn't have assets or employees, of course. It would be hard to imagine an industrial company functioning without them. However, it's often possible, even desirable, to decompose a business in such a way that a separable part of it can operate with almost no physical assets and minimal staff.

An example was given by Adam Hartung,[7] a managing consultant with whom I once worked. He had consulted with a company that provided petroleum product storage and transmission capacity management at a major port. The facilities and workforce for its operations were extensive. It

4 https://www.uber.com/us/en/s/d/kochab
5 https://www.lyft.com/
6 https://www.airbnb.com/
7 https://adamhartung.com/

happened that his client had developed a particular genius for managing and juggling the schedules for the port's facilities to maximize throughput at the port and the pipelines it fed, and this created financial rewards for the client's customers as well as efficiencies for all involved.

The client was looking for opportunities to unlock value from its business and Adam helped them to realize that its special logistical genius was creating value and the physical assets it owned at the port were creating a drag on it. By creating a technology- and knowledge-based service and separating it from the corporation and the existing assets and workforce, the client reaped a substantial reward. The new business unit had a completely different financial profile from the original company and divorcing itself from the assets and existing workforce resulted in explosive profitability while detaching itself from the risks of owning, depreciating and maintaining the utilization rate of the port's facilities.

Process automation can displace people, even high-level people

Robotic Process Automation is replacing human interaction with software application systems. AI-driven Robotics is making inroads into tasks that have traditionally been performed by knowledge workers. Medical scans are now read by software and any that show atypical findings are referred to a doctor to review. At some point, the doctor may get pushed out of the loop. Similarly, contracts and legal agreements are being constructed by software programs and only the most sensitive and non-standard of them are crafted by hand.

Cloud infrastructures level the playing field between startups and established companies

Cloud infrastructure with a pay-as-you-go cost structure provides opportunities for early-stage businesses to implement automation supporting business models that require vast computing power previously beyond their ability to acquire. Advanced, off-the-shelf AI-based services such as natural-language processing or machine learning, that were previously beyond the reach of nascent companies are now available for them to apply to the creation of new services and products that can compete with almost anything that an established company can achieve.

Your company's valuation depends on your keeping up with these trends

All these trends hit your company's financial statements. Traditional, asset-heavy business models are driven by fixed investment and Capital Expenses (capex), in which the company invests in assets that appear on the balance sheet, and writes off depreciation, which appears as a non-cash expense on the Profit and Loss (P&L) statement, where it offsets profits and reduces income taxes. Newer approaches eschew capex in favor of Operating Expense (opex)-driven models. These business models require less upfront investment, allow 100% of the expense to be deducted from taxes immediately and allow for an easier transition from fixed assets if circumstances warrant. For example, instead of buying or leasing a large computer server and running it in a company's datacenter, running workloads on a public cloud provides numerous benefits—processing capacity can be turned off when it is not in use, and it can be terminated with minimal exposure when it is no longer needed.

Societal changes

Deindustrialization of first-world economies is accelerating. The ratio of services to manufacturing in the US economy tilts more and more toward services and jobs in the manufacturing sector migrate offshore. Political considerations and risks ebb and flow as our relationships with various countries to which our manufacturing has migrated weaken and the vast sums we spend in them engenders wage growth, reducing the cost advantage they originally had. Supply chain and third-party risks are now becoming more of a consideration than ever.

Splintering of American society along political, class and urban vs. rural lines exacerbates the difficulty of creating public policy and creates opportunities for self-dealing that undermine Americans' faith in their government. Businesses increasingly focus on the easiest market segments to reach, often those in urban areas or those populated by customers and clientele most comfortable with internet-driven sales models, and abandon those who don't have broadband access, don't spend time online where they will be exposed to their advertising and who don't spend money purchasing there.

The costs of the major financial obligations of life—shelter, health care, education and retirement have spiraled out of control for many. Schisms in policy beliefs between political parties obstruct government intervention and business, the only other economic entity with the wherewithal to make an impact, seems disinclined to wade into peoples' lives, at least for now. Ultimately, changes are likely, and businesses will have to adapt to them.

The entire institution of higher education is likely to be upended. Many colleges will go under and opportunities for less capable or well-funded students to attain a degree will evaporate. The ability to get an education remotely will offset some of this but remote learning during the pandemic has not proven to work for many. It will evolve and improve, but when will that happen and how that will play out with prospective employers?

COVID is creating immediate impact, in the form of business closures and unemployment, and is driving knowledge workers to work from home.

Many of them may never return to their office environments, which could have profound impact on urban office buildings and the many businesses that served the workers that populated them. Similarly, expensive, close-in suburbs in which many of these workers live may lose their attraction and salary arbitrage between remote workers living in low-cost areas and those living in high-cost areas may push businesses to employ ever more dispersed staff that they can pay less.

In the absence of government intervention, health care and retirement will only become more and more divisive issues for the country. If health insurance were to be offloaded from employers and replaced by programs offered by the government, gig-economy business models might proliferate and structural changes in taxation might be enacted to fund them while the costs of today's employer-paid health insurance shift.

How can you prepare to compete?

Responding to these forces and others will require considerable change in how you organize and run your company. Assumptions, such as a lengthy life and planned evolution for your anchor products, are less valid now. Investment returns predicated on long-term depreciation of dedicated assets and streams of product revenues will be squeezed as products and whole lines of business can succumb to new competitors at any time. More than ever before, your business and its risks need to be managed actively.

The transformation journey you must prepare to undertake has much in common with past transformations of comparable scope, such as major acquisitions and consolidations; however, there are critical differences. The management and governance structures you'll need are going to be a major departure from what you're probably comfortable with and many of the assumptions and metrics on which you used to rely to understand the status of your business will have less validity and applicability than they once did. Instead of trying to reach a new stable state of equilibrium, you are aspiring to drive your business to a new state of dynamism. It can be very disconcerting ... and fraught with risks.

So, now seems a good time to reconsider how risk management is being performed at your company. I propose a more structured, multi-disciplinary approach, starting with Enterprise Architecture (EA) and Business Architecture (BA) and others, all of which will be discussed in some detail in due course. I believe that application of these disciplines would result in:

- Better identification of risks,
- Better understanding of the interplay of factors that create or amplify risks,
- Better prioritization of risk management and mitigation efforts,
- More informed sequencing of transformation initiatives (programs or projects), perhaps even more willingness to evolve quickly and

iteratively by proof-of-concept experiments involving trial, error, learning and revision in which termination is not failure, it is experience to be built upon,
- More nuanced understanding of the costs and benefits of risk management and greater ability to improve it and
- A basis for adding automation to your process for adjusting risk management to your business as it evolves, increasing responsiveness and agility.

Implementing Agile ERM

Briefly, implementing Agile Enterprise Risk Management (AERM) requires that you establish certain metadata repositories, such as the EA and BA models, implement the processes necessary to maintain them, staff the teams necessary to execute the processes and implement the processes required to respond to events as they occur and act on information as it is discovered. These artifacts and processes include:

Agile ERM Artifacts

To reiterate, the goals of AERM are continuous operation and comprehensive coverage. Both of these goals are achieved by tying them to repositories of prospective or highly current metadata—EA and BA models, process documentation and others. You simply cannot implement AERM without the foundation in place. I view these things as necessary for good management practice anyway, so you will not be implementing them just to support AERM.

These precursors include:

- Working models, and established metadata repositories,
- Operational processes that ensure the metadata repositories are maintained,
- The Taxonomy, which will dictate how the data in the repositories is tagged to ensure that it is both usable and useful,
- Knowledge Management processes that ensure that the data flowing into the repositories is categorized and tagged properly and
- Transfer, or linkage and consolidation of risks from the existing risk register to the new repository to ensure that they accounted for.

Agile ERM operational processes

Once the elements on which it depends are in place, AERM requires the following processes:

- Processes for monitoring the repositories, recognizing and then acting on triggering events,

- Triage—ERM must have a process to review and prioritize events to determine the urgency with which they should be addressed,
- A standard approach to risk appraisal and treatment and control formulation,
- A standard process for disseminating and activating the treatments and controls it determines are necessary and
- Compliance monitoring.

My recommendations are premised on the notion that you have to undertake a Digital Transformation and that this will generate massive change in your company. Disciplined transformation, itself, requires many of the same artifacts and processes that AERM does, so this represents an opportunity to perform both together and reap the benefits. The remainder of the book addresses WHY, WHAT and HOW—why you need to transform, what you need to do to accomplish it and how to do it.

Where do we go from here?

The fact is, there is no one-size-fits-all target model for your company. There are several changes that must be made, both in parallel and in series, to get you to where you need to be. Given the scope of what you will need to accomplish, the chances are that by the time you could complete the initiatives that you might plan to effectuate the transformation, the destination will have moved. What you need to do is begin the journey and develop your change muscles to course correct continuously along the way. Your real and true target is to become an agile organization, capable of rapid adjustment to evolving circumstances.

In this volume, we will:

- Look at common current risk management practices and some of the management practices that impact on their effectiveness,
- Survey some of the authoritative organizations and their positions on risk management,
- Establish the vocabulary we will use as we talk about risk management,
- Cover each of the disciplines that should contribute to overall risk management,
- Present an approach to transforming risk management in organizations and
- Apply subsets of these disciplines in three case studies that illustrate their use.

The journey that you must undertake is long and winding. It is strewn with dead ends and cul-de-sacs and the destination will move while you are underway. What you need to do is to establish an anchoring set of artifacts and practices that will give you a stable base from which to work as you evolve your company. And, you will also need to grow your risk-based disciplinary muscles to help you manage risks, create policies and problem-solve along the way.

I am hoping that this book can provide you with what you need to conceptualize and execute the journey.

Chapter 1

Context

COVID, BLM and upheaval

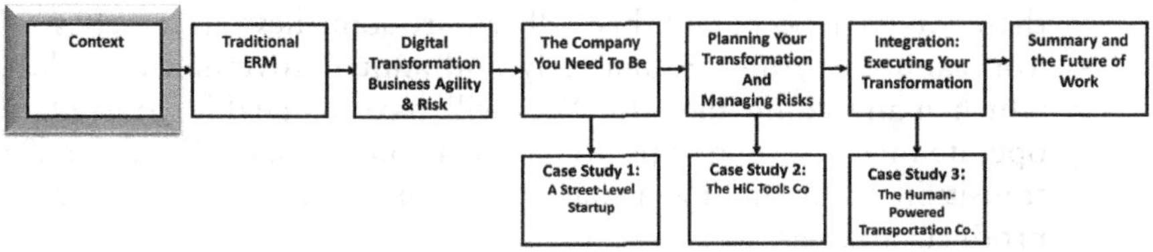

COVERED IN THIS CHAPTER

- **VUCA (Volatility, Uncertainty, Complexity and Ambiguity), our current state:** A variety of forces are conspiring to cause rapid changes in the environment and in the markets in which your company operates. You cannot expect to survive and succeed by employing the management approaches you have in the past.
- **Agile Is Not Agility:** Agile is a family of system development approaches, which have fractured into numerous sects, each with their own adherents. The term Agile is misapplied and misused to imply that it creates *Business Agility*, the ability to react rapidly when a business requires it. It doesn't.
- **Business Agility, the One Thing You Need to Survive:** In a world of change, you must be able to evolve and adapt. Preparation is what will enable you to achieve business agility.
- **The Challenges You're Facing:** Your approach to business strategy must change. A lot of the things that used to protect you from competition no longer do and the emergence of new technology and business models make it possible for much smaller competitors to invade what were formerly protected niches.
- **The Pressure to Execute a Digital Transformation:** You will have to create a digital presence and add digital products and services to your repertoire. These may either be side-by-side with existing products or independent digital products in their own right.

DOI: 10.1201/9781003188605-2

- **Managing Your Business and Risks as You Transform:**
  - You will have to adopt 'Value-Stream,' product-centric management approaches to focus your energy on constantly increasing the value that you offer to your customers. This will require significant changes to almost everything about how you run your business.
  - You will need to create, incubate and groom a portfolio of prospective businesses, much like a venture capital firm does. You will have to develop the skills required to rapidly evolve, test and evaluate them, culling the ones that aren't going to succeed and reallocate your resources.
  - You will have to embrace new workforce acquisition and management models. You may become more reliant on contracted expertise than you have been, and this will require some new approaches.
  - You cannot operate on quarterly and annual governance models, which many companies do. You will have to enable yourself to operate on something approximating a continuous basis. You must transition from funding projects to managing evolution of your products and services.
  - Transformation has its own risks. You will need to apply multiple planning and execution management approaches to minimize risks to your progress.
- **Traditional Management Practices No Longer Work:** Many legacy management processes will not serve you well as you go forward. Trying to govern in quarterly and annual reporting cycles is particularly at odds with the agile operations required for sustainability. If you are operating this way, you will need to reformulate and integrate your operational and risk management processes to enable the agility you'll need.
- **All management is risk management:** Risk-based thinking, decision-making and problem-solving must be incorporated into every management and governance process within your business. It's more intuitive than you may think.
- **Traditional risk management practices, as performed at many companies, are out of step:** You will have to evolve your risk management (RM) practices to focus on sources and root causes of risk, probabilistic assessment methods and increasing your abilities to identify, appraise and treat risks at the rate your evolving business creates, morphs or eliminates them.
- **Why you need integrated, multi-disciplinary risk management:** Risks arise from decisions you make and actions you take. A variety of management disciplines inform and guide how you make decisions and execute your operational processes. Not having RM tightly integrated into your core management processes is like trying to inspect quality into a product instead of designing and building it in. Your RM can't succeed if it's not as intrinsic to how you run your enterprise as your other disciplines.

- **The disciplines you will need to achieve your controlled transformation:** If you begin to make the changes that we discuss without careful planning, you will create emergent architecture, in which redundancies create inefficiency and constrain agility. You will need transformation disciplines to avoid this.

VUCA: OUR CURRENT STATE

VUCA is an apt description for the prevailing environment in which companies are operating today and will likely be for many years to come.

PESTLE is an acronym that identifies major external forces that act on and create risks for companies. It stands for Political, Economic, Social, Technological, Legal and Environmental. There are structural changes going on in each of these areas that should be of major concern to anyone who runs a company. Events are occurring at such a high rate that developing business agility is the only path to sustainability. 'The next big thing' will not be sufficient to attain or maintain a predominant competitive position that can last longer than it takes for the one after that to come along. If you make cars, the lead time from designing them to building a manufacturing facility to delivering them to customers may provide some cushion from prospective new competitors. If you deliver digital services, that cushion is vanishingly slim. New car models are expected once a year; updated web services can be delivered via DevOps literally every minute.

The implications of the increasing VUCA in your operating environment are profound. More than ever, it is imperative that you be able to add to, evolve and enhance your product and service offerings to meet the changing needs of your current or prospective customers. At the same time, you must continue to improve the interface and experience you present to them. Finally, you must enable your company to evolve with maximum velocity to grasp opportunities and respond to threats as they arise, or you will quickly become uncompetitive.

A great deal of traditional management thinking has gone by the wayside, particularly, notions about how to build barriers to entry to protect a company's market positions. Early in my IT career, custom-built application systems were depreciable assets with a financial life of seven years. Now, many applications are accounted for as operating expenses, and not capitalized at all. They are built iteratively and updated as frequently as *every minute*, and they may be abandoned or replaced in a moment if the product or service they support is superseded. When a company's customer base is more easily repurposed than its operating assets, a whole new way of thinking is required.

Allocating resources to experiment with new offerings and constructing rapid proof of concept projects hoping to get to minimum viable products with commercial potential is how companies will grow. Willingness to transition away from assets and the part of the workforce attached to a line of business that may not make sense in light of a changing marketplace is a painful but necessary discipline.

AGILE VS. AGILITY

These days, the word 'Agile' seems to appear everywhere in business-oriented books, publications and the press. Its first use was around 2001 as a descriptor of a software development paradigm and it has been widely co-opted and misused since. The prevailing systems development approach at the time was 'Waterfall,' in which projects proceeded through a prescribed set of steps, each flowing to the next. Several factors which we will cover later deterred any deviation from the original project plan, even if things changed to the point that the project didn't make sense anymore.

Agile supposedly provided an alternative that allowed for mid-course correction, accelerated delivery, time and money savings and improved quality: a panacea! Would that it were so but, alas, Agile has not improved on the failure rate of IT projects of any size, which remains at a stubborn 70%, depending on how you count and who you ask. It's simply not the magic wand many business product owners and stakeholders have been led to believe it was.

Two factors conspire to cause project failures under the waterfall approach: (a) product owners are never able to figure out exactly what they want and need at the outset of a project and (b) legacy funding practices lock in the scope (features and functions), schedule and budget when a project is approved. As users come face to face with what is under construction, enhancements and changes occur to them or the business environment in which the project would operate evolves. This invalidates the original plan and forces all involved through a painful process of contorting the product to finish with the resources remaining in the original plan, slashing some of the desired features or functions or fessing up and going back for more resources, money or time.

Agile was supposed to address this failing by reducing time spent documenting and the amount of documentation produced and by providing a path to course correct as users developed a better understanding of what they really needed. Unfortunately, if a Scrum (an Agile variant) project is managed using a Waterfall governance approach, 'Water-Scrum-Fall,' described here[1] and here[2], results. In the end, it is no different than an impaired or failed waterfall project.

[1] https://stefanedbrittain.medium.com/the-insidious-institutionalisation-of-water-scrum-fall-4af7de8865b9

[2] https://www.plutora.com/blog/water-scrum-fall

Agile Enterprise Risk Management (AERM is more than a project methodology or approach. It is intended to enable you to exploit various disciplines you should already be using to position yourself to identify and react to opportunities, events, threats and changes rapidly. The only thing it has in common with Agile software development approaches is the name. The goal of adopting AERM is ***Business Agility***.

BUSINESS AGILITY, THE ONE THING YOU NEED TO SURVIVE

Given the VUCA in which we will all operate for the foreseeable future, agility, ***business agility***, is the crucial capability that you must develop and nurture. Where does business agility come from? It comes from thoughtful design and preparation. We will talk about the Observe, Orient, Decide, Act (OODA) loop later in the book but the important concept you should consider is that designing for agility improves your performance in each step in the loop.

By identifying where risks may occur in your operations, you increase your awareness of them. If you are aware of them, you should have identified a set of possible responses for them, which should reduce your decision latency and accelerate your predetermined action or mitigation response. If you have considered and designed a response, you should be prepared to execute it at speed.

So, by creating and maintaining a sufficiently detailed model of your enterprise, you are establishing a foundational framework that will help to focus your attention on developments to which you must prepare to react and respond. This enterprise architecture (EA)-driven approach, which should be at the heart of how you manage and transform your business in any event, is also at the heart of AERM.

THE CHALLENGES YOU'RE FACING

Within your enterprise, there are three categories of businesses:

- Established businesses, which you must defend,
- Prospective businesses, whose viability you must determine and which you have to develop, mature and establish in the marketplace and
- Aspirational business opportunities, which are those in successful markets already occupied by other competitors.

In *The Nine Situations*, Sun Tzu[3] has said:

> "When a chieftain is fighting in his own territory, it is **dispersive ground** ... When he has penetrated into hostile territory, but to no great distance,

[3] https://suntzusaid.com/book/11

> it is **facile ground** ... Ground the possession of which imports great advantage to either side, is **contentious ground**.
>
> ... On dispersive ground, therefore, fight not. On facile ground, halt not. On contentious ground, attack not."

Your established lines of business are on *dispersive ground*, close to home and its comforts, representing distractions to your army. Sun Tzu advises that you fortify yourself to avoid fighting too close to home.

Your prospective businesses are on *facile ground*. You are designing them, validating them while restricting their external exposure, so as not to give competitors ideas that they can run with, and preparing to roll them out. Once you have matured your nascent businesses to the point that they become public facing, Sun Tzu advises that you throw all you can into maturing and developing them and do not stop until they become established.

The market of established products and services is *contentious ground*. Sun Tzu advises that you not attack in this space.

You will need to prepare yourself to defend or attack in each of these categories and your posture toward managing risks will contribute mightily to your ability to do so. Sun Tzu placed considerable weight on planning and RM; risk-based decision-making and risk-based problem-solving are exactly that.

Increasing volatility and time compression is undermining the model on which Sun Tzu predicated his advice. It is becoming increasingly difficult to fortify existing businesses so as to make it unnecessary to fight off competitors. It should also not be taken for granted that entering mature markets is not a viable option. Many of your competitors are looking at them and may not feel so restrained about the challenge.

Any endeavor worth pursuing, whether it is a business, a non-profit or a governmental organization, must compete for its share of rewards, financial, reputational, psychic or otherwise. The ground is shifting underneath you and you will have to develop the ability to adapt, respond and change at speed to maintain your competitiveness and viability for the longer term. As you do, new risks will develop, and existing ones will change. It is incumbent on you to prepare yourself to manage risks at the speed at which they evolve. Doing so is more than a matter of self-preservation, it is inherently bound up with your understanding and managing your business and the knowledge required is intrinsic to the successful evolution of your organization.

The pressure to execute a digital transformation

You have probably been reading and hearing a lot about Digital Transformation. If you are not familiar with the topic, this article on the subject[4] from Red Hat is an excellent overview and here is another from TechTarget.[5]

[4] https://enterprisersproject.com/what-is-digital-transformation

[5] https://searchcio.techtarget.com/definition/digital-transformation

Simply put, digital transformation is the process of integrating digital technologies into all areas of your business to achieve maximum agility and efficiency and to allow better interaction with and among you, your customers, workforce and external stakeholders. However, it's a lot more than just implementing some new technology and migrating all or part of your infrastructure and operations to the cloud. If it were that simple, there wouldn't be armies of consultants and product vendors out there offering to help you do it.

Remember, ***Business Agility*** is something without which you are unlikely to sustain your company. Instead of an efficient organization designed to produce a set of products and services under a command-and-control organizational structure, the goal is to create an organization that can gear up to create and deliver new services with great speed, transitioning away from anything that does not add to delivering value to customers or creating efficiency for the enterprise. It means operating as a portfolio of narrowly focused, minimally interdependent groups (highly cohesive and loosely coupled, in tech-speak), tolerating some redundancy if it enables velocity and developing new perspectives on measuring performance.

For instance, instead of a hierarchical product management and marketing department at the division level in a multi-line company, a set of empowered and enabled product management teams integrated with the technical resources focused on individual or closely related groups of products will be better situated to understand the markets for them and evolve them through iterative experimentation. In a hierarchical command-and-control structure, the drag and overhead on decision-making would serve only to slow things down.

Your goal is not to create and roll out a new product or two; it is to remake your company so that you can do it at will with a minimum of ramp-up time. You are in a shootout with numerous other competitors, and you must develop both a quick draw and the ability to fire rapidly. Many of your shots will miss the target but the more you fire in a short time, the more likely you are to hit something and slow the incoming fire.

As you can probably well imagine, managing risks in this type of organization will be a challenge, one that I think cannot be met the way that many, if not most, enterprises' RM functions operate today.

MANAGING YOUR BUSINESS AND RISKS AS YOU TRANSFORM

Traditional approaches to strategy are losing validity

Traditional thinking about business strategy focuses on attaining predominant market share, increased margins and, as markets mature, reduced competition. In 1980s cutting-edge thinking, companies were advised to adopt a portfolio model with businesses distributed across a range of market maturities (from emerging to mature) and use the profits from the '*Cash Cow*' products (those in mature markets in which the company had high market share) to fund investment in '*Question Mark*' products (those in growing markets) to grow the next wave of cash cows. This article[6] by Australian strategy consultant Allen Roberts is very much on point.

Vertical integration and proprietary capabilities were tools that could help retain profits and maintain cost advantages over competitors. Horizontal mergers of companies in different lines of business created diversification, supposedly smoothing corporate earnings, mitigating risks and supporting high share prices, which could fund acquisitions while serving as a defense against takeover attempts by others.

It worked quite well for GE until it didn't. GE went from a shining star to tattered old dame in a frighteningly brief time. During that time, it divested numerous lines of business and today is a shadow of its former self, though it is rebuilding. Pre-eminent retailers—Sears, Kmart, Neiman Marcus, to name a few, were tied to real estate and it dragged them down. The advantages they once had in purchasing power, the ability to obtain exclusive merchandise or to undersell their competition couldn't save them. People stopped going to the malls where they were located, and it killed them as well as the smaller businesses that had grown around them. Now, mall owners are desperately looking for alternative uses for properties that are no longer viable retail platforms. Some of them are being repurposed by online retailers as distribution and delivery hubs.

The stock price charts, below, illustrate the fortunes of these companies over the past few years. GE has lost substantial value over the past five years, Sears Holdings acquired KMart and seems to be on a path to receivership and Neiman Marcus has 'gone dark' and is no longer publishing its financial results to the public.

There's no question that there is still some truth in the strategic thinking of the past. Market share still brings benefits and there is still some validity to the portfolio approach and multi-line business management. However, one of the major factors that drove the portfolio model is under attack—the lower risk and higher profitability of the cash cow. The notion that a company can rely on natural barriers to competition and comfortably focus on optimizing performance (minimizing investment while maximizing profit over time) of the cash cow is no longer valid to the degree it was. If there's profit in it, you can expect competition from technology-enabled companies looking for their share. There is plenty of startup capital to fund disruptive companies and self-funded entries from established competitors are streaming into markets new to their parents. The relative costs and risks of 'taking a shot' decrease constantly.

Amazon's pre-eminent position in e-tailing hasn't entitled it to sit back, pay huge bonuses and engage in stock buybacks. Few of the products it sells

[6] https://www.strategyaudit.com.au/2021/05/24/how-do-you-manage-multiple-parallel-cycles/

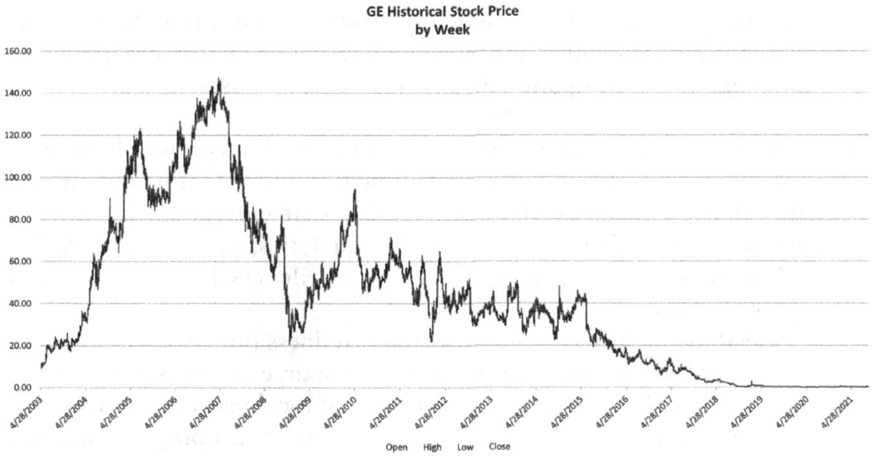

Figure 1.1 GE historical weekly stock price.

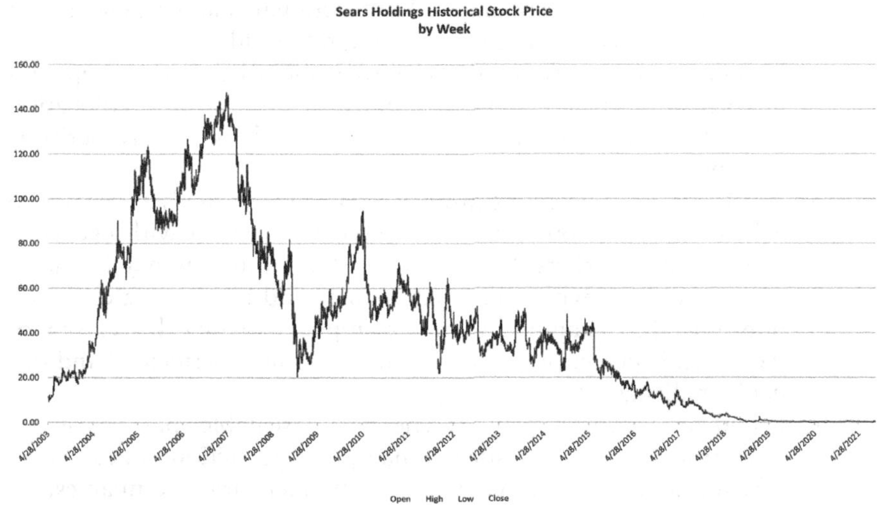

Figure 1.2 Sears holdings historical weekly stock price.

are unique to it. What is, though, is customer focus and relentless innovation that prevent it from being leapfrogged by a competitor leveraging a new technology or a novel business model.

Forces driving the need for new strategic approaches

A lot of the historical advantages of bigness can now be liabilities if they obstruct agility. Established companies with business models that incorporate large workforces, expansive real estate and substantial physical asset bases once benefited from them as barriers to entry; now they can be anchors that drag companies under. A wide range of factors compel us to rethink managing our companies and their attendant risks:

- Technology is the elephant in the room in any discussion of how business has changed and is evolving. Jeanne Ross[7] has identified five major areas that characterize the environment that enterprises must navigate now—SMACIT: Social, Mobile, Analytics, Cloud and Internet of Things (IoT). Each of them presents challenges from without and within the enterprise.
  - Social media brings us greater connectedness but also disintermediates traditional information and news sources, creates polarization and generally furthers the destruction of local press and news organizations. It is exploited by governmental and non-governmental actors to interfere with other countries' politics and elections and allows companies to create disinformation campaigns about their competitors' offerings. It has also created an explosion of new communication, advertising and promotional channels, mastery of which are critical to success in the digital world.
  - Mobile apps are becoming the new standard in how companies interact with their customers. Many of these apps' geolocation capabilities have significant implications, such as 'big-brother' surveillance concerns.
  - AI/ML-driven algorithms are going to be increasingly necessary to achieve the decision velocity required to keep up with events in a company's markets. Lack of algorithmic transparency is one of many problems with which companies and society are currently wrestling. For example, wringing implicit, opaque biases out of AI-driven decision processes is proving to be a pernicious and difficult challenge.
  - Cloud architectures provide cheap and scalable 'pay-as-you-go' infrastructure and sophisticated pay-per-use functions and services, which enable startups to compete with much larger companies.
  - Internet of Things (IoT) online sensors enable real-time monitoring and responses however, there are some significant security and privacy challenges that remain to be addressed.
- The average life span of companies is plummeting. According to a 2017 CNBC.com article,[8] *Is Technology Killing Off Corporate America*, "The average age of a company listed on the S&P 500 has fallen from 60 years in the 1950s to less than 20 years now." The lead time you have between recognizing an event that requires a response and executing

[7] https://mitpress.mit.edu/books/designed-digital

[8] https://www.cnbc.com/2017/08/24/technology-killing-off-corporations-average-lifespan-of-company-under-20-years.html

the response has shrunk dramatically. Anything that obstructs market surveillance, including short-sightedness on the part of management, or hinders rapid reaction can be the undoing of your company. Rapid reactions can range from the trivial, such as adding some functionality to an app, to re-envisioning the company, restructuring lines of business, acquiring another business or divesting parts of yours.

- Enterprise-level financial engineering approaches, such as the horizontally integrated portfolio model discussed earlier, are increasingly irrelevant. Every line of business must be optimized independently, though skills, knowledge and supporting infrastructure may be shared and repurposed to produce synergies. This means that instead of managing one business, you may need to manage several independent ones while trying to exploit opportunities for synergy by reusing infrastructure, application components and processes and minimizing redundancies and inefficiencies.
- The interface between companies, employees, clients and stakeholders must support increasing intimacy. Employees, clients and stakeholders are expecting, no, demanding, personalized services focused on their individual needs. Digital transformation is necessary to enable companies to provide this level of service and a host of competences are required to accomplish it. Many will require domain knowledge and skills new to your company. In all, overhauling your organization and acquiring new skills and implementing new processes will be needed to become and remain competitive. Rapid change with myriad interdependences has inherent risks that you will have to recognize and manage.
- Many, if not most, companies do not have the plethora of the diverse skills and knowledge required for digital transformation in-house. What various advisory firms, consultancies and product and services companies have to say about this right now is contradictory and troubling. There is no one-size-fits-all blueprint for this. It is incumbent on you to select advisers and partners, to design, sequence and execute your transformation and to determine how you will manage the risks along the way.
- Inherent in obtaining and maintaining employees', customers' and stakeholders' data are increasing risks associated with data privacy and protection. Data is what feeds digital strategies and managing risks associated with protecting it in an increasingly hostile environment requires its own evolving and specialized set of knowledge and skills.
- Operational efficiency and consistency are increasingly facilitated by process automation. Business Process Automation (BPA) tooling and Robotic Process Automation (RPA) have great benefits but also attendant risks. Implementing these technologies can mean substantial reorganization of your staff and their work roles and hands-off

decision-making embedded in their design must be monitored for continuous accuracy, validity and appropriateness.

- Artificial Intelligence and Machine Learning (AI/ML) will ultimately play an important role in how business is managed. The ability to recognize event patterns, adjust and respond rapidly enough to be competitive may soon be beyond the capability of manual or semi-automated decision processes such as are common today. While it becomes ever easier to build and deploy AI models, most companies have a large gap in the knowledge and experience required to realize value from them. To the extent that they require a lot of what may be sensitive data and can produce results that lack transparency, there are risks associated with AI that must be managed carefully.
- Everything that used to be a project, such as developing an application system, needs to be viewed more holistically as a transformation initiative. You will need to move away from waterfall-ish governance and project management (PM) processes that can't keep up. You will need to learn to architect and manage the evolution of shared resources concurrently with continuous revisions to customer- and stakeholder-facing services that rely on them. New knowledge, skills and processes will be needed and without question missteps will be made along the way to transforming how your company must work.
- The need for agility will bring about a multitude of strategies for increasing return on assets by employing approaches to minimize what a company owns. Mostly, this will mean outsourcing or contracting for asset-heavy services, like manufacturing, and labor, where it's possible. More and more, work will be performed by contractors and contracted employees. This will change how financial risk is measured and, therefore, how companies are rated with respect to borrowing and how their debt and equity are valued.
- The push to decouple from permanent employees will shift a lot of risks for career development onto contractors and gig workers, themselves. The COVID virus and economic pressure will force changes in our system of higher education and entice entrepreneurs to leap into gaps to provide alternatives to traditional university degrees. While the most obvious effect of the employee-to-contractor shift will be the need to replace benefits that used to come with employment, such as healthcare and retirement funding, it may bring education into play as a valued benefit. Once upon a time, large companies ran substantial training and education programs to develop employees' skills, but this had waned. Now, major tech employers are developing their own curricula and delivering training to employees and independent workers again. Going forward, generalized education and training may become an attractive strategic component of companies' value proposition to prospective employees and contractors.

Traditional business management practices that no longer work

Many holdover management processes will not serve companies well as we go forward. Governance processes tied to quarterly and annual reporting cycles are particularly at odds with the level of agility required for sustainability. Governance processes must be formulated with RM in mind, so addressing some of the following issues should be linked to your overall AERM transformation plan:

- Legacy funding approaches tied to annual capital budgeting cycles are completely antithetical to agile organizations. Traditionally, projects have been proposed and funded (or not) annually but this all-or-nothing approach has all kinds of downsides, including:
  - Creating zero-sum games out of projects in which the sponsors, stakeholders and developers compete to expand or constrain the features and functions implemented while remaining within the original budget and schedule and maintaining the quality of the final work product.
  - Inhibiting experimentation and forgoing opportunities that may require course correction or even termination before they are complete. If the business changes or new or better approaches to delivery are discovered during the course of a project, fixed funding and the threat of having to rerun the gantlet of the approval process to change course inhibit revising what was originally proposed.
  - Incentivizing sponsors and implementers to ignore or underreport project risks so as not to jeopardize the potential for obtaining funding for their projects.
- Management approaches to governing projects and initiatives have historically alternated between centralized and decentralized, usually determined by which one failed most recently. Decentralized oversight of projects is necessary to achieve agility but adherence to standards, which requires at least some centralized oversight, must be maintained at the same time. A middle ground must be achieved, and a lot of companies seem not to have the appetite for the organizational redesign necessary to reach the necessary balance.
- Traditional command-and-control management structures don't distribute decision-making authority sufficiently to achieve agility. Overbearing governance impedes change and renders many companies unresponsive to threats and opportunities.
- System Development Lifecycles (SDLCs) have become a battleground. Waterfall, Agile, SAfE, Scrum, LeSS, XP, Kanban and on and on … Various SDLCs have been (and in some cases still are) viewed as panaceas to provide velocity, predictability and agility but they don't work unless they are executed under enlightened leadership, performed

competently and embedded in complementary governance and oversight structures. Needless to say, this is often not the case.
- Cliff Berg and group of eminent practitioners have undertaken an in-depth look at Agile's failings and written a book on the subject.[9] Insofar as it is important for you to build agile/DevOps development capabilities, it is worth your while to look at what he and the team has to say.
- Inconsistent or inappropriate balance between in-house and contracted expertise can result in companies with gaps in their ability to manage day-to-day operations and make rapid course corrections as they may be required. Companies that are not intentional about managing their skills inventory may find themselves lacking agility.

Traditional risk management practices are seriously flawed

As you evaluate the changes to these practices in the context of your prospective AERM transformation, you will also need to consider how you will manage the transformation program risks as well as how you will transform your operational ERM approaches.

In his book *The Failure of Risk Management: Why It's Broken and How to Fix It*,[10] Doug Hubbard presents a cogent view of how traditional RM is practiced at most companies today. The most important failings he identifies are:

- Companies employ risk analysis methods that are not only not defensible, they often produce misleading results.
- The methods employed, ranging from intuition to arbitrary rankings and weightings are highly susceptible to biases that are not understood, acknowledged, assessed or accounted for in the analysis of risks.
- Companies do not conduct retrospective analysis to determine whether the results of past assessments were accurate and often fail to update predictive models with recent performance information that could improve them.

In the opening of the book, Hubbard asks (with respect to RM commonly in use today):

> Do any of these methods work?
> Would anyone in the organization know if they didn't work?
> If they didn't work, what would be the consequences?

He concludes:

> For most organizations, the answers to these questions are all bad news.

[9] https://agile2.net/

[10] https://www.howtomeasureanything.com/riskmanagement/

This book is not about probabilistic techniques; however, proper application of them is intrinsic to good RM practice and where it is appropriate, I will include them in the observations and recommendations I present. Keeping in mind that RM involves (a) identifying risks, (b) analyzing them, (c) formulating preventive measures and responses to them and (d) evaluating the results of the process and improving it continuously, applying appropriate statistical analysis is critical to success. The agile part of AERM is intended to improve your ability to identify risks rapidly (a, above) but also to facilitate your ability perform b, c and d. As such, thoughts and material from Hubbard will find its way into various chapters of this book.

All management is risk management

Your company may have a formal RM function and from the outside, it may appear to be a mysterious discipline with its own set of abstruse approaches and processes. Nonetheless, RM is just another management discipline, one that should be integrated with others to improve your company's operating results.

Business results should be judged in light of the level of risk that was assumed in achieving them. If you engage in venture capital or oil and gas exploration and achieve a return similar to what would be expected from a commodity manufacturing business, is it a good thing? You may not have lost money (this year) but you're likely to in the future. Risk/reward analysis is intrinsic to evaluating performance and if you don't identify and account for risks properly, you will misjudge your success or failure. Your management challenge is to optimize your risk-adjusted results; therefore, recognizing, understanding and controlling risks is intrinsic to management.

Hubbard spends Chapter 5 in his book examining the use of terminology and it's worth paraphrasing several definitions that I will use throughout this book:

- Uncertainty: The lack of complete certainty about an outcome, state, result or value. This is measured by a set of probabilities for various outcomes.
- Strict Uncertainty: Uncertainty for which we have identified outcomes but do not have probabilities to assign to them.
- Risk: The probability of loss or a negative event. Hubbard asserts that this can only be applied to situations in which you have something at risk. The outcome of a dice roll, or card draw might produce a loss in a game, but it would not represent a risk to you unless you had made a bet.
- Risk/Reward Analysis: An analysis that takes account of the possible upside and downside of an investment.
- Ignorance: A state of Uncertainty in which we have identified neither outcomes nor probabilities—a case of 'unknown unknowns.'

Well-managed, organized enterprises:

- anticipate potential impediments to reaching their goals,
- have plans in place to overcome obstacles or navigate around them,
- exercise the maturity and discipline required to discontinue efforts that are unlikely to achieve their targeted benefits and
- apply ongoing efforts to analyze and account for uncertainties that create risks and then mitigate them.

Mature, well-managed and organized enterprises demonstrate a conscious approach to RM. In fact, most day-to-day decisions are guided by risk considerations. When we perform a set of tasks in a specific order to ensure, we achieve the result we're aiming for, that's RM. When we select a specific restaurant to dine at with some friends because we think they'll enjoy it, that may well be also. The only difference between these examples is that day-to-day RM in our personal lives is more likely to be unconscious than conscious. Unfortunately, a lot of RM in commercial and professional settings is performed unconsciously, which can lead to sub-optimal, if not downright disastrous, results.

YOU ALREADY MANAGE RISKS—YOU INTUITIVELY KNOW HOW TO DO THIS

Why do you put your wallet, keys or purse in the same place every night? So that you can find them when you leave in the morning. By doing this, you mitigate the risk of having to scramble for things you need to take with you when you are under time pressure to get out of the house the next day.

Homeowner's insurance, retirement savings, spare tire in your car? All implement RM strategies—transfer, avoid and mitigate, respectively.

You establish processes and procedures in your business to mitigate the risk that 'things' won't be done properly. Software development methodologies are intended to make the development process more predictable and less prone to creating flawed software that will require time, effort and money to fix. Supply chains are diversified to provide alternatives if the primary source of an input fails. Manufacturing facilities are dispersed to be closer to the markets they serve, minimize shipping costs and provide fault tolerance.

In some cases, you are trying to avoid the costs of negative events, such as not being able to find your wallet or having a prime supplier fall behind on delivery, and in others, you are trying to realize upsides, like minimizing costs or increasing revenues and profits.

But are we actually any good at it?

How do we measure the success of RM efforts? It's complicated. If we design a process or a product to avoid specific problems, we can measure their (hopefully decreasing) rate of occurrence. We can set targets to limit them and assess how well we are doing at avoiding them. Can we relax the constraints we implemented in our design and achieve the same results with reduced cost or impact? Cost-effectiveness is also a crucial target in RM. Lenders may test their lending criteria by making loans that just fail their credit scoring models' criteria to see whether they are overly restrictive or not. If enough of the test loans are repaid in a timely fashion, then they re-evaluate their criteria and models.

To assess our success, we must also acknowledge and analyze failures. Have we had negative events for which we were not prepared? Were they foreseeable? If so, why and how did we miss them and fail to prepare for them in advance? Did the provisions we made for specific events work as planned when they occurred? If not, why not? Did we find unanticipated correlated problems when events occurred? Did we not anticipate a chain of events that caused a much bigger impact than we planned for? If so, why and what should we do about it?

It is fair to say that planning to address isolated risks in the abstract can be relatively straightforward. Dealing with complex interactions, however, can be far from it. First, if you fail to identify a risk, you will certainly also fail to prepare for it. Secondly, if you do not recognize ensuing effects that a negative event may create, you will not prepare for them, either.

So, managing risks requires that you recognize them and that you identify correlated risks related to them, explicitly assess them and select and implement treatments—preventative steps or mitigations for their effects. Doing this efficiently, with reliability, comprehensiveness, effectiveness and with minimal costs, requires senior management commitment, dedicated staffing, knowledge and repeatable processes and procedures.

As we go forward, we will examine and make suggestions on all these issues.

WHY YOU NEED MULTI-DISCIPLINARY, INTEGRATED RISK MANAGEMENT

By this point, it should be obvious that we are advocating for your transformation to a more agile organization. Probably, you're already begun—created internal collaboration capabilities and customer-facing, web-enabled services. But you probably have a long, long way to go before you have reached an optimal level of business agility.

Wherever you are in the evolutionary process, ERM must evolve and become more agile at the same time, or you can impair your ability to recognize and manage risks as they are created or transformed by your evolving business.

Why multi-disciplinary?

The disciplines alluded to earlier—Enterprise and Business Architecture, Business Process Management, Transformation Portfolio, Program and Project Management—as well as Scenario Analysis, Strategic Planning and Transformation Road mapping, are intrinsic to your managing your company. There are, or should be, planning, operating, quality-controlling, monitoring and performance management processes and practices associated with each of them. In addition to informing, guiding and governing how you do what your company does, you collect a great deal of valuable, raw information while executing them.

ERM is an information-intensive discipline; if you cannot see things that should be addressed, you will not address them. Assembling a group of people with indeterminate levels of insight into the company and its operations in a conference room and having them try to build an inventory of these things is a sure way to miss some of them. Extracting what is passively generated from your governance processes and day-to-day activities and experiences is a good way to be more comprehensive. You're already doing it, more or less, but you need to develop a focus on root sources of risks, which may not be obvious to you. So, looking at your company through the lens of each of the disciplines you use to run it will provide perspective that can enable you to put together a (more) complete and deeply nuanced picture of where you should focus your RM efforts.

If you have an EA team and it focuses on documenting as-built, after-the-fact results of change and is not integrated into the process of helping to fashion it, then it is less likely to help you identify emerging or morphing risks. If you evolve the design of your business processes and then involve your business process management team to automate them, then you're missing an opportunity to prepare to manage new or evolving risks so that your treatments can be applied as the revised processes and automation are going into operation. If you are not road mapping and transforming in a disciplined fashion, you could easily be missing cases in which changes you are making propagate risks unbeknownst to you.

Why integrated?

Risks arise from decisions you make and actions you take. Ideally, risks attached to actions you take—execution of Business-as-Usual (BAU) operations—are addressed via policies, practices, processes and procedures. It should be OK, once these are running smoothly to lower the scrutiny level. Decisions, other than those integrated and embodied in BAU operational processes, may occur regularly or irregularly and your RM team must be present for you to manage the risks associated with them.

In the case of higher-level decisions, such as an acquisition, you would expect RM to be an intrinsic component of the analytical process and it probably is, up to a point. In acquisitions, due diligence is an important RM tool, perhaps the acquirer's only opportunity to identify and assess non-obvious risks that don't appear in the acquisition target's financial statements or that may involve differences in governance or operational processes or culture.

A Corporate Taxonomy, as defined in this Wikipedia article,[11] is

> "… the hierarchical classification of entities of interest of an enterprise, organization or administration, used to classify documents, digital assets and other information. Taxonomies can cover virtually any type of physical or conceptual entities (products, processes, knowledge fields, human groups, etc.) at any level of granularity."

An example of a commercial taxonomy is the WAND Banking Taxonomy,[12] which

> *"… has 1,717 terms with 1,540 synonyms covering banking processes, retail banking, regulations, products, fees, risk management, banking documents, and much more. The WAND Banking Taxonomy is specifically designed to help banks tag and organize their unstructured information with relevant, industry-specific concepts, processes, subjects, and document types."*

Your taxonomy is an important lens that you can apply to focus due diligence and analytical efforts. When you apply your taxonomy to risks that you identify, you classify them with respect to characteristics that you have determined as being important to managing them properly, and this facilitates your ability to recognize and treat them. In performing due diligence on an acquisition, what you see as a risk, with a presumed cause or source, your acquisition target may view as something entirely different, something which didn't rate mentioning to you or enacting a prescriptive treatment in the course of their operations.

For example, a *third-party risk* is defined by Awake[13] as "… the potential threat presented to organizations' employee and customer data, financial information and operations from the organization's supply-chain and other outside parties that provide products and/or services and have access to privileged systems."

[11] https://en.wikipedia.org/wiki/Corporate_taxonomy
[12] https://www.wandinc.com/taxonomies/wand-banking-taxonomy
[13] https://awakesecurity.com/glossary/third-party-risk/

SecurityScorecard[14] has a more comprehensive definition, which includes factors other than just those relating to privileged data.

If you apply your taxonomic tag 'third-party' to some of your risks, you will be able to identify similarities among them and this should facilitate your identifying reusable treatments, controls and policies that you can employ to manage similar risks. This will accelerate your ability to react and respond to them as they are created by your evolving operations. Thus, if you decide to outsource a process, adding the supplier as new Enabler to your EA model should trigger a risk review and if you've tagged the supplier as third-party, it should point you to where you will need to look to see whether you have already figured out how to deal with the associated risks.

In the case of BAU-related risks, decisions crop up when a case arises for which there is no prescribed action or when there is a need to revise the business process. If your RM team is not integrated to the degree necessary to recognize and respond to either of these events, then your RM comprehensiveness will slip, just that little bit. Obviously, if you amass enough of these cases, your control over your risks can be seriously compromised.

Depending on a periodic review process to identify new or morphed risks is a bit like driving while looking in the rear-view mirror. It's OK for a few seconds while you are on a straight road but fails spectacularly when a curve comes along. The process you will go through while you compile your starting risk inventory, which may be well stocked with risks from your existing risk register, will hopefully be a one-time thing. However, many existing risk inventories are structured around avoiding undesirable outcomes more than they are identifying root causes. Revisiting the risks in the register to refocus on source-of-risk and risk/reward analysis is an important task and crucial to reorienting your RM posture. Once you have refocused and developed intuition about risk sources, you can apply continuous RM best by integrating your risk team in tight collaboration with operating units whenever decisions are being made.

Any transformation has risks

So, you need to transform to maintain your competitiveness, you need to acquire the information and expertise to do it in a controlled fashion and you need to be able to update your risk controls in parallel with all of it. You must understand that transformation itself creates risks that you must control so that you can execute it in a choreographed and disciplined manner.

As opposed to the way things may work at your company now, job roles, processes, disposition of assets and other elements of your anatomy will change:

[14] https://securityscorecard.com/blog/six-types-of-vendor-risk-that-are-important-to-monitor

- There may be a substantial effort to re-architect the company's transactional (administrative) systems.
- There will be a substantial investment in analytics, AI and ML. This will become incorporated into product management processes and, in some cases, products, themselves.
- Product Management will fuse traditional product managers with technologists that enable integration of digital offerings and user experiences.
- The velocity with which your products and services evolve will increase dramatically. There is no way that traditional, centrally managed IT can sustain this. Some IT staff will migrate into business units.
- The rate at which business systems evolve will increase dramatically. The integrated product management/development team will acquire operational responsibilities in addition to their development responsibilities.
- Authority for product-level decisions will be dispersed to executives with P&L responsibility for them and Product Management teams will gain increasing discretion over investments relating to features and services that can make the products for which they are responsible more competitive and profitable.
- A portfolio of experimental, developmental businesses will be implemented and actively managed. Ideas will be funded, tried out and terminated within three to six months if they do not meet performance targets.
- Corporate-level annual budgeting and legacy initiative funding will disappear for all but the largest initiatives. Even then, the all-or-nothing paradigm will disappear in favor of continuous review.

So, you can see that your organization, responsibility and authority structures will have to change. Your approach to investment vetting and management will need to change. You may need to rethink your product and service portfolio. You will need to adopt new thinking about how technology management is integrated into the organization. All of these have interdependencies and represent substantial challenges with significant risks. Just trying to transform, then, is a process that is fraught with risk and, given that this is tied to your ability to be competitive, doubly so.

CONTROLLED TRANSFORMATION IS KEY TO MANAGING TRANSFORMATION RISKS

Many companies have (and suffer from) ***Emergent Architecture***. ***Emergent Architecture*** is what happens when an organization evolves in an unplanned fashion, and it becomes more likely to happen as the need to evolve accelerates. With decreasing lead time and increasing urgency to make decisions, acquiring missing information or accounting for subtle yet important interactions and dependencies across the organization frequently take a back seat to expedient implementation. Risk considerations are often left for later, when the train has already left the station. Make no mistake, emergent architecture is a risk, to agility most of all.

Controlled Transformation helps prevent emergent architecture. Performing it requires that you have collected and maintain sufficient information about the architecture of your company (EA and BA models, at a minimum) and can enable you to identify the implications of all the changes you will need to make to all the elements of your enterprise to achieve the result you intend. Uncontrolled transformations contribute to emergent architecture and ***Technical Debt***.

Technical Debt accrues from design decisions that favor urgent needs to the detriment of longer-term considerations. For instance, ***Technical Debt*** may arise from applications built expediently to respond to imminent threats but aren't architected to be enhanced easily later, that burden future enhancement projects with extra work that could have been avoided. Dumping a new set of responsibilities on an existing department when it is not structured or trained to support them adequately creates organizational or process debt.

Every transformation and every system implementation requires that your enterprise find an appropriate point on the continuum between knowing everything and doing nothing (paralysis by analysis) and knowing nothing and doing everything (shooting from the hip.) Ideally, your company will have invested sufficient time and resources to enable you to avoid short-sighted, sub-optimal designs when faced with a need to transform.

THE DISCIPLINES YOU WILL NEED TO EXECUTE YOUR CONTROLLED TRANSFORMATION

Preparing for and executing a transformation this all-encompassing will be a significant challenge. You will need to define:

- The target (to-be) state of your transformed company,
- A roadmap of how you will get there—what initiatives you will execute in what order, what interim states you expect to achieve along the way,
- The operational architecture of your target-state company, keeping in mind that the to-be target you started with will continue to evolve as you execute your transformation.

Defining and structuring your transformation will require an enormous amount of information and disciplines that most companies employ, whether consciously or unconsciously, are an excellent place to obtain it. These disciplines[15] include:

- **Strategic and Competitive Analysis**
  How Strategic and Competitive Analysis is performed is unique to each company and possibly even among business units. What is important is that your company's EA be consistent with and appropriate for your strategy. If you articulate strategy so that you can relate it to the elements of your EA model, it will facilitate your identifying important dependencies that can indicate areas that warrant scrutiny for potential risks.
- **Enterprise Architecture**
  Performing EA involves creating a model of your company. The elements or building blocks of this model include:
  - the Markets and Segments in which you compete,
  - the Products and Services you sell,
  - Value Streams—the portfolio of capabilities (see below) you exercise to produce the things you sell,
  - Capabilities—the things you must be able to do to produce the things you sell, which are bundled in value streams through which they are delivered, and
  - Enablers—the people, processes, technology, physical assets and information assets required to enable your capabilities.
    What is important about this model is that it shows how the elements of your enterprise are interconnected and interdependent in enabling your company to fulfill its strategic mission. Understanding the relationships among the elements is critical to identifying risks in your operations and should inform the transformation plan to ensure that nothing falls through the cracks in the process.
- **Business Architecture**
  BA is focused on the products and services, value streams and capabilities that are (or should be) represented in the EA model. The two models are strongly intertwined and must remain synchronized to provide the value that they are supposed to.
- **Transformation Planning and Road Mapping**
  When change is required, transformation planning and road mapping should be employed to define a program to accomplish it. Rather than simply updating a system supporting a capability, planning and road mapping accounts for the impact of the contemplated change across related elements of your company's EA, allowing you to create a comprehensive RM plan and identifying opportunities to avoid creating technical and other forms of debt. It should be tied to the EA and BA

[15] These will be covered in greater detail in section on Integration.

models, allowing a full picture of what will be added or deleted, how the models will change and what the impacts on existing, transitional and future risks will be.

- **Capabilities Enablement— People, Processes, Technology, Information and Physical Assets**
  Understanding how your company does what it does requires understanding what it has in place and how it's structured to deliver or execute on its capabilities.

The following disciplines are associated with various enablers:

- People: Organizational Change Management (OCM): When changes to your organizational structure are required, organizational change management should be applied to define the process by which they will be executed and integrated into your organization. Changes in organization structure, roles and responsibilities, job content, knowledge requirements and reporting structures must all be handled appropriately to ensure a smooth transition. Many, if not most, transformations that fail can be traced back to people issues that were not handled properly. Effective OCM is an important transformation risk mitigation tool.
- Process: Business Process Management (BPM): Efficient business processes are critical to the cost-effectiveness and quality of your operations. Business Process Automation (BPA), Robotic Process Automation (RPA), Digital Process Automation (DPA) and Business Process Re-engineering (BPR) are all employed to improve reliability, increase process throughput and improve the user experience with your operations. This article[16] is a good introduction to these methods and tools.
  Processes are critical elements to evaluate for RM requirements. Many employ decision criteria or implement defined policies and business rules that can be sources of risk or require review of assumptions.
- **Technology: Technical Architecture (TA):** Technical Architecture includes all of your systems, your networks, your infrastructure and the architecture of your data. Optimal TA is a balance involving capacity, performance, scalability, elasticity, security, agility, costs, risks, technical debt and numerous other considerations. Because technology is evolving so rapidly, aspects of TA are overseen by a number of specialist architects, focused on solutions, infrastructure, data and others.
- **Information: Data Architecture and Data Governance (DA and DG):** Data is a strategic asset of your business and critical enabler of the business analytics, AI and ML that will drive your business. As you progress through your digital transformation, you will begin to

[16] https://searchcio.techtarget.com/tip/Process-automation-technologies-evolve-RPA-vs-BPA-vs-DPA

amass diverse raw data at a furious rate. Data Architecture and Data Governance are the disciplines that will enable you to structure, manage and exploit the data you're collecting.

- **Physical Assets and Facilities:** Even if you are in a totally digital services business, your physical assets and facilities are intrinsic to enabling your operations. Often, risks arise from dependencies that are not recognized when changes are considered or when operations are restructured. Mapping the relationships among elements of your EA model and physical assets and facilities will help ensure that these connections are not overlooked.
- **Program and Project Management** (PgM, PM)
  Transformations are normally executed in defined scopes that form Programs and Projects. PgM and PM discipline is employed to ensure predictable execution, based on comprehensive portfolio management, planning and monitoring. As more and more digital services are managed via an Agile SDLC supported by DevOps, PM approaches are changing to make them manageable.

In the next chapter, we will explore what business agility looks like and the interplay between strategies for the digital age and the need for Digital Transformation.

CHAPTER SUMMARY

Key concepts addressed in this chapter:

- VUCA, our current state—A plethora of forces are creating change and uncertainty in the environment in which you run your company. You will have to adapt to the new reality by becoming more agile.
- You must execute a Digital Transformation if you are going to compete successfully in today's markets. Adding digital products and services is table stakes in the new game, even if you sell traditional physical products or personal services.
- You need a new perspective on strategy and execution. Product and company lifespans are becoming shorter, and you must be prepared to pivot rapidly to exploit new opportunities or react to threats from new and smaller competitors. Your risk profile will grow and change rapidly as you navigate your environment.
- Given how fast things are changing, traditional management practices will not enable you to steer and control your company's evolution at the pace required for you to maintain your competitiveness. They are simply too slow to execute and cannot accommodate the distributed authority and accountability structures that a digital business requires.

- You will need to transform in a planned and controlled manner, not just change. Changing without proper planning exposes you to the risks of emergent architecture and technical debt.
- Business agility and RM can only be achieved if you integrate RM with the other management disciplines you probably already use on a day-to-day basis. The disciplines that you need to ensure that you transform on a predictable and controlled trajectory are the same ones you will need on an ongoing basis.
- RM as it is commonly practiced is flawed, often based on incomplete discovery, qualitative not quantitative analysis and periodic updates. A new approach to RM is needed. It must become more distributed, continuous and quantitative and be supported by appropriate automation.

Chapter 2

Enterprise risk management today

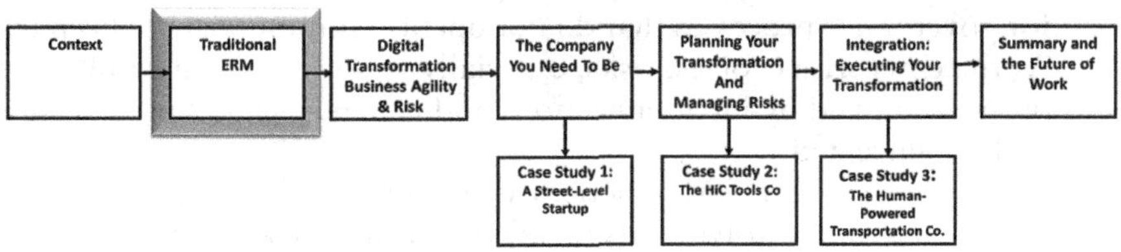

COVERED IN THIS CHAPTER

- Before attempting to manage risk, we must come to a common understanding of what it is. In this chapter, I address some seminal questions: What is risk? How is it measured and how do we deal with it? What are Risk Appetite and Risk Tolerance?
- Traditional Risk Management (TRM) practices incorporate several steps, from articulating the context in which risk management (RM) will be performed to defining, executing and monitoring risk treatments. Enterprise Risk Management (ERM), which differs from TRM in scope and comprehensiveness, may employ similar processes, just at a holistic enterprise level as opposed to a siloed or domain level.
- The processes many companies employ to identify and assess risks are often practiced unevenly across domains and may not be particularly comprehensive. This can be the result of who performs risk assessments. Also, many companies employ simplified risk ranking and rating approaches not based on appropriate quantitative methods. Finally, many company's assessments fail to properly identify and scrutinize decision processes, a potent source of risks, which then go untreated.
- Using qualitative measures like 'low-medium-high' and heat maps as proxies for probabilistic analysis can be a significant source of error and omission in the RM process. To the degree that AI, ML

DOI: 10.1201/9781003188605-3

and Business Analytics will become more everyday tools, the people, knowledge, experience and skills necessary to become more quantitative should become more readily available than they may be today.

- Traditional RM (TRM) and Enterprise RM (ERM), as they are practiced by many companies, will run into the same issues that other processes already are. Change will accelerate, and the inflow of events requiring responses will increase and become denser. Pressure to do more with fewer people will hit RM teams, just as it has every other operational team. Automation is the only way that this can be accommodated. RM as it is often done now, even where it is done well, is not a sustainable model.

  To remain competitive, the enterprise will have to change too fast for governance processes that do not operate continuously to keep up. As the enterprise evolves, risks, especially subtle ones that result from or are amplified by interconnections and dependencies, will be missed and go untreated.
- A benefit of better RM practices is an improved ability to identify developing and evolving risks *while* business transformations are being analyzed and planned, which can contribute mightily to their success. In much the same way that better quality is realized when processes are designed to achieve it than when inspection is applied to weed out flawed output after the fact, better RM is realized when risk-based discipline is integrated into business management disciplines and processes.

INTRODUCTION

Prior to delving into how RM has traditionally been practiced, it's reasonable to say that little can be more frustrating than trying to get your head around how you should do this from scratch. If you do a search on the Internet for 'Risk Assessment' what you will soon learn is that it is a free-form exercise. You will be advised to:

- Identify hazards,
- Decide who will be harmed and how,
- Evaluate risks and decide on precautions,
- Record your findings and implement them and
- Review your assessment and revise, if necessary.

Really!

This same advice is repeated, in one form or another, on site after site. It's much more of *what* you should be doing but tells you virtually nothing about *how* to do it.

This advice boils down to:

- Identify risks,
- Figure out what to do about them,
- Review results (evaluate lessons learned) and
- Repeat as things change.

Obviously, what you don't know about, you can't deal with. Therefore, identifying risks is absolutely necessary (but not sufficient) to address them comprehensively. Merely convening a meeting of the minds in a conference room and making a list, no matter how extensive, is unlikely to surface all your risks.

The Delphi Method was developed by the RAND Corporation in the 1950s and is still practiced today. It is intended to elicit unbiased input on a subject of interest or concern from multiple expert sources and help converge on a consensus. It involves getting experts to ponder independently from one-another and then collect their thoughts, suggestions or solutions, collate and distribute the unattributed collection back out to the group for another round of consideration. The cycle is repeated until the participants or the leader feel that they have made as much progress as is possible. It is described here.[1] It's useful but isn't sufficient to fully identify and articulate all your risks, either.

There are alternative methods described in this paper,[2] such as *Environmental Scanning*, *Issues Management* and *Emerging Issues Analysis*. The *Nominal Group Technique* is described in this paper.[3] The fact is, any or all of these methods can work; the question is—will they work in your company? What determines the comprehensiveness of any risk identification effort is the information that is available and accessible, the knowledge levels of the people involved, the time available to conduct the process and, perhaps, a little imagination and creativity. Without these things, risks will be missed and, if you are fortunate, they will not be major ones.

Ultimately, this is one of the main motivators for this book—you need a framework to apply to help understand your company, its anatomy and the interdependencies of its components to even begin to create a comprehensive ERM program. If you believe that you have a good framework and an effective ERM program, and you might, then you must still consider how you will evolve your ERM capabilities to accommodate increased volume and complexity as the pace of change increases.

If you are establishing or re-establishing your framework, you will need to plan how you will employ it to maximize the probability of achieving

1 https://www.rand.org/topics/delphi-method.html
2 http://158.132.155.107/posh97/private/research/methods-delphi/LANG.html
3 https://www.ncbi.nlm.nih.gov/pmc/articles/PMC4909789/

positive outcomes, prevent negative outcomes and how to do so in an optimally efficient and cost-effective manner. But how do you do that?

The framework you should use for this should account for your strategy—the markets you sell into and the products and services you sell, and your internal anatomy—your Enterprise and Business Architectures. The thorough discovery and documentation required for these will ensure that little is likely to fall through the cracks and result in unidentified risks. If you are familiar at all with Enterprise and Business Architecture, you may think of them as pernicious time, effort and cost sinks that produce voluminous reams of shelfware and walls full of colorful diagrams of questionable value. As many practice these disciplines, you wouldn't be too far wrong. However, we propose to perform them at a level of detail that will not be onerous to maintain, and which will provide invaluable information to guide RM processes.

With this in mind, let's examine where RM as a modern corporate discipline came from, how it has evolved into ERM and how it is commonly practiced today.

THE EMERGENCE AND EVOLUTION OF RISK MANAGEMENT

This article by Georges Dionne[4] is the most frequently-cited reference on this topic. He identifies that formalized study of RM dates to the end of World War II and it was originally focused on insurance and insurable hazards and risks. Dionne identifies that soon thereafter,

> Other forms of risk management, alternatives to market insurance, surfaced during the 1950s when market insurance was perceived as very costly and incomplete for protection against pure risk. The use of derivatives as risk management instruments arose during the 1970s, and expanded rapidly during the 1980s, as companies intensified their financial risk management. International risk regulation began in the 1980s, and financial firms developed internal risk management models and capital calculation formulas to hedge against unanticipated risks and reduce regulatory capital. Concomitantly, governance of risk management became essential, integrated risk management was introduced and the chief risk officer positions were created. Nonetheless, these regulations, governance rules and risk management methods failed to prevent the financial crisis that began in 2007.

[4] https://scholar.google.com/scholar_url?url=https://www.cirrelt.ca/documentstravail/cirrelt-2013-56.pdf&hl=en&sa=X&ei=PKYfYd_RLNvSsQLVl42ACw&scisig=AAGBfm3V-oGqBNYKMxiiOPy8sdYvCmpnVg&oi=scholarr

In the 1960s to the 1990s approaches to manage insurable and non-insurable hazards evolved substantially. Initially, financial risks and operational or hazard risks were treated as two separate disciplines. In the 1970s and 1980s tools for addressing financial risks, such as futures, derivatives and portfolio management techniques, developed and matured. In the 1980s, companies began to look for alternative protections to overpriced insurance and prevention and self-insurance instruments and other practices arose and matured. Around that time, coverage for operational business activities, such as work-related illnesses and accidents appeared. In the early 1990s, integrated operational and liquidity management approaches emerged. In the late 1990s, Boards became more involved in Integrated Risk Management and the Chief Risk Officer (CRO) emerged.

> Dionne observes, "The goal of corporate risk management is to create a reference framework that will allow companies to handle risk and uncertainty. Risks are present in nearly all of firms' financial and economic activities. The risk identification, assessment and management process is part of companies' strategic development; it must be designed and planned at the highest level, namely the board of directors."

This provides some historical perspective on where the divide between RM and ERM originated. Based on what I have read and critiques I have received, I have come to believe that what many call RM is performed below the enterprise level and addresses risks that are specific to the business unit, mostly operational ones. ERM is integrated, addressing all forms of risk that may impact a company's ability to realize its goals, regardless of the context in which they occur.

Like so many other management disciplines, everyone has their own idea of what the definitions of these two things are. I believe that for our purposes, this one will be more than adequate.

RM VS. TRM VS. ERM VS. AERM

In order to avoid ambiguity, it seems a good idea to establish the usage we will employ.

According to Ideagen,[5] Traditional Risk Management (TRM) is "… primarily concerned with loss exposures generated by hazard risk. This method excludes from its remit all exposure attributed to business risk and instead prioritises managing health and safety, purchasing insurance and controlling financial recovery."

---

[5] https://www.ideagen.com/thought-leadership/blog/traditional-risk-management-vs-enterprise-risk-management-which-approach-is-best

and Enterprise Risk Management (ERM) is

> … an extension of traditional risk management to elevate it to a strategic organisational level in response to a rapidly changing risk climate. Not only does it assess risk through a much wider lens but it also facilitates a more holistic approach that looks at opportunities as well as threats.

According to the Cowell James Forge Insurance Group,[6] the difference between TRM and ERM is "… the focus on insurable versus non-insurable risks. TRM focuses solely on risks that can be insured."

In this article,[7] the Blackburn Group states that

> In a traditional risk management service structure, the effort is departmentalized and focused primarily on hazard risks. Using this approach, an organization rarely makes relative comparisons among its risks to determine how they interact with one another or to evaluate their cumulative effect on the organization. Conversely, in an ERM environment, there is a senior executive or Chief Risk Officer (CRO) who compares and evaluates all of the risks the organization faces in a more holistic way.

and they differentiate ERM and TRM with the following observations:

- "**Strategic application**. An ERM approach is integrated into an organizations [sic] business decisions. Because the effort is enterprise-wide, it supersedes any departmental or functional autonomy to encourage continuous review and support of the organizations most value-based objectives.
- **Risks considered**. ERM involves managing all of the risks affecting an organization's ability to meet its goals, regardless of the types of risks being considered. This carefully reviewed and benchmarked approach allows organizations the ability to stay focused on key areas of prosperity and survival.
- **Performance metrics**. ERM emphasizes results-based performance measurement throughout the organization. Results indicate whether a risk management technique helped to achieve a business goal, such as return on investment or return on assets. All forms of risk management, including ERM, are intended to help minimize the adverse effects of missed opportunities and losses. The specific benefits of ERM include

6 https://cjfig.com/blog/the-difference-between-risk-management-and-enterprise-risk-management/

7 https://www.blackburngroup.com/newsroom/enterprise-risk-management-erm-versus-traditional-risk-management-best-practice

> maximizing the possible opportunities for growth, minimizing the expected organizational losses and therefore increasing the expected income and asset value, and reducing the residual uncertainty in all areas of the enterprise."

In a 2016 whitepaper,[8] Mark S. Beasley, Deloitte Professor of ERM and Director of the ERM Initiative at NC State University, observes that the objective of ERM is to "... develop a holistic, portfolio view of the most significant risks to the achievement of the entity's most important objectives. The "e" in ERM signals that ERM seeks to create a top-down, enterprise view of all the significant risks that might impact the business. In other words, ERM attempts to create a basket of all types of risks that might have an impact – both positively and negatively – on the viability of the business."

while in TRM,

> "Each of these functional leaders is charged with managing risks related to their key areas of responsibility. This traditional approach to risk management is often referred to as silo or stove-pipe risk management whereby each silo leader is responsible for managing or elevating risks within their silo"

I am sure that if you performed your own search, you would find any number of alternative definitions, most of which would boil down to:

- RM and TRM are much the same thing. They are siloed within specific domains, address mainly operational risks and are overseen by people within them that are domain experts.
- ERM is a more inclusive discipline that focuses on the risks that TRM does, but also includes risks at the corporate level that have to do with the company achieving its strategic goals. ERM is managed at the corporate level by executives that report to the company's executive management and/or the board of directors.

Going forward, we will assume that a company practices either TRM or ERM and will refer to them, generically as RM, when specific scope and the discipline's niche in the organization chart is not an issue.

The recommendations that I offer in the book are geared toward your company's migrating from TRM to ERM, if you have not already done so, and beyond that, from ERM to Agile ERM or AERM.

8 https://erm.ncsu.edu/az/erm/i/chan/library/What_is_Enterprise_Risk_Management.pdf

CURRENT STATE OF RM

Before we make any effort to explore how RM should transform, we need to establish a common understanding of how it begins, evolves and operates in most places. The steps, below, are a common path by which RM emerges and evolves.

- **Set Context in Which RM Will Operate**
  RM design must be specific to each organization. It must account for the markets in which you operate, your organization's business strategy, how it's constructed to execute on that strategy and its appetite and tolerance for risk. Then, you must identify who in your organization will be responsible for RM, who will be responsible for governance and how the function will integrate and work with the rest of the organization. Establishing and evolving the ERM function will require articulating each of these things before you can create a framework to identify and manage risks.
- **Establish Risk Appetite and Tolerance**
  Managing risk is always a balancing act and if the right balance is to be struck, your organization must articulate its willingness to experience negative outcomes as you strive for returns. If you cannot delineate what you are willing to accept and what you are not, then you cannot articulate what you are willing to do to avoid or at least mitigate what you cannot accept.
- **Identify Risk Sources**
  A map of the organization that will guide the *risk assessment* is required to create an actionable RM plan. A discovery process can then be conducted to assemble an inventory of risks, the comprehensiveness of which will ultimately determine the overall success of your ERM effort. This step is more about identifying where the risks are than it is about identifying individual risks.
- **Conduct a Risk Assessment:** Inventory and Analyze Risks and Develop Management Strategies
  The map will guide the process of conducting the risk assessment to identify, inventory, analyze and develop plans to treat (prevent to the degree possible and prepare to react where prevention is not possible) and manage risks. Comprehensiveness is crucial because if you don't identify risks, you certainly can't plan for them, and it is often unforeseen and unplanned-for risks that do the most damage.
- **Establish RM Controls and Processes,** Integrate into Management Processes
  The steps outlined to this point will produce a baseline or a starting point for RM, which should include an inventory of risks, the signals that you will use to alert you that an event that requires a response has occurred and the mitigation—the action that is prescribed. In this

step, you will put in place controls, people and processes to monitor and respond to events as per your plan when required. ERM must be integrated with your organization's management and operational structure. It cannot be effective if it operates in a vacuum independent of decision processes and operations.

- **Implement, Execute and Monitor ERM Performance**
  Once established, your ERM function should operate on both a day-to-day or business-as-usual basis and at higher strategic levels. You should be monitoring whether systematic operational processes are performing within the specifications defined for them as well as whether higher-level decision processes are incorporating risk considerations properly.
- **Evolve and Improve ERM Performance**
  Part of establishing the ERM function should be specifying a process for monitoring and assessing its performance. It is important to know whether relevant events are addressed adequately by your controls and whether the responses you specified for them are producing the results you expected. It is equally important to be able to identify when your controls are excessive—eliminating negative events but at too high a cost.

In the following section, we will explore each of these steps in more detail.

THE ERM PROCESS

Set context in which ERM will operate

As we said, above, the context in which your organization operates is specific to it. Articulating and documenting relevant aspects of your context consists of four tasks:

- Developing an understanding of the markets and environment in which the enterprise operates, its strategic goals and how it is constituted to enable it to achieve them,
- Understanding the organization culture in which ERM will function,
- Articulating the enterprise's risk appetite and tolerance and
- Inventorying the enterprise to identify where risks exist.

Just as your context is specific to you, your company's is specific to it. Things that are of little concern to you may be vitally important to others. If your company doesn't operate in a specific regulated industry, you don't need to spend time worrying about regulatory risks in that space. Defining and articulating the context is the only way to ensure that the ERM function addresses known and relevant risks comprehensively and serves to guide and inform the workplan for implementing it.

Establish risk appetite and tolerance

Every business has risks. No outcome, good or bad, is guaranteed and, as we've already observed, management is all about maximizing positive results and minimizing negative ones. To do this competently, it is necessary to establish what level of risk is acceptable and how much the enterprise is willing to stretch its risk limits to reach for an opportunity and then manage so as to remain within the limits.

At some point, even the potential for an outsize return is outweighed by the risk of an unacceptable outcome, such as bankruptcy. Pursuing such opportunities either out of ignorance of or disregard for risks or transcending the accepted risk appetite or tolerance is simply management malpractice.

Independent of any other ERM steps, the business must establish its ***risk appetite*** and ***risk tolerance***. These are measures of how much variance in performance, financial or otherwise, the enterprise is willing to accept in the normal course of business and how much deviation from that is acceptable. To paraphrase a definition on this site,[9] ***Risk Appetite*** might be represented by the speed limit on a highway, determined in consideration of capacity, throughput and safety. ***Risk Tolerance*** might be represented as the range of speeds outside of which, motorists will be ticketed.

Some businesses are inherently riskier than others—venture capital investing vs. commodity manufacturing, for example—though neither is without its risks. Venture Capitalists (VCs) invest millions in startups, hoping that one out of ten will succeed. If and when they find a Google, a Microsoft or an Amazon, they do very well, indeed, and more than cover the 90%+ of their investments that go bust. No one running a business that manufactures commodity products could bear a 90% risk of failure and, commensurately, the return on investment in such businesses is far lower than what VCs must achieve on their successful businesses to keep themselves in the game.

What is risk?

Risk is the *probability* that things will not turn out as you expect them to or as you hope they will and that you will incur some type of loss or other sub-optimal outcome. **Risk** is tightly related to ***variance***.

Consider the following:

You can buy books wholesale. You can pay $12 for a $25 book. You buy four books for $48 and then set off to sell them. You now have $48 at risk. There is a distribution of probabilities for the number of books you will sell, your net profit if you sell that many and the probability weighted expected outcome shown in the Table 2.1, below:

[9] https://www.fairinstitute.org/blog/risk-appetite-vs.-risk-tolerance.-whats-the-difference

Table 2.1 Data for the probability example.

Case	*Probability*	*# Sold*	*Cost*	*Revenue*	*Net Profit*	*Probability-Weighted Outcome*
Base	10%	0	$48	$0	−$48	−4.80
Base	20%	1	$48	$25	−$23	−4.60
Base	35%	2	$48	$50	$2	0.70
Base	25%	3	$48	$75	$27	6.75
Base	10%	4	$48	$100	$52	5.20
With Adv	5%	0	$53	$0	−$53	−2.65
With Adv	20%	1	$53	$25	−$28	−5.60
With Adv	25%	2	$53	$50	−$3	−0.75
With Adv	35%	3	$53	$75	$22	7.70
With Adv	15%	4	$53	$100	$47	7.05

The five rows labeled Base contain the Base case. In this case, you have a 10% chance of selling no books, which would result in a $48 loss. This would contribute -$4.80 to the aggregate expected value of your venture. The remaining rows are treated similarly. If you pursue this venture, then, your expected net profit (the sum of the probability-weighted outcomes for the case) would be $3.25, which equates to a return of 6.77% on your $48 investment.

How can you improve your prospective results from your book sale? You can:

- Find a cheaper place to buy the books, reducing the value you have at risk. If you can buy books for $10, you can reduce your value at risk to $40.
- Find a way to increase the probability of selling books, increasing the chance that you will make a profit. If you were to spend $5 on advertising and this improves your chances for selling books, you would reduce your probability of loss, but your results would be impacted by the $5 you spent to do it.
- Obviously, if you can do both, you can do even better.

Let's say that you decide to spend the $5 on advertising. The five rows labeled *With Adv* contain this case. In this case, you have lower probabilities of selling fewer books and higher probabilities of selling more. Your cost is higher by the price of advertising, but your probability-weighted outcome is better. Your expected net profit would be $5.75, which equates to a net return of 10.85% on your investment of $53.

Here is a graph of the results, with and without advertising:

Financial leverage—borrowing money to increase the size of an investment you can make while adding interest payments to your cost—does exactly the same thing. It increases the variance of your returns.

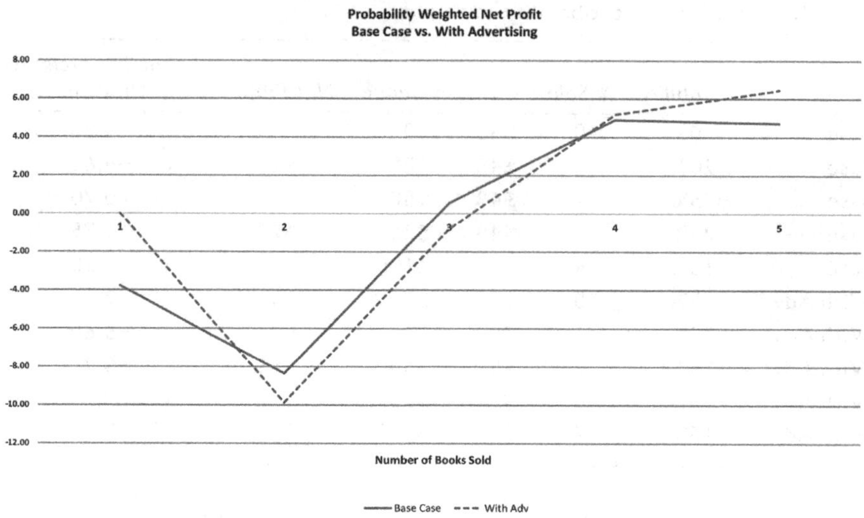

Figure 2.1 Probability-weighted returns.

The point to be made here is that the **risk** is not in the variance of your potential sales, it is the probability that you will not sell enough to recoup your investment. No matter how high the variance gets, if the mean or expected value does not change, the expected result of your investment will remain the same. However, as variance increases, the possibility of an extreme outcome increases and the impact of it must be considered.

Now, imagine two games. In the first, players pay \$10 to play and then flip a coin and receive back \$11 if they get heads or \$9 if they get tails. In the second, they pay \$10 to play and then receive \$15 if they get heads and \$5 if they get tails. If the coin is fair, the ***expected value*** of both games over repeated trials is the same—\$10 or 0% return—but the second game clearly has greater ***variance*** and exposes the player to greater risk. Which game would you rather play?

It's worth noting that if you play the second game and lose twice in a row, you're out of money to play again. You could lose the first game a number of times and still be able to stay in it. These possible outcomes must figure into your thinking. You might tolerate the former but not the latter. That is, your ***risk appetite*** would accommodate the game with the smaller risk and variance but the one with the larger risk and variance would exceed your ***risk tolerance***. There's a great difference between having a down quarter or two and losing the company on a 'bet the farm' investment while trying to become a unicorn.

Your company must make this decision in each endeavor in which it engages. In a multi-line business, some lines may be quite risky and others, much less. As with the VC vs. manufacturing example, some businesses are inherently risky and simply choosing to be in them comes with risks that cannot be mitigated or diversified away.

Creating a consolidated company out of diverse lines of business can smooth out the bumps in earnings in one business with returns from another. Similarly, choosing to fund a group of projects in which some are risky, and others are not, can help to reduce the overall risk profile of them as a group. Portfolio Theory involves optimizing returns from diverse investments to achieve higher returns with lower risks in aggregate. Portfolio Theory is beyond the scope of this book, but it is important that your ERM efforts be calibrated to account for your ***risk appetite*** and ***risk tolerance***—the levels of risk that your organization is willing to accept, both for individual lines of business and for the company, in aggregate.

We'll focus on some elementary statistics later in the book, but it is worth mentioning *correlation* in relation to portfolio theory. Correlation between two variables is determined by the degree to which they tend to be above or below their means together. For instance, crop yields are usually *positively* correlated with sun and rain—the more of both (up to a point), the greater the yield. Variables that are *negatively correlated* demonstrate the opposite, when one is below its mean, the other tends to be above it and vice-versa.

For instance, when the number of rainy days, which keep people from coming out of their offices to get lunch, during the work week is higher, the sales of food from street carts that serve them will be lower. If you owned a car wash, in which business increases following rain, its returns would be *negatively correlated* with your street food business. Sunny days favor the food cart and rainy ones favor the car wash. If you own both a food cart and a car wash, you might have a fairly predictable stream of income, as one of them would be likely to be doing well when the other wasn't.

So, if you construct a portfolio of businesses in which at least some of them are *negatively correlated* with one another, you expect to smooth out your earnings, lowering your overall variance, because some would be up when others are down. This is a product of diversification.

This digression aside, what does ***risk appetite*** look like? How is it described?

First and foremost, every investment must be viewed in terms of its risks and rewards, how it compares with alternative uses to which funds could have been put and what fraction of the overall investable capital it represents. There are financial measures that account for expected returns and risks (such as Net Present Value (NPV) and Risk-Adjusted Internal Rate of Return (IRR)) but they are also out of scope for discussion here. None of them alone can provide a complete picture of how an investment fits into the overall structure of your company. Several moderately sized lower-risk investments might be wiped out by one large high-risk, high-return investment that goes bad. Portfolio analysis can produce aggregate measures of your company's expected returns and riskiness, based on which you can adjust your investments to suit your goals for financial returns, your risk appetite and your risk tolerance.

For each line of business you are in, you need to specify two measures—what return you expect to make on it and the maximum loss you're willing to tolerate to try to achieve the expected return. It makes little sense to take your entire pool of investable capital and make a single venture investment in just one company; you could win but you're much more likely (nine or ten times more likely, at least) to lose all of it. However, if you made ten venture investments and one or two broke even or even did a little better and one returned 1,000 percent or more, you would have done quite well for yourself. Overall, VCs expect 25%+ aggregate returns on their investment portfolios.

How does this apply to RM? How you decide to treat risks can have a great deal of impact on the financial results of your business. For example, say you have a factory that is efficient, productive and low-cost but is in a country that is politically unstable. If you believe there is a five percent possibility that the factory could be nationalized by the government and that you could be forced to sell it at a large loss, how much would you be willing to pay for insurance that reimburses you for it? The greater your risk tolerance, the more willing you would be to accept a partial loss and the smaller the insurance policy you would buy. Insurance, after all, can be expensive and foregoing it would increase the return you achieve on your business, but only if the political environment stays stable.

So, your risk appetite and tolerance will help to determine both what business lines you're comfortable being in, how much you're willing to invest in them and how you deal with the business-as-usual risks of operating them.

Finally, it's worth pointing out that ***not identifying or not managing risks may be the riskiest strategy of all.***

Inventory risk sources

If you are to do a comprehensive job of identifying risks, you will first have to identify the sources of risk inherent in your enterprise and its operations so that you will know where to look. There are numerous frameworks and accompanying mnemonics that describe approaches for this. **PESTLE**, which we mentioned earlier, includes six potential categories of external risk to be explored. **SWOT**[10] is an acronym for Strengths, Weaknesses, Opportunities and Threats, which describes a framework often used to identify candidate strategic initiatives based on what the enterprise does well or not so well and where there may be exogenous prospects or pressures that require a response.

[10] https://en.wikipedia.org/wiki/SWOT_analysis

However it is accomplished, setting a road map for detailed analysis is required to guide a comprehensive risk assessment.

It would be nice to define an approach to managing each and every risk at your company. It is, however, completely unrealistic and, perhaps, not even desirable as it would require an unending supply of dedicated resources to keep up with both structural and day-to-day changes. There are two approaches to contemplate in this regard—take a snapshot of the business and then determine how to manage the risks you identify or establish an approach to managing risks dynamically as things change and then apply that approach continuously until all or most risks have been addressed.

As you might expect, a combination of both makes sense. Any analytical activity that requires a highly granular picture of even a simple business will require extensive discovery and documentation that could well be outdated by the time it is assembled. Therefore, a big-bang approach alone probably isn't going to be the way to go.

However it is done, an inventory of elements of the business must be created to inform a plan to find, evaluate and treat risks. Thereafter, execution of the plan can proceed and a larger evergreen process to maintain the currency of your ERM controls can be defined and implemented.

So, a hierarchical picture of the company is the place to start. We recommend that Enterprise and Business Architecture (EA and BA) inform the priorities of discovery and guide the development of an information repository that will form the backbone of ERM efforts. In the chapter entitled '*Integration: How to Get There*,' we'll look at these disciplines in some detail, but for now you should consider that these models are comprised of Products and Services, Business Capabilities, Assets, People, Processes, Systems and information Repositories—an anatomy of how your company is designed to do what it does. Once in place, these models should guide you through planning a prioritized agenda of where to look first for risks to evaluate and treat.

Identify, map and prioritize where general operating risks occur

This is a precursor to a traditional risk assessment—identify where anything can go wrong, assign some measure of importance or criticality to it and plan to review it in the assessment process. Depending on who is doing this it can range from highly naive to extremely insightful and from scattershot to thorough.

What is more important than anything is that no significant risks are missed because they will not then be analyzed, so how this is attacked may determine its success. Many organizations rely on people within each operating area to identify the risks in it, which is fine if they are attuned to the process but not so fine if they haven't done it before or are not sufficiently familiar with the full scope of the unit's operations. Others apply a framework in which they walk backward or forward through elements of the business, following dependencies and connections to ensure comprehensiveness. This, I believe, is preferable as it makes it less likely that risks may be missed.

Overall, establishing the roadmap for the assessment can be one of the major weaknesses in TRM practice if it is not done comprehensively.

Identify external drivers or forces that create risks and opportunities

Strategy and execution: a chicken and egg problem

The success of your business is ultimately determined by your strategy ***and*** your execution. For our purposes, we propose that strategy be represented by the market segments you choose to serve and the value proposition (the products and services that they are willing to pay for) that you deliver to them. Your execution is determined by how you configure your company to create and deliver the value.

These are two separate things, though obviously tightly coupled to one another. As Eric Ries, author of *The Lean Startup*, says[11]

> Too many startups begin with an idea for a product that they think people want. They then spend months, sometimes years, perfecting that product without ever showing the product, even in a very rudimentary form, to the prospective customer. When they fail to reach broad uptake from customers, it is often because they never spoke to prospective customers and determined whether or not the product was interesting. When customers ultimately communicate, through their indifference, that they don't care about the idea, the startup fails.

This applies equally well to the ongoing operation of any established company. If you're not selling something people want, it doesn't matter how efficiently you're making it. Doing the wrong thing right is worse than doing the right thing wrong. In the latter case, at least, you may have a chance to course correct and save your business.

Strategy, more often than not, is driven by ***outside-in*** challenges—what are our competitors doing and how do we compare? These are linked to execution issues which become ***inside-out*** challenges:

- Outside-In: Our competition is now offering next-day delivery and we currently don't.
- Inside-out: How can we change our operating processes so we can match what they are doing? Can we do that and sell profitably at a competitive price point?

---

[11] https://theleanstartup.com/principles

Yes, you can come up with innovative products and services that you then take to market and succeed with. I am quite sure that if you developed an internal combustion engine that achieved 150 miles per gallon, people would want it. However, it certainly appears that the internal combustion engine is on its way out, to be displaced by electric vehicles (EVs) in the not-too-distant future. Would it be worth tooling up to make your high-efficiency engine knowing it might only have a 20-year life? Maybe and maybe not. It would depend on the cost and how fast you can get it into production. And ... you still need to validate that the demand you assumed for it would materialize as a reality.

- Inside-out: We have something no one else does—a 150 MPG engine!
- Outside-in: We need to be sure that people will want it, given that it may be expensive, and everyone may be moving to EVs in the 15-20 years

This raises an important RM issue—you must identify the critical success factors (CSFs) in your operations without which you cannot deliver on your strategy. The more a strategic target depends on your operational capabilities, the bigger a risk factor they become. This is an important criterion that, among others, should inform priorities as you focus your ERM efforts.

Beyond market risks, there are concerns that fall into the PESTLE categories—political issues, regulatory issues, environmental issues, legal issues and so forth. These must be accounted for in your contextual model and tied back to your strategic and operational risk inventories. For instance, the European General Data Protection Regulations (GDPR)[12] may have profound implications for companies doing business on the Internet in the geographies it covers. Some countries may make it illegal to store their citizens' data outside the country.

Modifying execution capabilities to accommodate the requirements will be expensive, cause dislocation for many companies and may force changes in business models that limit their profitability or even their feasibility. Given the magnitude of potential fines for unintended disclosure or proscribed use of customers' data, the risks associated with certain businesses could ramp up and require substantial changes to operating models or operational architectures to accommodate.

Identify recurring and ad hoc decision processes

Multi-path business processes driven by decisions are common sources of risk. Deciding whether to make a loan, sell an insurance policy, recommend one product option vs. another can all determine overall success in the lines of business in which they take place. Making bad loans or selling insurance

[12] https://en.wikipedia.org/wiki/General_Data_Protection_Regulation

to bad risks can have very swift and negative outcomes. Making poor product recommendations can mean lost sales opportunities.

It happens that all three of these examples are the kinds of things to which companies are beginning to apply Robotic Process Automation[13] (RPA) and Artificial Intelligence (AI) and having some success. However, as these technologies are relatively new at many companies, novel and unforeseen problems have surfaced. For one thing, AI models can be completely opaque—the logic behind the results they produce may not be easy to discern or validate and they may implement and reinforce implicit biases perpetuated from the training data that was used to build the models.

Technology aside, your company is likely to have numerous processes in which your staff make decisions on a case-by-case basis. Some of these may be based on policies or codified historical practices and some of them may be ad- hoc and dependent on the experience and judgment of individuals. Presumably, there is a better and worse outcome to be realized in each case and you should be cognizant of and monitor all such decisions to minimize the chances of sub-optimal outcomes and maximize the chances for better ones.

Finally, your comfort level with the status quo of your operations and the explicit and implicit decision processes it incorporates is more than likely tied to the degree to which you believe that you have an innate understanding of it. As I've opined, things are going to change, keep on changing and change faster and faster. You're going to consolidate roles as you automate business processes and this is going to cause you to have to reconfigure where, on what basis and maybe by whom decisions will be made. If you haven't identified them, who's making them and what the basis for them is now, you will have to slow down your evolution efforts to go back and develop the understanding you will need to redesign, re-implement and risk-manage them later.

PERFORM A RISK ASSESSMENT: INVENTORY AND ANALYZE RISKS AND DEVELOP MANAGEMENT STRATEGIES

Having mapped the strategic and operational landscape of your enterprise and identified the sources of risks, you can then inventory them, explore them and plan responses for them.

This often proves to be more complicated than managers expect. There are innumerable approaches and techniques for this and most of them amount to "create a list of all the risks that you can think of, then categorize, analyze and define treatments for them." If the right people are involved, it may be possible to identify a fair majority of them. It's the few that fall

[13] https://en.wikipedia.org/wiki/Robotic_process_automation

through the cracks that are a concern. Some of them may be reasonably innocuous but others may not be. It's also the case that changes in the enterprise or the environment in which it operates can attenuate, eliminate, amplify or generate risks that can go unrecognized until an event occurs, or a periodic review or new initiative causes reappraisal.

Given the relentless increase in the rate at which forces in your business environment change, the frequency at which reappraisal and course correction on RM must occur will increase and continue to do so.

Identify risks

Within each of the areas that were identified for exploration, you must identify each of the risks that are inherent to them so that they can be analyzed. There are innumerable approaches to this. How you do it should be informed by who will be doing it and what their background and knowledge level is. Someone who is conversant with the nuances of the operations of the unit is best positioned to perform this task. This article, *8 Ways to Identify Risks in Your Organization*,[14] is pretty representative of common advice offered to those charged with RM.

Traditionally, this has been focused on "what might go wrong?" Now, it needs to be focused equally on that and "how might we make things work better?" Instead of evading or responding to events that create negative outcomes, you should focus equally on understanding how to obtain the best possible results from your operations and an important part of this is to do some scenario analysis to think about what could happen to induce changes in your business. As I have said previously, "***All management is risk management***" and this is one of the ways that RM has to change.

In any event, as risks are identified, they should be entered into a repository from which they can be extracted for analysis. The data you choose to maintain in the repository should include whatever is relevant to downstream analysis, whether it is qualitative or quantitative. For instance, the capacity and throughput of a production process and the costs of ramping it up, might be useful information. Certainly, the presumed costs of outages of varying lengths would also be useful if the information is available to you.

Analyze risks

The traditional way

This is the area that critics of TRM approaches justifiably focus on most. Understanding risks and losses is best informed by statistical analysis and many practitioners go out of their way to oversimplify it. Where the right approach to modeling a potential event is a probability density function,

[14] https://www.clearrisk.com/risk-management-blog/8-ways-to-identify-risk-0-0

Likelihood		Impact / Consequence				
		Negligible	Minor	Moderate	Major	Catastrophic
	Highly Likely	Moderate	Major	Critical	Critical	Catastrophic
	Likely	Moderate	Moderate	Major	Critical	Critical
	Possible	Minor	Moderate	Moderate	Major	Critical
	Unlikely	Minor	Minor	Moderate	Moderate	Major
	Very Unlikely	Negligible	Minor	Moderate	Moderate	Major

Figure 2.2 A typical risk heat map.

this is often reduced to a single measure—low, medium or high. Where the impact of the outcome should also be a probability density function, it is similarly reduced to a single measure. Typically, risks are classified on a nine- or twenty-five-cell heat map[15] based on their likelihood and impact. For example:

While it makes sense that risks that fall into the cells at the upper right (high probability, high negative impact) should receive the earliest and most careful consideration, it's really not clear about everything else. All of the classifications are arbitrary and there are other shortcomings, which we will cover later. For the moment, this heatmap can be used legitimately to inform the first step in the analysis: prioritizing risks for further study.

The second step is to evaluate each risk to understand its dynamics and underlying drivers. Whether the organization is willing and able to undertake formal statistical analysis of risks or not, the process they have been employing often imputes the results of having done so. For instance, a company has a supply chain that involves sourcing a critical input from outside of the country and it's delivered via container ship. Every so often, there is a cyclone or hurricane that interrupts delivery by some number of days. This occurs with a relatively predictable frequency and has a predictable impact in terms of late fulfillment of orders and delays in cash flow. Based on this information, the company can articulate and compare options for dealing with the risk. Presumably, some quantitative analysis will be applied for this purpose.

Many companies use this heat map to assess how well they are doing at managing risks in aggregate. If their mitigations result in reclassifying risks from the upper right toward the lower left, it is their feeling that they have accomplished something to address their risks. Probably, they have, but I don't think that this is an appropriate way to assess the overall value of their RM efforts.

[15] https://en.wikipedia.org/wiki/Heat_map

A better way: quantitative analysis, incorporating uncertainty and variance

Many people think about risk as the potential impact of an exogenous event, like a hurricane or an auto accident. However, it is much more nuanced than that. If you have value at risk, risk emanates from uncertainty with respect to attainment of a desired outcome from a process which may result in either a more positive or negative outcome than expected. Focusing only on avoiding negative outcomes ignores important aspects of the nature of variance and stems from an incomplete understanding.

To ensure that we have a common baseline of understanding about important concepts, we can adopt the following definitions:

- Trial
  A ***trial*** is a process or an event that produces an outcome. For instance, when you flip a coin, it will land as either heads or tails. If you throw it five times, that could constitute five trials. You may also consider a set of throws as a trial. For instance, you run a trial of five tosses and observe four heads.
- Probability
  Probability is the chance of a specific outcome occurring. A fair coin flip has a .50 (50%) probability of heads or tails and the probability of rolling any specific number on a fair die is 1/6 or .167.
- Mean, Expected Value
  The ***Mean*** is the average result from one or more trials—the sum of results divided by the number of trials. The ***Expected Value*** (EV) is what you would predict, based on what you know about the system generating results. For instance, if you run a trial in which you throw a fair six-sided die, in which each side has an equal chance of coming up, the ***Expected Value*** of the roll should approach 3.5, which is the sum of the probability of each outcome (.167) times the value of the outcome (1-6) or .167 x 1 + .167 x 2 + .167 x 3 + .167 x 4 + .167 x 5 + .167 x 6 = 3.5.

  The ***Expected Value*** in this case is the ***Mean*** outcome of the throws. That is, if you had to predict what the value of any given throw would be in advance, you would guess that it would be the ***Expected Value***.

  I used the term ***approach*** above because it's highly unlikely that six throws would result in each side landing exactly once. If you conducted a trial of six throws and got 1, 2, 2, 3, 4, 6, the ***Mean*** for the ***Trial*** would be 3. However, if you conducted a large number of such ***Trials***, the resulting ***Mean*** would tend toward or ***approach*** the ***Mean*** that we project from the structure of the system we have created.

  In the system of fair die rolls, all possible outcomes have an equal likelihood of occurring. In many other systems, there are discrete outcomes in which the probabilities differ. In these cases, the ***Mean and Expected Value*** are:

$$EV = \sum_{i=1}^{n} p_i V_i$$

Where:
EV is the expected value,
n is the number of all discrete possible potential outcomes,
p_i is the probability of outcome i and
V_i is the value of outcome i

Where would we apply this? One important candidate is adjusting estimates for risk and determining what we are willing to do or pay for to mitigate them. We seldom know exactly how many widgets we're going to sell in the coming quarter, but we may have identified scenarios in which we apply several factors to make an estimate. If each scenario is assigned a probability, then we can use the formula to calculate an ***Expected Value*** for the number of sales.

For example, we run an ice cream stand at a local beach. If there's sunny weather, then our ice cream stand will sell 100 cones. If it's cloudy, then only 70. Our weather forecast for the next quarter indicates that over the next 90 days there's a .25 probability of 60 sunny days, a .40 probability of 50 and a .35 probability of 40. Thus, there is:

- a .25 probability of 8,100 cone sales ((60 x 100) + (30 x 70)),
- a .40 probability of 7,800 ((50 x 100) + (40 x 70)) and
- a .35 probability of 7,500 ((40 x 100) + (50 x 70)).

The EV is 7,770 cones, not any one potential outcome but the weighted average of all of them.

- Independent and Dependent Variables
  The goal of employing statistics as in the previous example is to predict the future. We are using the expected number of sunny days to predict how many ice cream cones we will sell.

  We will use that information to guide decision-making, for instance, given our expected sales and the expected number of days we will not be able to operate due to power loss to evaluate options to avoid, mitigate or transfer the risk of loss due to power outage. In this example, days of sunshine and potential power outage are *independent variables* over which we have no control and our sales are a *dependent variable*, which we believe to be determined by the independent variables.

- Impact

  Impact, for our purposes, is the change in outcome *if* a specific event occurs. In the case of our ice cream stand, a power outage that shuts us down for five days would create an impact of 428 lost sales. (7,700 expected sales over 90 days = 85.6 cones per day x 5 days = 428).

  Now, we should also account for how many of those days would have been sunny and how many not, but that is a complication not worth pursuing at this point. We'll just use the mean, as calculated above.

  Just to delve into a little RM, let's consider what we might do about this risk. First, the potential event we must plan for is not whether there will be five-day outage or not. It is the risk of there being an outage that lasts for *n* days. We can reasonably assume that the distribution (see below) will have a decreasing probability for longer and longer outages, i.e., the potential for a 1-day outage is greater than the potential for a 10-day outage. To perform the analysis, we will have to assume a distribution for the potential for outages of varying lengths throughout our operating season. Then we can obtain a quote for business disruption insurance from our carrier (who is also doing these calculations) and see whether the cost of the insurance exceeds what we think our expected potential loss is.

  Given this information, we have four potential strategies:

  - Avoid

    Avoiding the risk means restructuring the operation of our stand to make the issue of power outages moot. On a practical basis, it's not possible to run the stand without electricity, so we can assume this option is not viable.
  - Mitigate

    Mitigation would involve taking steps to minimize or eliminate the impact of a power outage. Buying a generator, for instance, might be an option. We would need to assess what that would cost and compare it with other options.
  - Transfer

    Transferring the risk means finding someone who is willing to share or accept it, for a price. Insurance transfers the risk from us to an insurance carrier. We will need to assess the costs and benefits of this, and they are based on the statistical probabilities of outages of varying lengths and the lost sales that would result.
  - Accept

    If we accept the risk, we basically do nothing. If an outage happens, we will bear the loss. If the potential loss, based on the expected value of the distribution of a potential outage is less than the cost of a backup generator or business disruption insurance, then this may be the best option.

I should point out, here, that the strategy you select should reflect your risk appetite and tolerance. The mitigation and transfer options have a cost, which will lower profits but also offset losses due to a power outage, thus lowering variance of your returns on owning and operating the stand. The accept option eliminates the costs of either of the other options but provides no protection against losses due to a power outage, which increases the variance and risk of your returns. So, if you have limited appetite or tolerance for risk, mitigate or transfer it. If you have a higher appetite and tolerance, just accept it.

- Distribution

  A **distribution**, or a *Probability Density Function*,[16] describes how potential outcomes may fall. The chart, below, shows the decreasing probability of outages of increasing length at our ice cream stand. It shows that there is a .25% (one in 400) chance of a one-day outage and a .05% (one in 2,000) chance of a five-day outage. This information would inform our decision-making as to what we might be willing to pay to treat the risk.

  You are probably familiar with the 'bell curve' of the normal ***distribution***. Outcomes fitting this ***distribution*** cluster around the mean and tail off in either direction as they get farther and farther from it. The normal distribution is symmetric—the probability of observations or outcomes of equal magnitude above or below the mean are equally likely.

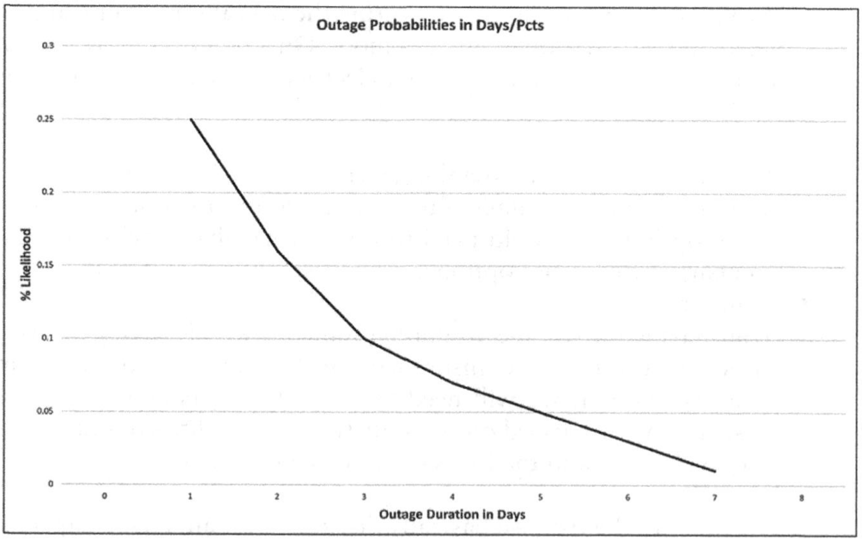

Figure 2.3 Outage probability distribution.

[16] https://en.wikipedia.org/wiki/Probability_density_function

Continuing with our ice cream stand example, we should note a couple of things—the ***distribution*** of our cone sales is unlikely to be normal or so smoothly distributed. Why? It will be determined by some number of discrete factors, in the case above, the number of sunny days and probably a few other things for which we haven't explicitly accounted. Even though there may be quite a few of them, there will be only so many ways that they can combine and, therefore, our distribution will be determined by a relatively small number of potential outcomes, and each will not be equally likely. Some will be likely, and others will be pretty unlikely. Some will be one-in-a-million, 'black swan' events, like the COVID-19 outbreak.

- Variance, Standard Deviation
  Variance and ***Standard Deviation*** are statistics that describe the distribution of expected outcomes. In a normal distribution, the ***variance*** is the ***standard deviation*** squared. In the distributions, pictured below, the one in the black line has a greater ***standard deviation*** and is, therefore, spread farther out then the one depicted with the gray line.
  In the normal distribution:

  - 68% of observed values will be within one standard deviation of the mean,
  - 95% of observed values will be within two standard deviations of the mean and
  - 99% of observed values will be within three standard deviations of the mean.

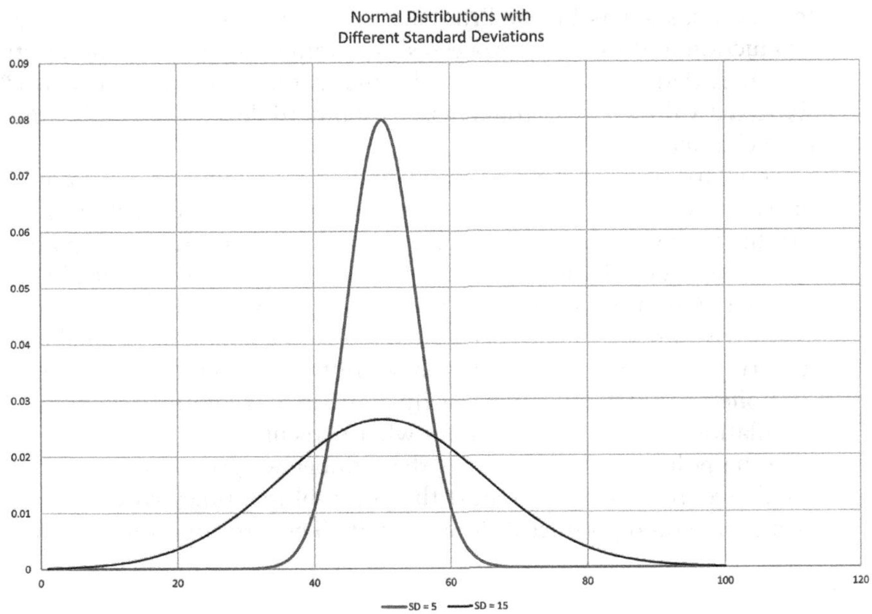

Figure 2.4 Two normal distributions with different standard deviations.

- Correlation and Covariance
  Correlation measures relationships between variables. In our example, the number of cones we expect to sell in a season is *positively correlated* with the number of sunny days that occur. That is: **more** sunny days, **more** cone sales. Cloudy days would be *negatively correlated* with sales: **more** cloudy days, **less** cones sold. Independent variables that are *strongly correlated* with dependent variables have high predictive value, those that are *weakly correlated* have little or no predictive value.
  Correlation is determined by *Covariance*, that is the degree to which two variables vary together—that both are above or below their means simultaneously. If an independent variable varies little, it will probably not be a good predictor. For instance, the height of the roof of our ice cream stand is fixed. We sell more or fewer cones as a result of other factors and including the height measurement in our calculations will add nothing to our ability to predict our sales.
- Variance, Standard Deviation and Risk
  Ultimately, our goal is to understand the interplay of factors that determine a likely outcome. Based on relationships among our variables, the predicted Expected Value will have its own distribution and standard deviation. If the estimate has a large standard deviation, it will have less value as a basis for making decisions. In business school, I studied Operations Research (OR), a discipline in which various techniques, such as Linear Programming,[17] are employed to optimize production and business processes. A common joke about the utility of OR is that it tells you to "build one factory, plus or minus two." Expected Values with extremely large standard deviations can be similarly characterized.
  Standard deviation in our predictions can be reduced in a number of ways, depending on how we are calculating it. One starting point for this is simply using more data. You may have noticed that polling figures are quoted with an error of estimate, e.g., some result plus or minus a margin. This margin of error relates to what is called *sampling error*, which represents the degree to which the people we polled may not truly represent the population we're trying to characterize. So, if we polled 1,000 people living in zip codes in and around a city with a population of millions to find out what percent of them were in favor of some policy, it's unlikely that the number we got would be 100% predictive. If we were to repeat the poll multiple times with different groups, it would produce different results. The error of estimate relates

[17] https://en.wikipedia.org/wiki/Linear_programming

to the variance of these results and is primarily a function of the number of respondents in the poll. If we poll more people, the margin of error will decrease.

Now, polling costs money and takes time. Whether it's worth increasing the resources expended on polling depends on how we're using the results and what the cost of being wrong is. In recent elections, the polling results were quite inaccurate. It's possible that campaign decisions made based on them could have cost some candidates the offices for which they were running. Should their campaigns have done more or something different? It's currently the subject of a lot of introspection.

- Conditional Probability

The example of our ice cream stand had an implicit *conditional probability* imputed into it: ***if it is sunny out, then we will sell 100 cones in a day***. If you think about it, a lot of the risk-based decision-making commonly done now implicitly relies on exactly this—*if* the factory has to shut down for more than one day, *then* we will lose two days' worth of sales. If [some risk], then [some outcome].

Many, if not most, RM departments employ the *heat map*, depicted earlier, to categorize risks. What do the terms Minor, Moderate, Major and Critical mean? How are we to interpret the scales on the axes? How does a risk classified as Possible and Moderate equal an impact of Major? What do the colors signify?

It's pretty clear that a risk that's likely to occur and could have a tremendous negative impact on our company should be high priority for attention. But what should we do with it and what should we be willing to spend to avoid, mitigate or transfer it?

More importantly, other than potential impact, what does this really tell us about our business that is actionable? What does it mean if many of our risks are in the gray or light gray cells? Should it be a goal to try to move our distribution more toward the white cells at the lower left? What if that is inconsistent with our strategic goals?

And finally, where do opportunities for improving outcomes appear? There really isn't anywhere to accommodate the risk/return calculation that drives investment in this chart.

The heat map may help us to prioritize on high-likelihood/high-consequence risks, but that is about all it is good for. We really need to go much, much further.

- Bayes Networks and Inference

Thomas Bayes was an 18th-century clergyman and statistician. He developed a technique for computing *inverse probability*, in which *causes* are inferred from observation of *effects*. A simple example involves a wet lawn, rain and a sprinkler. There is a relationship between the sprinkler and rain, such that when it's raining, the sprinkler is usually not run. Below, is a diagram of a Bayesian Network taken from Wikipedia[18]:

What this network tells us is that rain influences whether the sprinkler is run and both influence whether the grass is wet, which is something we can observe. Adjacent to each factor is a two-way probability table. For instance, the Rain/Sprinkler table tells us that if it has rained, then the sprinkler has a 40% probability of having been run. If it hasn't rained, then the probability that the sprinkler ran is 60%. The rain table tells us that there's a 20% chance that it has rained. Now, if the lawn's wet what is the probability that rain is the cause?

Just to save you the need to look it up, learn the math and solve, the answer is 35.77%.

What is the importance of Bayesian statistics to our RM efforts? To formulate a treatment for a risk, we must assume the probability of its occurrence and the expected value of its impact. Frequentist statistics[19] are based on observations of past behavior or results. For example, we observe whether a day was sunny or not and keep a count of cone sales. From this data, we calculate a mean and variance and we base our estimates of sales on these numbers. From the Wikipedia article: "**Frequentist inference** is a type of statistical inference that draws conclusions from sample data by emphasizing the frequency or proportion of the data. An alternative name is **frequentist statistics**."

But what if we have no data, no place to start? Then we can employ Bayesian inference. We arbitrarily select a best guess as a starting point and then refine it as new evidence is collected. From Wikipedia[20]

Bayesian probability belongs to the category of evidential probabilities; to evaluate the probability of a hypothesis, the Bayesian probabilist specifies a prior probability. This, in turn, is then updated to a posterior probability in the light of new, relevant data (evidence). The Bayesian interpretation provides a standard set of procedures and formulae to perform this calculation.

Don't get too wound up in all this. The important concept to take away is this: just because you don't have prior data to work with doesn't mean that you cannot apply statistical rigor to understand how your risks will behave. If you apply these techniques conscientiously, you will come to improve your ability to define cost-justified controls and treatments for your risks.

In many, if not most, real-world cases we will not encounter defined, discrete probabilities; rather, we assume or estimate distributions from which

[18] https://en.wikipedia.org/wiki/Bayesian_network
[19] https://en.wikipedia.org/wiki/Frequentist_inference
[20] https://en.wikipedia.org/wiki/Bayesian_probability

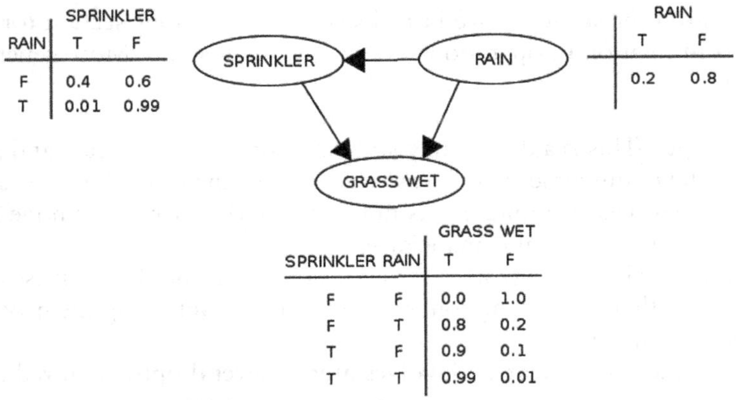

Figure 2.5 Bayes network diagram.

we derive the probabilities that we use to determine the weighted potential costs or impacts of the risks we seek to manage. Frequentist and Bayesian inference are two, among many, approaches that are used for this.

In sum, RM is all about accounting for events, assessing the likelihood of their occurrence and the impact that will result if they occur. When potential events have been identified and evaluated, we must decide what we should do about them. Generally, we may have options to **avoid them** (figure out a way to run our business that allows us to sidestep the risk), **mitigate them** (operate to reduce the probability or impact of a risk), **transfer them** (say, by buying insurance against them) or to just **accept them**. If a risk is, instead, an opportunity, we would look for ways that we can increase the probability for it to occur and the benefit it will create if it does.

This is the essence of risk-based thinking, risk-based problem-solving and risk-based decision-making. Instead of implementing an intuitive solution to a problem or guessing at what might work to optimize sales or productivity, risk-based discipline is applied to understand and weigh the factors underlying the dynamics with which you are confronted and make reasoned decisions about how best to proceed.

Throughout the remainder of this book, we will focus on applying risk-based discipline to identify risks, evaluate and assess them and their potential interactions and to select among alternative options for treating them.

Evaluate strategies and alternative treatments for each risk

Treating a risk means to select and implement a strategy for dealing with it—avoiding or reducing the probability of it occurring and minimizing the negative consequences if it does.

There are four strategies we introduced in the previous section for treating risks in relation to operations of our ice cream stand. More generically, these are:

- **Accept**—This is a do-nothing strategy. Continue to operate and accept whatever outcomes may be associated with the risk. This makes sense where a negative outcome is not particularly onerous or none of the other strategies make financial sense.
- **Avoid**—This strategy involves either restructuring the business operation so that the risk no longer applies or discontinuing the process or operation entirely.
- **Mitigate**—This strategy involves any of several options to reduce the probability of an event or its impact. For instance, a company might take over services that were previously outsourced and move them in-house to eliminate contention with the former provider's other customers.
- **Transfer**—This strategy involves paying someone else to accept all or part of a risk, for instance, by purchasing commodity futures, buying insurance or contracting with a third party to provide a service with a performance guarantee to ensure that the provider continues to meet the standards required or pay a penalty.

What you may be willing to accept will be determined by your ***risk appetite*** and ***risk tolerance***. How you might choose to implement a risk treatment involving Avoiding, Mitigating or Transferring risks should be informed by a statistical analysis of the probability and costs associated with the risk.

Select treatment for each risk

A Risk Treatment encompasses the strategy that you have selected to deal with a risk. For instance, you may have decided to transfer the risk by purchasing insurance or avoid the risk by changing how your operations are performed, obviating the need to bear the risk.

Based on your analysis, you select and implement a strategy and treatment for each risk. You can then reclassify your risks based on post-mitigation parameters. For example, if you have purchased insurance for a shipping delay caused by a cyclone, the potential financial impact should be lower by the amount of the benefit you will receive from the carrier. However, you will be out the premium you paid for the coverage and while the financial loss will be reduced, your customers will still receive their orders late and your cash flow will be impacted. In this case, then, the probability of an event hasn't been reduced (we're talking about nature, after all), but the impact has. This may be sufficient to downgrade the risk in future assessments.

Document your plan

Once you have selected a treatment strategy for each risk, you must monitor for occurrences and enact any response that may be required, such as filing an insurance claim and initiating the process of repairing damage.

Ultimately, the data underlying the plan is multi-dimensional—business unit, risk type, risk class, mitigations chosen, cost of implementation, etc. How you choose to structure your documentation is up to you. You must consider who will use it and how it will be used. There are several purposes for the plan:

- Monitoring the status of your progress through the discovery, analysis and mitigation process.
- Keeping track of your backlog, the new risks or changes you've identified but not yet pushed through the process for assessment or re-assessment,
- Serving as a playbook to guide the response if a risk event occurs,
- Serving as a knowledge base that informs future ERM efforts and, if historical actions and events are included, can be used as the starting point for assessing effectiveness.

ESTABLISH INTEGRATED RM CONTROLS, POLICIES AND PROCESSES

The steps outlined to this point will produce a baseline or a starting point for ERM. You will have identified risks and developed treatments or responses for them. In this step, you will have to put in place people and processes to execute these responsibilities:

- Monitor the enterprise to capture changes that warrant a risk assessment and initiate the process of identifying, analyzing and defining treatments for new or morphed risks,
- Monitor the business environment for changes that may have an impact on your identified risks and trigger a re-assessment or re-appraisal, as required,
- Monitor events to identify when something has occurred that requires a response and execute it. ERM cannot be effective if it operates in a vacuum, independent of decision processes and operations,
- Enact and operate processes to monitor and record ERM activities to produce a repository of data that can be used to assess results and performance and
- Review historical data to identify opportunities to improve ERM performance.

Day-to-day or Business as Usual operations, such as processing and shipping orders, are likely to require only that procedures formulated with risk-based thinking be executed as specified. For example, sales orders with a value less than a threshold will be automatically approved without a credit check, as this will avoid compliance costs that would exceed a potential loss. This is an example of a policy- or business rule-based risk treatment. If the net benefit of accelerating order processing and saving on the time required to perform credit checks does not result in increased orders or causes increased losses exceeding the saved expenses, then the policy needs to be reviewed and modified. Perhaps automation can be applied to increase screening without requiring additional manual review or perhaps the threshold should be reset. If expectations are met, the workflow can operate without intervention as long as defined procedures are followed and controls enforced.

On the other hand, higher-level decision-making processes, such as planning for a new line of business should be informed by a thorough evaluation of the risks involved. If the decision to go ahead is made, risk-based thinking should be applied to designing operational monitoring and management review processes and embedding them in the operations of the new business.

IMPLEMENT, EXECUTE AND MONITOR ERM PERFORMANCE

At this point, ERM should be operating at two levels—intermittent monitoring of day-to-day execution and a higher-level involving policy and procedure creation and integration into the enterprise's management decision processes.

At the day-to-day level, most RM-informed practices are based on assumptions and hypotheses, and you should monitor them regularly to ensure that they are producing the results you intended. For instance, consider the policy of eliminating credit checks for orders below a specified threshold, from the previous section. You assumed accepting orders below a certain dollar value without taking the time to conduct credit checks would result in writing off no more than 5% of their value as bad debts. Is this expectation being met? If not, the limit may need to be reset. On the other hand, is the ability to simplify and accelerate the order process resulting in higher order volume that offsets the write offs?

Several factors go into the initial analysis of how this risk should be treated:

- The percentage of all orders that will fall below the threshold,
- The percentage of such orders that default on payment,
- The average loss on orders that default,

- The cost of a credit check,
- The presumed increase in orders that would result from making it faster and easier to order and
- The presumed average order value of such orders.

Having identified, analyzed and specified treatment for this risk, you are now positioned to monitor and assess how well your controls are performing. If they are not working to your expectations, you will at least be armed with the information necessary to re-evaluate and adjust them.

At the higher level, have any of your business units suffered an adverse event? Had you identified the possibility and prepared for it? Were your expectations about the effectiveness of your planned response met?

Were you able to keep up with managing risks across your evolving enterprise? Are there business units undergoing transformations for which you haven't had the chance to conduct a risk assessment?

You need to continuously check the validity of your assumptions and hypotheses about how your enterprise is working and ensure that you are maintaining appropriate risk policies as it evolves. Unexpected and unplanned for events, lack of defined responses and falling out of step with the rate of change of the company will compromise your ERM function to the point at which its value proposition could be called into question.

RISK AUDIT AND RISK ASSURANCE

As with any number of other business functions, a company's management and board may employ an internal unit or an outside auditor, or both, to monitor and report on how well RM is performing. This can be applied to both the ERM function, itself, and the efficacy of the controls, policies and procedures it enacts. Some of the questions that senior management and the board should be asking include:

- **ERM efficacy**—How well is the company doing at managing risks?
  - Is the company experiencing losses for which it was unprepared?
  - Is RM contributing to risk-based thinking and risk-based decision-making within the company?
- **ERM currency, efficiency**—How well is ERM doing at keeping up with changes in the business or environment, assessing risks, defining controls and treatments for them and enacting them?
- **ERM cost-effectiveness**—Are ERM costs excessive? This is complicated as it involves many dimensions:
  - Direct ERM staffing and other expenses,
  - Impact of prescribed policies, practices and procedures on operating departments,
  - Costs of mitigations implemented and

    - Costs vs. expectations for recovering from loss occurrences.
- **ERM integration**—Is ERM participating in and making a positive contribution to operational decisions where it is appropriate?
- **ERM improvement**—Does ERM have a defined program of performance measurement and continuous improvement?

Risk Audit and Risk Assurance serve the company's management and board to ensure that ERM is being conducted properly and is effective.

Risk Audit involves monitoring and reporting on the performance of ERM. It may be performed by different groups, depending on the size and complexity of the enterprise; however, separation of responsibilities is required to ensure objectivity. (No operating function should be charged with monitoring and reporting on itself, which could create conflicts of interest.)

This position paper[21] by the UK Chartered Institute of Internal Auditors recommends a collaboration model for IA and ERM. Essentially, ERM does its job and IA reports on and provides assurance to management and the board on it.

The paper mentions the ***Three Lines of Defense*** model.

This model, which was formulated by the Institute of Internal Auditors in 2013 and updated in 2020, describes three layers of oversight of risks in the enterprise:

- Operational Management Controls
- Risk and Control Monitoring
- Independent Internal Auditing

Implementation of the Three Lines Model is described succinctly in this article.[22]

This recent article in the Journal of Accountancy[23] describes updates to the Three Lines Model, shown above:

- In the previous model, the three lines of defense were represented by management control as the first line, risk and control monitoring as the second, and independent assurance through the internal audit function as the third.

[21] https://www.iia.org.uk/resources/risk-management/position-paper-risk-management-and-internal-audit/#:~:text=Internal%20audit%20should%20not%20manage,taking%20risk%20management%20decisions%20themselves.

[22] https://cviewllc.com/insights/risk-advisory/using-the-three-lines-of-defense-model-to-manage-risk/

[23] https://www.journalofaccountancy.com/news/2020/jul/3-lines-of-defense-model-for-risk-management-gets-major-update.html

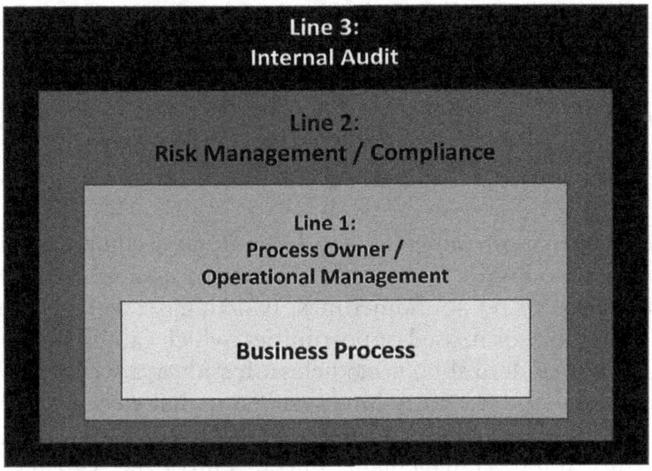

Figure 2.6 The three lines of defense model

- The new model is designed to better identify and structure interactions and responsibilities of management, internal audit, and those charged with governance to achieve more effective alignment, collaboration, accountability, and objectives.
- Roles are clearly defined in the new model for various leaders within an organization, including oversight by the board or governing body; management and operational leaders including risk and compliance (first- and second-line roles); and independent assurance through internal audit (third-line role).[24]

Risk Assurance is usually performed by an independent auditor. In it, various processes, functions and results are audited and reported on to the company's management and board. The Sarbanes Oxley Act of 2002 (SOX) prescribed formal responsibilities among companies' managements and boards to document and sign off on the accuracy and reliability of certain governance processes and external auditors were enlisted to review and issue opinions on them. Boards used these opinions as a basis for personally certifying their reported financial results, which is a requirement of SOX. Risks, other than those that could impact what appeared on financial statements were not explicitly addressed; however, the assurance aspect is the same—boards want to be able to represent that they are managing operational risks systematically.

[24] https://www.journalofaccountancy.com/news/2020/jul/3-lines-of-defense-model-for-risk-management-gets-major-update.html

This paper,[25] a practice guide by the IIA, describes the relationship among the various groups involved in risk governance, including the subject of assurance.

EVOLVE AND IMPROVE YOUR ERM

Bad things happen, sometimes to good people and companies and sometimes to not so good ones. It's not always easy to assign blame and it's not always productive to do so. Sometimes, bad things take the form of sub-optimal performance or missed opportunities, which can be less painful than actual losses, but undesirable, nonetheless. It's always worth looking back in retrospect to see if there's anything systematic that we are either doing or not doing that can be changed or improved upon to produce better results.

Long-Term Capital Management, Enron, Hurricane Katrina, the tragically botched US response to COVID-19, the World Trade Center attack and Collapse on 911, the Bhopal gas leak, the loss of two NASA space shuttles and their crews, the Exxon Valdez oil spill ... the list is long. The failure was not only the event, such as a natural disaster that occurred, but that reasonably foreseeable risks were not factored into designs or processes and their impacts were avoidable or could, at least, have been attenuated.

How good are we at this? It's not a simple question to answer. Often, we skate by on substandard management practices just because a random (and, maybe, not so random) event hasn't occurred. We may not know that this was the case because of a blind spot—we never saw it coming and since it didn't happen, we never saw it, period.

Measurement is difficult. There are innumerable statistical subtleties, and it isn't straightforward to determine whether your estimate that an event had a three percent chance of happening was accurate if it didn't happen. Probabilities are not derived from single trials, they are estimated from many of them and, usually, the more the better. Not having a catastrophe that you believed had a three percent probability this fiscal year is a good thing but if you're in business long enough, it's possible, if not probable, that it eventually will happen. Your job is to identify the risk, assess it and do something to reduce the probability of it happening or the loss if it does.

> Therefore, it is important not to attribute, ex ante, the absence of a negative event that did not occur with the efficacy of your efforts to prevent or mitigate it.

Again, measurement is difficult. You need to be able to adjust or tune your mitigation costs to appropriate levels to avoid wasting money, time or

[25] https://gDivisional.theiia.org/certification/Public%20Documents/Coordinating%20Risk%20Management%20and%20Assurance.pdf

resources. No one should be willing to spend $1,000 to avoid a loss of $100 regardless of the probability it will occur. If you purchased insurance against a loss from your supposed three percent probability event priced as if it had a five percent probability, you would have overpaid for it. If you had merely ranked the risk as 'high' and the impact as 'moderate,' it would not have helped you to determine the appropriate level of insurance to buy or what it should have cost. The chances are that the insurance underwriters at your carrier were in a position to make a determination of your probability for loss, after all, that's their job, but they are usually more than happy to have your business either way. They don't make money by not selling coverage, but they do protect themselves from losses by identifying risks that are too dangerous to insure.

Causes of substandard risk management

There's a lot of substandard RM being done out there. Here are observations from several industry sources about some of the causes:

This article, *5 Common Risk Management Failures*[26] by Corporate Compliance Insights describes five symptoms of RM failure:

- Poor Governance and 'Tone of the Organization'
- Reckless Risk Taking
- Inability to Implement Effective Enterprise Risk Management
- Nonexistent, Ineffective or Inefficient Risk Assessment
- Not Integrating Risk Management with Strategy Setting and Performance Management

This post[27] by Protiviti includes those in the Corporate Compliance Insights article plus:

- Falling Prey to a 'Herd Mentality'
- Misunderstanding the 'If You Can't Measure It, You Can't Manage It!' Mindset
- Accepting a Lack of Transparency in High-Risk Areas
- Ignoring the Dysfunctionalities and 'Blind Spots' of the Organization's Culture
- Not Involving the Board in a Timely Manner

This paper[28] from Cornerstone Research reiterates the causes cited by Corporate Compliance Insights and describes how they manifested themselves in the failure of Long-Term Capital Management, which famously

[26] https://www.corporatecomplianceinsights.com/5-common-risk-management-failures/
[27] https://www.protiviti.com/US-en/insights/bulletinv3-i6
[28] https://www.cornerstone.com/Publications/Research/Risk-Management-Failures.pdf

almost brought the US and Global Capital Markets to a standstill and necessitated the largest bailout ever made up to that point in time.

This paper[29] by René Stultz of the Ohio State University in the Journal of Applied Corporate Finance lists five common causes of failure:

- Failure to use appropriate risk metrics
- Mismeasurement of known risks
- Failure to take known risks into account
- Failure in communicating risks to top management
- Failure in monitoring and managing risks

Now, the failures described in most of these papers and articles were in financial markets—related mainly to trading activities—but the issues are equally applicable to general business operations.

There are some common themes in these papers. Bad RM almost always involves some or all of:

- Misaligned corporate culture with respect to risk appetite or tolerance
- Failure of governance
- Failure to identify risks
- Failure to evaluate them properly
- Failure to implement systematic RM practices and employ risk-based thinking and problem-solving

Your goals for improving your risk management

Your company's culture is unique to it. If the company is led by 'swing-for-the-fences,' 'risks-be damned' types (think, Enron), then the chances are that there won't be a lot of attraction or willingness to focus on managing risks. Then again, the company might not be around long enough to benefit from a comprehensive RM approach, anyway. Governance requires discipline, so if your company falls into this category, it's unlikely that there will be interest in implementing and assuring competent execution of processes you don't have.

For everyone else, these are your goals:

- **Comprehensiveness**—reliably recognizing existing risks, new ones as they are created or morphing ones as they change,
- **Rapidity**—staying ahead of risks as the company and its business evolves,
- **Accuracy**—application of appropriate statistical techniques to ensure that prevention and mitigation efforts will be effective and properly calibrated,

---

29 https://cpb-us-w2.wpmucdn.com/u.osu.edu/dist/0/30211/files/2017/02/Risk-management-Failures-1l5due1.pdf

- **Repeatability**—employing mature, repeatable processes to identify, assess and treat risks and
- **Evolution and Improvement**—continuously improving your ability to do all the above with efficiency and effectiveness.

To achieve the evolution from TRM to ERM to AERM, you will have to:

- Integrate ERM with the other management disciplines you exercise and processes you execute to run your business,
- Employ qualitative and quantitative techniques,
- Identify the underlying causes of risks, not just try to manipulate the outcomes from your business activities and
- Establish systematic approaches to RM, backed up with automation to support the analytics you will need for AERM.

WHY WON'T TRADITIONAL APPROACHES TO MANAGING RISK WORK GOING FORWARD?

In the earlier section on *Agile and Agility*, we discussed how the evolving world is making it imperative for companies to achieve business agility if they expect to survive and thrive. In this section, we've discussed how RM is currently practiced at many companies.

Like many management practices, RM as a formal practice developed at a time when companies and the environments in which they competed evolved more slowly than they do now. Then, and in some measure even now, companies operated on a quarterly and annual rhythm. Financial reports and tax filings are produced on that schedule, projects are funded largely on that schedule, employees are reviewed on that schedule, board meetings occur on that schedule and important decisions are often made on that schedule.

It seems likely that many initiatives are even planned (whether consciously or not) to fit in units of the quarters that they will require to execute. This fits nicely into the mental Gantt chart[30] that senior executives keep in their heads of what to expect quarter by quarter.

Now, that schedule is largely out the window. Things evolve much too fast for an arbitrary tempo to drive a company's evolution.

A lot of this is motivated by an inherent psychic need for most managers: ***predictability***—what will happen, when it will happen and how much it's going to cost. Hitting those measures has historically been viewed as the mark of a well-managed project or business unit and missing them has been viewed as an indicator of mismanagement. This is espoused by the Project

[30] https://en.wikipedia.org/wiki/Gantt_chart

Management Institute (the PMI)[31] and other organizations and has been drilled into the heads of their certificate holders from the time the organizations sprung up and began issuing them.

In 2001, *the Agile Manifesto*[32] was written, and the idea of iterative software development began to proliferate. Soon thereafter, Agile adherents began creating proprietary versions of it, each with their own vocabulary, processes and ceremonies, most of them more alike than any of them would be willing to admit. The Agile Industrial Complex (the AIC)[33] was born!

While it was an improvement over the Waterfall approach, Agile was force-fitted into the same ***triple constraint*** (scope, schedule, cost) project management framework. So, you were free to evolve your product as long as the project completed on time and within budget. Hopefully, the sponsors and users got something beneficial out of it and positive business outcomes were realized.

If you research the subject, you will find estimates that anywhere from 15% to 70% of software development projects fail or fail to deliver what they were expected to. The wide variance is attributable to how failure is defined. Where it's tied to the traditional measures of project success (the triple constraint), the estimate tends to be higher. Reported failure rates seem to be stable over time, though. Agile seems not to have had a gigantic impact on software development project success rates so far.

This should tell us something important—many organizations have not changed their mind set about how transformation should be executed and managed. It comports with my experience that ***many companies' senior executives want to improve their businesses and are willing to do anything but actually change to achieve it.***

*So, **Agile, as prescribed by the AIC, frequently fails to facilitate business agility***. It does, however, formalize and, in some instances, increase collaboration between business users or 'product owners' and the development team—a positive step. Unfortunately, decision-makers from the business side often assign a mid-level staff member to represent their interests, undercutting the value that should be realized from continuous exposure to and on-the-spot resolution of questions and issues.

As the Agile Industrial Complex evolved, the notion of rapid, iterative transformation escaped the confines of software development activities and began to spread to other areas of management. New approaches in all sorts of areas are emerging, motivated largely by an increasing rate of change in technology and business models driven by the Internet, Cloud technologies, DevOps development techniques and the need to evolve or die.

---

31 https://www.pmi.org/

32 https://en.wikipedia.org/wiki/Agile_software_development#The_Manifesto_for_Agile_Software_Development

33 https://martinfowler.com/articles/agile-aus-2018.html

So, traditional approaches to RM, as practiced by many companies, will not work because they cannot keep up with the rate of change required today. Attempting to manage rapidly evolving risks on a quarterly or annual calendar will certainly lead to missing and failing to mitigate many of them and it will also shortchange the repository of historical information that should power continuous improvement. It's pretty much as simple as that.

What values can we take from Agile to apply to transforming ERM to AERM? Agile is a project-oriented, systems development approach and AERM is intended to facilitate identification of changes in risk resulting from changes in your environment or operations. While they partially share a name, they are two different things.

However, like Agile, AERM employs:

- Tight integration among the various parties involved in transformation and evolution,
- Application of technology-enabled tooling to support it, and
- Implementation of models and information repositories that contribute to accelerating recognition of changes that require attention and adoption of ever-more efficient approaches to execution.

You must enable risk managers to identify rapidly and reliably ***what*** is being changed as the enterprise is evolved, ***what*** it's connected to, ***what*** it's dependent on, ***what*** connects to it and ***what*** depends on it. If you know all that, you have a fighting chance of maintaining awareness of the scope and domain of internal changes as they are being made. Then, if risk managers can collaborate with their colleagues and identify ***why*** changes are being made and trace them to the internal and external forces that are driving them, there is a chance to perform RM at the speed required to keep up with the business.

That is the underlying premise of Agile Enterprise Risk Management.

CHAPTER SUMMARY

Key concepts addressed in this chapter include:

- Traditional ERM practices include eight steps:
  1. Set Context
  2. Establish Risk Appetite and Tolerance
  3. Inventory Risks
  4. Perform a Risk Assessment
  5. Establish Integrated RM Controls, Policies and Processes
  6. Implement, Execute and Monitor ERM Performance
  7. Conduct Risk Audit and Risk Assurance
  8. Evolve and Improve

- The traditional approach has failings that will be exacerbated by the transformation companies will require to remain competitive as markets evolve. Specifically:
    - Failure to identify risks, especially those relating to interdependencies, comprehensively,
    - Application of qualitative methods to what are quantitative problems,
    - Failure to identify and assess decision processes and
    - Inability to operate at the velocity required to keep pace with business changes.
- What Is Risk?
    - Risk is the *probability* that things will not turn out as you expect them to or as you hope they will and that you will incur some type of loss or other sub-optimal outcome in circumstances in which you have something of value at risk.
    - Risk is ideally judged as a cumulative probability that the value that determines the outcome being measured will fall outside of a desired cutoff. This means that estimating a probability density function for the value is required—for example, the probability that you will fall short of projected net profit in a future period.
- Understanding ***risk appetite*** and ***risk tolerance*** are baseline requirements for formulating your risk treatments. You must know what you can tolerate before you can determine what you are willing to do to mitigate risks.
- ERM governance involves ***Risk Audit*** and ***Risk Assurance***. Your updated ERM process should be designed to facilitate these executive and board-level processes.
- The five goals of your ERM function are comprehensiveness, rapidity, accuracy, repeatability and continuous evolution and improvement.
- Traditional ERM is not a sustainable model. However, if you can implement a new model integrated with the disciplines with which you manage your business, you can enable yourself to manage risks more comprehensively, transform more rapidly and reliably and achieve better business results.

Chapter 3

Digital transformation, business agility and risk

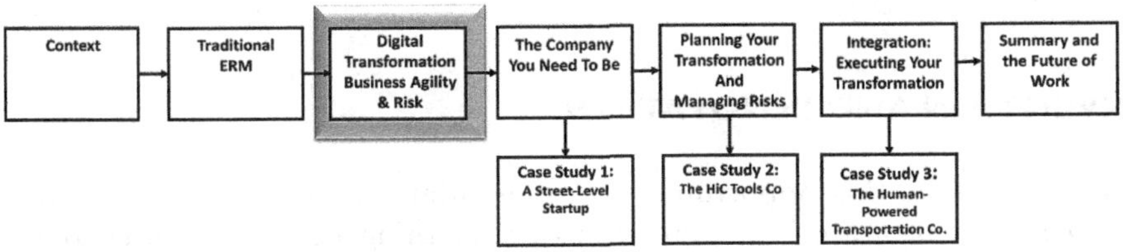

COVERED IN THIS CHAPTER

- *Invention* and *Innovation* drive change and produce recurring market cycles. A model with four phases is common to many industry strategists:
  - Introduction—offerings emerge,
  - Maturation—offerings are customized for individual purchasers,
  - Growth—competition increases, and offerings become productized and
  - Decline—product evolution slows, marginal sellers leave the market, major players realize higher profits with less investment required to preserve market share, becoming 'Cash Cows'
- As the rate of *innovation* accelerates, the length of market lifecycles decreases. The life of Cash Cows gets shorter and shorter. Also, cloud-based services are making it possible for smaller players to build technology-enabled products that were formerly possible only for larger companies.
- Traditional products and services are increasingly delivered side by side with innovative digital services and products. GE and Caterpillar are excellent examples of this. The implication is that you will have to transform to enable yourself to deliver digital products and services if you expect to sustain your business, even if you have a traditional product line, such as earth-moving equipment or personal care products.

DOI: 10.1201/9781003188605-4

- To remain competitive in the evolving digital landscape you will have to undergo a Digital Transformation, acquiring a lot of new skills, modifying your organization and governance structures, developing new processes and exposing your company to a very different set of risks than you are probably used to.
- If your approach to ERM relies on quarterly and annual updates to a static risk register, then it will not be adequate to keep pace with the business you are aiming to become. If that is what you're doing, you will need to step up to manage on a continuous basis.
- *Agile Enterprise Risk Management* will be required to manage the risks inherent in the highly dynamic environment in which you will be operating.

INVENTION AND INNOVATION

We should take this opportunity to differentiate the terms *invention* and *innovation. Invention* is the creation of something new, most often these days, technology driven. *Innovation* is the creation of value from the invention. Teflon®[1] was discovered/invented by DuPont in 1938. In 1954, French and American engineers innovated by applying it to cookware and labware and it has become a common element of many products since then. In this case, the lag between invention and productization of the innovation was uncommonly lengthy. Such windows of opportunity are certainly not the case today. However, because Teflon has so many applications, there remain hundreds of companies that are still profitably producing products that employ it, from consumer cookware to industrial applications.

Invention and innovation cycles drive markets

Markets operate in natural cycles:

- An invention—a technology or an application of it—is developed.
- Early adopters take the invention, innovate around it and produce early-stage commercial offerings based on it that provide substantial advantage to customers,
- The invention and innovations mature, becoming more widely produced, accessible and cheaper to more companies and more and more competitors jump on the bandwagon,
- The market matures; evolution of the inventions and innovations slows; they become more commonly available and accessible and competitors with greater market shares and staying ability thrive while

[1] https://en.wikipedia.org/wiki/Polytetrafluoroethylene

marginal competitors exit the market, perhaps by selling to a more competitive company or by simply shutting down,

- The inventions and innovations become commoditized and the market growth for products incorporating them slows to the point at which almost all competitors move on. The chances are good that something will have come along with better features or price-performance, obviating the value or advantage of the aging inventions and innovations.

Consider the Sony Walkman®, which first appeared as a cassette player (1979) and has transformed many times since:

- Slimline redesign and rechargeable batteries
- Digital audio tape (1987), recorder/player (1990)
- Sports version (1988)
- Minidisc model (1992)
- Slimmer/smaller form factor redesign (1996)
- CD Walkman (1999)
- Solid-state flash memory-20Gb (2000-2003)
- MP3 Walkman (2004)
- Sony-Ericsson phone Walkman (2007)
- Touchscreen version (2009)
- Hi-res version (2013)

By 1989, Sony owned about 50% of the market for portable players in the US and Japan. Now, the Walkman and other products like personal digital assistants (PDAs) are pretty nearly gone, all replaced by our smart phones.

Various models illustrate cycles' impact

Several people have described the phenomenon and developed approaches to business strategy based on its effects. These include the Boston Consulting Group (BCG) Growth-Share Matrix model,[2] Simon Wardley[3] and Mik Kersten[4] and many others. The diagrams, below, illustrate how this seminal idea appears in their work:

The BCG Growth-Share Matrix

In 1968, the BCG developed a portfolio management strategy for multi-line companies. The logic behind the approach is that a company should get into promising markets early and compete hard to establish substantial market share. As markets mature, marginal competitors exit, creating the

[2] https://www.bcg.com/en-us/about/our-history/growth-share-matrix
[3] https://en.wikipedia.org/wiki/Wardley_map
[4] https://projecttoproduct.org/the-book/

Figure 3.1 The Boston Consulting Group's Growth-Share model.

opportunity for survivors to realize high profitability with limited requirement for investment capital and a high cash throw off—a 'Cash Cow.' Cash would be recycled from the Cash Cows and be invested back into business lines involved in earlier-stage, more competitive markets. The point of the strategy behind the model is to manage the enterprise's businesses as a portfolio, with 'Cash Cows' (businesses with large market share in mature stable or shrinking markets) providing funds to invest in 'Stars' (businesses with small market share in growing markets) to increase their market share.

The Invincible Company: a portfolio of businesses

In a similar vein, the consulting company Strategyzer published a book called *The Invincible Company*,[5] advocating that companies look within themselves for innovation to create new business models, maintaining a portfolio of experimental prospective businesses, pruning it relentlessly in order to continually reallocate investment capital from projects that did not prove out to new ones. This diagram illustrates the cash-flow relationship between more successful, maturing business and the portfolio of experimental projects:

Note that this model is driven by the same market cycle-driven strategy as the BCG model—get involved early, establish a presence and achieve market share, reap the reward and recycle cash or exit early and preserve capital.

Parallels among the models

This diagram below shows the common elements of BCG's and Simon Wardley's models. The scale at the top (Startup, Growth, Maturity, Decline) is common to many market lifecycle models. The BCG business classes fit pretty well into this lifecycle.

[5] https://www.strategyzer.com/books/the-invincible-company

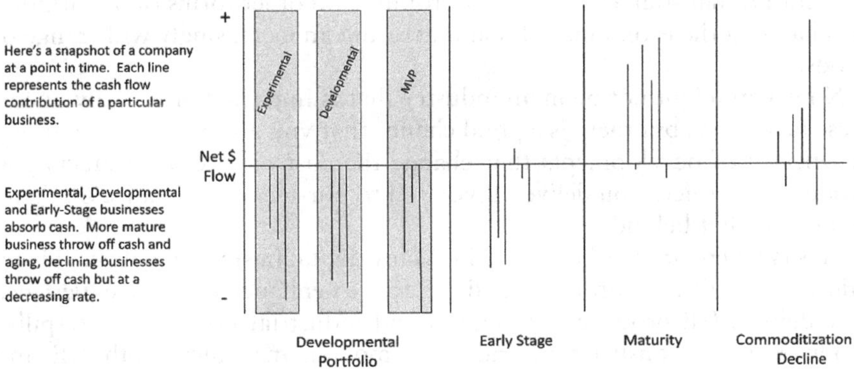

Figure 3.2 Typical cash flows across lifecycle stages.

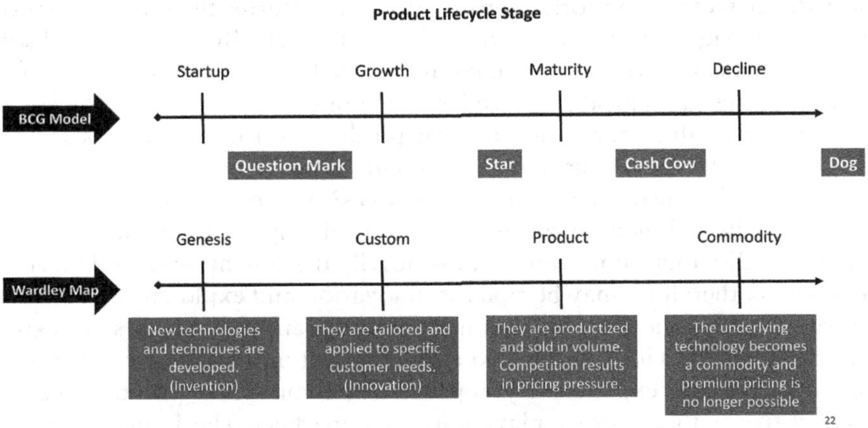

Figure 3.3 Comparison of the BCG and Wardley lifecycle stages.

Below that is Wardley's market lifecycle. His model is based on the same phenomena.

IMPLICATIONS FOR YOUR BUSINESS

Understanding the environment requires that you consider both *invention* and *innovation*. Yes, advancements are taking place in myriad industries, such as health care, energy and manufacturing. New inventions are enabling fantastic products and changing the economics of markets left and right. One only need consider the velocity with which new COVID vaccines were developed to have a sense of it. Similarly, renewable energy sources are being developed and evolved, driving prices down and making them competitive with traditional sources. Stereolithogrophy[6] and other forms of 3D printing are changing the economics of manufacturing an increasingly wide range of goods.

Now, you might not be in an industry that is impacted directly by one of these inventions but there is a good chance that you are, at least, an indirect beneficiary of developments that change the cost picture of products you produce or services you deliver. If you fail to pursue and capitalize on them, you will be left behind.

This is where *innovation* comes in. Many digital businesses deliver side by side with traditional products and services to enhance the user experience they deliver. GE produces jet engines and industrial products. Caterpillar produces giant construction and earth-moving machines. Both GE and Caterpillar have thrived by adding digital services to their products. These services monitor the usage, performance and condition of what they've sold, allowing them to anticipate customers' needs for maintenance services and provide telemetric monitoring information that informs their ability to proactively manage their inventory of replacement parts. By adding digital services to physical products, these companies help to prevent downtime for their customers and produce considerable savings for them in the process. It improves the value proposition of their products to their customers as well as deepening the bond they have with them.

Do you sell consumer products or services? You may, but you probably don't actually sell them to consumers. You probably sell them into a supply chain and distribution network that is heavily dependent on digital services and which, therefore, may be ripe for innovation and exploitation, whether by you or someone else. The online marketing and sales ecosystem exists side by side with what you sell and it's incumbent on you to make sure your offerings, the user experiences you provide and your value propositions are competitive with the other players in your markets. The brand equity of many name-brand consumer products has been eroded by me-too competitors willing to compete on 'good-enough' quality and cheaper prices. White-labeled house brands sold online may well be competing with your premium priced, top-shelf products.

Irrespective of product-specific digital enhancements, your customers and suppliers want to be able to work with you digitally. No one wants to have to get on the phone to get an account or order status if they can look it up themselves on a web app and none of your employees want to get stuck in a game of telephone tag with another if they can employ self-service to resolve questions or problems. No one wants to go to a bank branch to deposit a paper check if they can take a picture of it with their phone and perform the transaction remotely. You're going to want to employ technology such as Robotic Process Automation (RPA) to realize the benefits that

[6] https://en.wikipedia.org/wiki/Stereolithography

it can provide, and you can't do that if your processes are not properly structured and digitized.

Finally, there is the issue of decision velocity—how quickly you can decide how to respond to a situation. If you are going to be doing business digitally, your workforce is likely to be managing a much larger number of transactions per capita and each one may require a decision. If you are a bank, you could be using a web-based application to capture small-business loan applications and employing Artificial Intelligence (AI) to screen them before presenting them to a banker for review. If you are an insurer, you might be accepting applications for insurance and requests for quotes through an online portal and should be able to respond through automation that performs screening and policy pricing as well as upselling without involving an underwriter as long as the requested coverage is within acceptable limits.

Digital products and services will come to constitute a growing fraction of the total value of what is sold. In juxtaposition to the time it takes to revise the design of a car and produce next year's model, digital services can be upgraded from minute to minute. Amazon, Google and Netflix all release new software *thousands of times per day*.[7] While many of these are bug fixes or minor changes, a fair number of them are part of enhancements to their offerings or tests to help inform design decisions that will optimize performance or financial results. As you should well imagine, the lifespan of any business model will shrink in the evolving environment and the value and viability of your Cash Cow will diminish with it.

The bottom line is simply this: you have to become a digital business if you expect to remain competitive and profitable. You must achieve agility in order to survive and you will have to be able to deal with the risks attendant with this as you go.

DIGITAL'S STRATEGIC IMPACT IS FORCING ENTERPRISES TO RETHINK EXECUTION

Almost no offering can be considered stand-alone, even something like personal services. You can't get your hair cut without going to the salon, but you can use an online service to make the appointment and pay for it afterward. The salon can offer returning customers rewards or incentives from a diverse mutual referral network to which it belongs. The personal care products that the salon sells can be tied to manufacturers' incentive programs. All these things can and should be tied to various participants' web services and their online presence. Interactions can be analyzed to see if exposure, engagement and behavioral trends can inform new opportunities to communicate with and earn new business from customers and prospects. The

7 https://www.zdnet.com/article/devops-leaders-deliver-software-200-times-more-frequently-than-their-peers-study-shows/

customer experience your company provides and your online reputation are critical components of your value proposition and must be constantly monitored, managed and enhanced.

The breadth of changes you need to accommodate has grown. As you add features, functions or pricing changes to your products or services, you will have to synchronize them with your online presence. To enable your company to implement them, you need to take every opportunity to create efficiencies in your production and delivery processes. This means looking at how you can digitize your business as usual (BAU) and governance processes to improve communication and collaboration, remove bottlenecks and exploit information to improve decision-making.

SWOT is an acronym for Strengths, Weaknesses, Opportunities and Threats. It is an intuitive framework for looking at your company's competitive position. Compared to your competitors, relative strengths generally provide opportunities and relative weaknesses may expose you to threats. In this vein, it is important to view opportunities and threats from both inside-out and outside-in standpoints. If a competitor comes up with a novel and attractive offering you can't match, that represents an outside-in threat. If you come up with a new and innovative composite service, that represents an inside-out opportunity. Your relative strengths and weaknesses are what will determine whether inventions, innovations or other developments within your company or that occur in the markets in which you compete are threats or opportunities.

For example, remember your 150 MPG engine. Having the ability to build and deliver it is a ***strength*** relative to your competitors, one that confers an ***opportunity*** to acquire market share. From the viewpoint of a competitor, the inability to deliver such a product is a ***weakness***, which creates a ***threat*** of lost market share.

Here's the digital rub—you now, and increasingly will, have online product, service and user experience characteristics to monitor in addition to those of the products and services you provide today. Package delivery services offer the same service at mostly comparable prices. They are all competing to provide more convenient, comprehensive web-based services to go along with physical package delivery. The easier and simpler they can make it to schedule pickup, delivery or monitor the location of your package within their network, the more attractive their services are. Right now, they record when packages make transition points in their network—when it's received at a sorting center, when it's loaded onto a truck, when it goes out for delivery and so forth. Eventually, packages will probably have cheap transponders attached to them to allow anyone to track them continuously. Even if your company offers the same services as everyone else in your business, if you're not keeping pace online, you have a weakness that can threaten your survival.

So, whether you want to or not, you must widen the scope of what you monitor in your environment to include every aspect of your and your competitors' value propositions and maximize your ability to exploit opportunities or respond to threats at speed. Business Agility is crucial to enabling your business to survive and thrive. This means rapid change and that means rapid evolution of your risks.

A strategy that reflects today's digital realities demands revised operational capabilities

The rate at which markets and business models are evolving is now making some things that used to be considered strategic, tactical and there is a plethora of changes that go into being able to respond at that level. Business Agility demands that your organization must have a distributed responsibility and authority structure that will allow product managers to devise, implement and begin selling new offerings swiftly. You must have analytical capabilities and the data they require to inform your decision-making and, possibly, customize your product characteristics on a customer-by-customer basis. You must have governance and supporting functions, such as your audit and legal departments, organized to perform oversight and provide advisory services as and when they are needed. You must develop reusable processes that provide a playbook for product development teams to follow to accelerate their work. You must architect your information technology to make solution-building as close to plug-and-play as you can. And you must manage the risks of your business as continuous evolution happens.

It's a daunting list, one that implies a lot of changes in parallel for most organizations that have been around for any length of time. It's impossible to make all of them simultaneously, so careful planning is a key to succeeding at digital transformation, which at companies of any size, will probably require years.

There are a number of structural elements that distinguish a digital business from a traditional business, many of which have profound implications for risks. Some that stand out include:

- Distributed authority and responsibility structures,
- Management teams that integrate traditional product managers with technologists and anyone else required to design, produce and deliver digital products and services,
- Digital Product and Services development and delivery platforms, optimized for high-velocity, agile, DevOps development,
- Established, redeployable product development processes, supporting services and reusable components. As described by Mik Kersten, projects, and the governance models through which they are traditionally approved, must transition to value-stream, product development initiatives.
- Shared information infrastructure, optimized for accessibility, integrability, elasticity, security, availability, etc.

Traditional enterprise structural and management models that will have to change

A lot about traditional *command and control* management still in use in many businesses is antithetical to business agility and will have to change to be compatible with operating as a digital business. This article from Inc.[8] and this one from Forbes[9] speak to this issue. Some elements of traditional approaches that will be rethought include:

- Quarterly and annual governance cycles,
- Annual budgeting, review and approval for transformation initiatives,
- Legacy (all or nothing) project funding,
- Traditional project management practices,
- Traditional thinking about share price preservation which can create resistance to change or reluctance to writing off assets tied to waning business models and
- Business models that require substantial asset bases and work forces if there are alternative approaches available.

THE GOALS AND CHALLENGES OF TRANSFORMATION

Ultimately, your goal in transforming to adapt to the VUCA world we're now in is to enable yourself to create, deliver and evolve new business offerings and business models at great speed, in short—Business Agility. Invariably, most of these offerings will be digital in their entirety or will consist of a combination of a product or service paired with a digital services component. If you do not currently provide digital products or services, you will have to learn how and enable yourself to. You're going to need to identify opportunities to apply AI to increase your decision-making velocity and enhance your ability to provide customized offerings.

At the same time as you are developing these capabilities, you will have to rationalize and redesign your infrastructure, modify your governance models, transform your organization and quite possibly rework some of your current lines of business. You are going to have to change how you think about depreciable assets and become more willing to accept some technical debt to accelerate delivering or evolving solutions. And, you're going to have to revisit your approach to managing the risks that are inherent in running your business this way. We'll deal with this in more detail in a subsequent chapter—*The Company You Need to Be*.

---

8 https://www.inc.com/robert-glazer/command-control-leadership-is-dead-heres-whats-taking-its-place.html

9 https://www.forbes.com/sites/lizryan/2016/02/26/command-and-control-management-is-for-dinosaurs

The path to achieving agility such as this is not straightforward, nor is it in any way standard. There are six major architectural elements of a digital company—a rationalized operational infrastructure, API gateways, a distributed governance model, a digital product & service factory, business intelligence and analytics and a partner development platform. In addition to implementing this set of target-state elements, you will need to adopt what may be entirely new practices to you, such as value-stream product management and agile/DevOps development and delivery processes.

It requires parallel tracks, and in most cases, progress in two or three of them is required to achieve a minimal capability in a targeted area. Planning and road mapping the transformation process will be a complex challenge. Given the timeframe likely to be involved, a number of the assumptions you start out with are going to be invalidated, technologies will become superseded, and the business landscape will certainly change. Simply put, it's a process, not a project or even a program.

In her book *Designed for Digital*,[10] Jeanne Ross presents case studies of several companies' journeys toward becoming digital businesses and achieving the type of business agility you will need. Each of the businesses is quite different from the others, each pursues a different path and, taken together, they demonstrate a diversity of approaches that are available. Although these companies have been in transformation for years, none of them, as of the time the book was published, had 'landed' at a final to-be state, nor will they ever. The path on which you will need to embark is a process of continual evolution that will never end.

Charting a course forward is fraught with opportunities to err. You can easily go too big or too small, too fast or too slow. You can constrain yourself to the narrow domain of what you are already doing, or you can fling yourself into totally new waters. This article[11] from McKinsey identifies a number of mistakes that companies make in trying to accommodate the realities of competition in the digital realm. One of the biggest is to try to add a veneer of digital services over existing product and service lines without the substantially refactoring strategies, processes, organization and technology, which are all integral to success.

In this subsequent article,[12] McKinsey identifies four areas that differentiate companies that demonstrate markedly better economic performance from their peers:

- "The best performers have increased the agility of their digital-strategy practices, which enables first-mover opportunities.
- They have taken advantage of digital platforms to access broader ecosystems and to innovate new digital products and business models.

10 https://mitpress.mit.edu/books/designed-digital

11 https://www.mckinsey.com/business-functions/mckinsey-digital/our-insights/why-digital-strategies-fail

12 https://www.bcg.com/en-us/publications/2019/five-rules-digital-strategy

- They have used M&A to build new digital capabilities and digital businesses.
- They have invested ahead of their peers in digital talent."

Among the other recommendations in the article, they identify a need for companies to "increase the agility of creating, executing, and adjusting strategy." This is exactly what we have been espousing, throughout the book, thus far. However, the approaches they recommend all come with attendant risks, in many cases risks which may be entirely unfamiliar, that you will have to manage as you go.

In this article,[13] BCG has advised that "While there is no need to completely rewrite the transformation rule book when it comes to digital, some issues will need your attention—such as the rate at which the critical underlying technologies for your industry are evolving, and thus how often you should revisit the underlying strategy to refresh the transformation plan."

But, they also warn that " ...planning three years out can set you up for executional failure if changes in technologies and market dynamics shift more rapidly."

To address these concerns, they call out the need for speed in this article[14] "**Design for speed**. Traditional organizations separate strategy and execution. Agile, responsive organizations remove this distinction and create an ongoing strategic loop by making deliberate, appropriate changes to communication structures and functional silos."

In this Harvard Business Review article,[15] Benham Tabrizi[16] observes: "A recent survey of directors, CEOs, and senior executives found that digital transformation (DT) risk is their #1 concern in 2019. Yet 70% of all DT initiatives do not reach their goals. Of the $1.3 trillion that was spent on DT last year, it was estimated that $900 billion went to waste. Why do some DT efforts succeed and others fail? Fundamentally, it's because most digital technologies provide possibilities for efficiency gains and customer intimacy. But if people lack the right mindset to change and the current organizational practices are flawed, DT will simply magnify those flaws."

There are innumerable business thought leaders that are pretty consistent on several points:

- Digital Transformation is not solely about technology. You must set a strategy and remake your company thoughtfully in order to succeed.
- Digital Transformation, like any transformation is about people. If you do not manage the people side of the process, you cannot succeed.

13 https://www.bcg.com/en-us/publications/2019/five-rules-digital-strategy
14 https://www.bcg.com/en-us/publications/2019/fast-execution-needs-fast-strategy
15 https://hbr.org/2019/03/digital-transformation-is-not-about-technology
16 https://hbr.org/search?term=behnam%20tabrizi&search_type=search-all

- Velocity and business agility are crucial goals of your transformation.
- You cannot succeed without taking risks and selecting the right ones is critical.

HOW AND WHY RISK MANAGEMENT NEEDS TO CHANGE

Risk management challenges will accumulate. First, you will be going through a significant transformation for an extended time, which will have its own risks that require monitoring and management. Second, you will be moving into an operational environment with new expectations, assumptions and challenges, exacerbated by an increased tempo. The expected life of the products, services and solutions you will be creating, at least in their initial incarnations, will be shorter than those you're used to, and this may change the imputed impact of many risks, such as the cost of technical debt. *If a system supporting a new product with what you expect will be a two-year life has to be in production in three months for the product to be viable, is it worth stretching the implementation cycle to make it more reusable later?*

Annual, even quarterly assessment will not be adequate to keep pace with the rate of change for which you are preparing. If this is the basis you're working on, you need to transition to one that is as close to possible to being continuous.

Componentizing and distributing authority in your organization, as is required by a digital business, will complicate your risk management efforts. The diversity of processes and approaches to problem-solving that may evolve in your operations will only serve to increase the diversity of the risks you will have to manage.

The rate at which your markets change will increase the risk profile of your company. As cloud-enabled services enable newer and smaller companies to compete with you, it is probable that you will have to maintain surveillance on a much wider range of potential competitors than you do now.

Ultimately, then, you will need to evolve your ability to identify risk generators in your markets and operational architecture, understand dependencies and interrelationships among the components of your company's architecture and develop a strong sense of the key risk indicators that you will need to monitor to ensure that you can respond to risk events with alacrity. A new approach—***Agile Enterprise Risk Management***—is what you will need.

CHAPTER SUMMARY

Key concepts addressed in this chapter include:

- *Invention* and *innovation* drive the evolution of markets. The forces they generate are creating change with increasing rapidity and magnitude, with profound implications for businesses. You must pay attention to opportunities and threats relating to both *invention* and *innovation* if you are to keep your business in step with the markets in which you compete.

- Digital's impact will force you to rethink your strategy and execution. Just because you don't sell digital products today doesn't mean that you can't add innovative services to them. As you do that, you will have to transform your operating model to accommodate new ways of doing things.
- Traditional enterprise structural models that will have to transform include Information and Communication Technology (ICT) architecture, organizational structures, value-stream or product (not project) focus and governance processes. New sources of risk will emerge, and old ones will transform.
- Your primary goal for transformation is simple—***business agility***. You must strip away everything that impedes your ability to recognize threats or opportunities and act on them. The challenges and risks of transformation are many and you must pursue a path informed by risk-based thinking to achieve it.

Chapter 4

The company you need to be

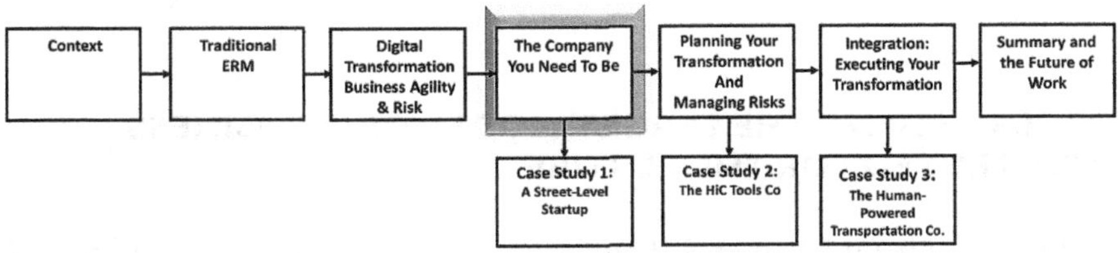

COVERED IN THIS CHAPTER

- A recap of the major forces that should inform the target design of your enterprise.
- Why do I need a Digital Transformation?
- The Anatomy of Your Company—Enterprise and Business Architecture frameworks describe how your company is constituted to fulfill its mission—how it will create and deliver value to your customers and much more. Creating, populating and maintaining this model will give you a vital tool to understand the implications of change on your organization, identify risks and manage them.
- The Anatomy of a Digital Business—the operational elements of a digital business are composed of Capabilities and Enablers, organized into Value Streams that deliver Products and Services to your Markets. A number of specialized entities enable your digital capabilities.
- Digital Transformation Means Transforming Your Enterprise Architecture.
- A preview of the transformation journey—Preparing to execute the transformation requires an as-is and a to-be enterprise architecture (EA)/ business architecture (BA) model that incorporates the Digital Business building blocks and accounts for change along many dimensions. Ultimately, there are two components of the transformation. You will need to do both to realize the benefits:

DOI: 10.1201/9781003188605-5

    - Implement the elements identified in the *Anatomy of a Digital Business*.
    - Evolve your company's architecture to exploit the capabilities that you will have enabled.
- Risk Management and the Controlled Transformation Journey.
- Haven't I already done some of this? You probably have implemented pieces and parts of the Digital Business Anatomy. You need to standardize them where it's possible and integrate them into a cohesive whole with your EA to realize the benefits.
- Agile Enterprise Risk Management (AERM) and the digital enterprise—given what you are preparing to do, how do you keep up with the risks?

FORCES DRIVING THE TARGET MODEL OF A BUSINESS ARCHITECTED FOR THE FUTURE

To summarize from Chapter 3 (*Digital transformation, business agility and risk)*, here are the most significant factors that should influence how you design or redesign your company:

- **Rapid evolution of business models:** Digital products and services are being layered on top of, next to or marketed and sold independent of traditional ones. Subscription models as diverse as Netflix streaming services and GE's monitoring and maintenance services are growing in popularity and volume.
- **Cloud-based architectures and pay-as-you-go infrastructure and services:** These make it possible for early-stage and smaller competitors to acquire and employ computing resources at price points that enable them to compete with much larger players.
- **Reduced ability to leverage Cash Cows:** As Cash Cows come under increasing attack, they require more investment to maintain their market position and throw off less cash for a shorter time to fund newer, investment-hungry businesses.
- **Novel risks will arise, and old ones will morph**: As your company and its business models evolve, the risk environment in which you operate will transform. Maintaining pace will require that you can triage at speed and make informed judgments about which risks to treat and which to accept.
- **Business Agility is crucial:** Your ability to pivot rapidly and your willingness to walk away from what has been working when necessary to keep pace or get ahead is absolutely required for sustainability. Netflix' transitioning from physical distribution of CDs and DVDs to

streaming its content even while it was beating its competition in the market for home movie viewing is a quintessential example of this.

WHY DO I NEED A DIGITAL TRANSFORMATION?

Digital Transformation touches almost all aspects of your business and while it's not necessary to have completed every aspect of it to get benefits, the synergies from a comprehensive transition are intrinsic to achieving the business agility that is the ultimate goal you should seek from the process. In the end, if you only partially transform your business, you will probably not fully realize this goal.

The benefits you might expect to realize from digital transformation include:

- Better interface and interactions with customers and external stakeholders from
  - Enhanced personalization and customization opportunities
  - Increased ability to apply AI to interactions, for example, by improving recommendations and upselling
- Increased speed to market for new or enhanced products and services by
  - Adopting value-stream product management paradigms, supported by Agile, DevOps development approaches
  - Iterating product features and characteristics rapidly, collecting user response data and analyzing it to guide and accelerate evolution
- Better integration and collaboration among members of your workforce and external partners by
  - Automating processes, which facilitates consolidating transactional data so that it can be exploited to evaluate and analyze them more easily.
- Streamlined business processes, increased operational agility by
  - Applying workflow and robotic process automation tools, enabling you to integrate AI to accelerate and improve decision-making and reconfigure processes rapidly.
- Better integration of technology
  - Standardizing approaches and toolsets makes it easier to reuse things that you have built. For instance, developing a consistent experiment, development, MVP lifecycle with a standard workbench of management and reporting systems obviates the need to reinvent them for each prospective product or business that you begin to incubate.

Hopefully, it makes intuitive sense to you that you should evolve with a purpose and employing entirely new tooling while continuing to do things as you have been will not get you to where you need to go.

In short, achieving the architecture of a digital enterprise:

- Will position you to reduce your dependence on your Cash Cows,
- Will position you to evolve your business model rapidly,
- Will be powered by cloud-based architectures and infrastructure,
- Will require that you ramp up your transformation muscles, increase your technical agility and revise your governance processes and
- Will require that you manage new and transformed risks that arise or morph as your business environment evolves and, if you have put the right metadata assets in place, facilitate your doing it.

THE ANATOMY OF YOUR COMPANY—ENTERPRISE AND BUSINESS ARCHITECTURE

A definition of enterprise

When you think of an enterprise or a business, you think of its brand, the products it sells and its reputation. The fact is, while they are all relevant to the enterprise, it is none of those things. The brand is an asset; products can be changed or discontinued and its reputation can wax or wane based on factors that the enterprise may not control completely. Actually, the enterprise is a portfolio of Capabilities and Enablers, all of which are included in the EA and BA models.

Capabilities are that which your enterprise is capable of doing. For example, auto companies design and build cars, banks assess applicants' credit and make loans and home builders construct houses. All of them perform administrative tasks, such as paying bills, filing taxes and managing their employees' benefits. To enable these Capabilities, the companies employ people with specific skills and enable them with places to work, application systems and equipment.

Enterprise architecture

An architect designing a building employs a palette that includes rooms, hallways, doors windows, stairways, electrical, plumbing and HVAC systems, among other things, to create a set of building plans. An architect designing an enterprise employs a palette that includes Products and Services, Value Streams, Capabilities, People, Processes, Technology, Physical Assets, Intellectual Property and so forth to create an EA model. A business architect designing how a business will deliver a product or service to the enterprise's customers will employ a palette incorporating elements of the EA model.

The diagram, below, depicts a schematic of an enterprise's architecture. It contains a limited number of entities but is sufficiently comprehensive for the purposes to which we will put it.

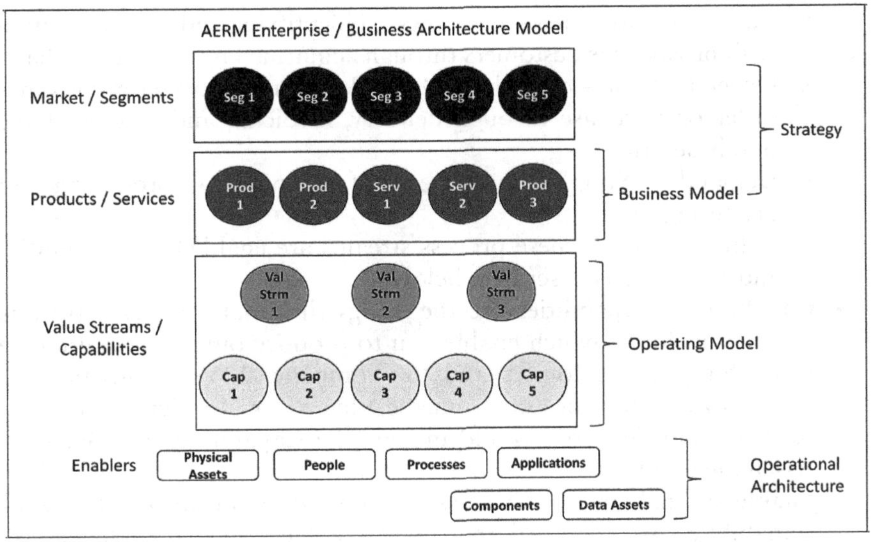

Figure 4.1 AERM EA/BA Architecture Model.

The entities contained in the model include:

- **Markets and Segments:** Market Segments are your enterprise's customers or potential customers, who may be broken into separate categories based on a variety of criteria. Individual customers or prospects may appear in multiple Segments if their demographics qualify them to.
- **Products and Services:** Products and Services are simply what your enterprise sells. Their characteristics, pricing and everything about the marketing and sales processes must be designed to optimize opportunities to sell to the Market Segments for which they are targeted.
- **Value Streams:** Value Streams contain the Capabilities required to produce specific outcomes that create value for your customers and your enterprise. For instance, if your company sells cars, it must design them, make or source parts for them, assemble them, publicize and promote them, finance them, sell them, deliver them and service them.

  This post[1] from the consulting company SYTE does a good job describing core and enabling business processes that comprise value streams common to most companies. The four core processes are:

  - Concept to Product—the heart of Value Stream product development. Ideation through development through productization to release.

[1] https://sytecg.com/erp-readiness-series-the-four-core-process-every-business-should-document/

 - Market to Customer—the process of identifying and communicating with prospective customers through acquiring an order or purchase.
 - Order to Cash—everything that takes place between a customer order or purchase through delivery, invoicing and receipt of the purchase price.
 - Demand to Supply—the process of planning for, producing and delivering products.

 In this model, these process streams are enabled by capabilities and enablers, as described, below.
- **Capabilities:** Capabilities are the things that that your enterprise is capable of doing, which enable you to produce outcomes that create value for your customers and the company. A Value Stream that addresses all that goes on from the time a car is ordered until it is paid for and delivered would include the Capabilities Sell, Finance, Assemble and Deliver.
- **Enablers:** Enablers are the assets required to produce what your Capabilities are designed to deliver. Enablers may include People, Processes, Technology (Application Systems, Technical Components and Information Assets), Physical Assets, Intellectual Property and so forth.

The EA model is organized into four levels:

- **Strategy:** The architecture of the enterprise must be driven by its strategy, that is—it must be optimized to deliver your products and services, to allow you to evolve the company to meet challenges and exploit opportunities in the foreseeable future. I define strategy, for the purpose of this model, as what the company will sell and to whom, and also which Capabilities you will develop and what Enablers will be required to support them. Strategy must be looked at from both outside-in and inside-out perspectives. The former represents what is going on in the markets in which you compete—what is creating opportunities and threats. The latter represents how you are planning to increase your competitiveness—how you will add or enhance Capabilities.

 Marketing disciplines often incorporate techniques that can inform strategy articulation. *Personas* are models of customers and prospects created to convey a rich picture of who they are, what they want and need and what is presumed to motivate their purchasing behavior. *Customer Journeys* are constructed to describe the process a customer goes through and the *Touchpoints* he encounters as he progresses from discovering a product to making a purchase decision.

 Representative techniques employed in strategy formulation include Trend and Scenario Analysis; Strength, Weakness, Opportunity, Threat (SWOT) Analysis.

Trend and Scenario Analysis focuses on external events, how they may play out and how your company should react to them. For example, in light of the expectation that new chips with 10 times the computing power of current chips will become available within the next 12 to 18 months, a computer manufacturer may revise expectations relating to the volume of its existing models it can expect to sell until then.

SWOT Analysis is focused both internally and externally to identify things the enterprise can do to play offense or defense. It is a useful framework to use in conjunction with the EA model because exploiting Strengths or offsetting Weaknesses in order to react to Opportunities or Threats will usually be accomplished by transforming Capabilities.

There are innumerable approaches to formulating and articulating business strategy, each with its own vocabulary and analytical rubric and illustrating and critiquing them is beyond the scope of this book. The definition we'll use here may sound simplistic, and it is, but it is sufficient for the purposes to which we will put this model.

- **Business Model:** The Business Model is the company's Product/Service portfolio as it relates to the Market Segment model that the company is using to define its strategy. You may think of it as what customers and prospects see when they look at what the company offers.
- **Operating Model:** The Operating Model encompasses the Value Streams and Capabilities that your company has in place to deliver value to customers and internally to itself. In a multiline company, Value Streams and Capabilities are likely to be shared among the lines and this creates interdependences that must be understood in order to manage risks prior to making changes in the EA model.
- **Operational Architecture:** The Operational Architecture consists of the Enablers: the people, processes, information, technology and assets that are employed to enable the company's Capabilities. These may include:
  - Physical Assets
    - Real estate
    - Plants and equipment
    - Offices, furniture, equipment
    - Data centers
    - Vehicles
    - Many others
  - Non-Physical Assets
    - Reputation
    - Brands, trademarks
    - Intellectual property, patents, copyrights
    - Financial resources, lines of credit
    - Business relationships, partnerships
    - Existing customer base

- Organization (People)
  - Employees and contractors
  - Roles, responsibilities and reporting relationships
  - Their skill sets, both general and role-specific
  - Their experience and know-how
- Processes
  - Standardized, defined
  - Monitoring practices
  - Automation supporting them
  - Rule repositories or decision engines
- Technology
- Architecture
  - Application systems
  - Infrastructure
  - Others
- Information Resources
  - Transaction history
  - Internal work product
  - Data generated from web interactions
  - Others

The image below is taken from a labeled property graph database that depicts the EA of a generic business that makes and sells two products to two Market Segments. Sales are encompassed within two Value Streams, in which a number of Capabilities, enabled by a number of Enablers are exercised. Note that many of the Capabilities and Enablers are shared between Products and Value Streams.

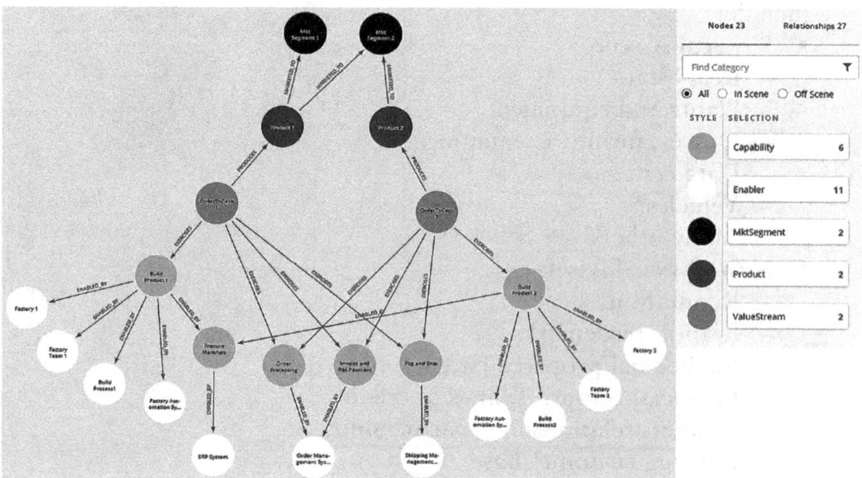

Figure 4.2 Graph representation of a generic company's EA.

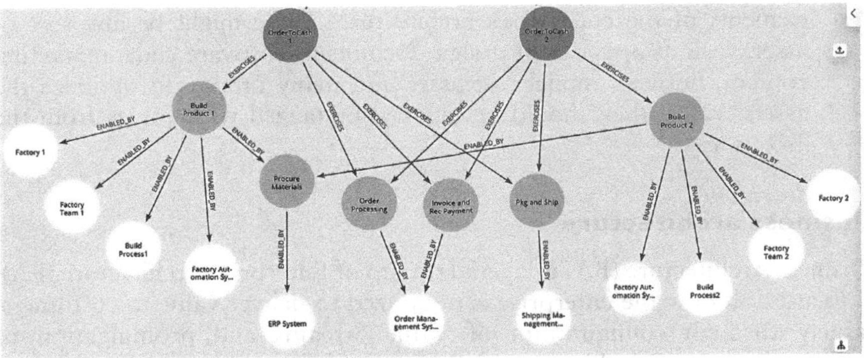

Figure 4.3 Detail showing Value Streams, Capabilities and Enablers from the Graph in Figure 4.2

This EA model shows how entities and elements of your enterprise are linked and combined to create value. If external events create opportunities or threats or if innovation creates an opportunity to deliver new or improved products or services or streamline operations, it is crucial to be able to comprehensively identify what you will need to change, what these entities are connected to that might be impacted and plan to effect the transformation while mitigating the risks of doing so. This, in a nutshell, is the connection between the EA discipline and AERM. If the EA model does not exist or has not been maintained, then you will be stuck planning for change without assurance that you are accounting for all that you should be or trying to create as much of the model as you can under the stress of exigent circumstances. Neither is optimal and with discipline, the situation is wholly avoidable.

There are two additional elements of the model that contribute to its purpose that are not depicted in the diagram:

- **Taxonomy:** If entities in the model are not referenced in a standard way, then it will impede the ability to identify relationships reliably, which will undermine the value of the model. A Taxonomy is used to enforce naming conventions and control labeling and tagging of data in the model to ensure that it conforms to standards.

  For example, consider an insurance company. One enabler it certainly must have is a payment system; however, it probably has three—one to pay claims, one for payroll and one to pay operating expenses. In the taxonomy, these would appear as a parent class—payments systems—and children, which would facilitate our finding them if we were searching the model for, say an existing enabler for a new business unit.
- **Pattern Library:** Asset reusability contributes to consistency and efficient use and reuse. The Pattern Library is a repository of potentially reusable assets that can accelerate designing, implementing or renovating

elements of the enterprise's architecture. These might be any sort of asset, such as application design documents, software code, marketing content, business model canvasses and many others. To optimize the assets' value, they should be indexed or tagged with values from the Taxonomy.

Business architecture

Business Architecture (BA) is layered on top of Enterprise Architecture (EA). It focuses on how the enterprise is organized to deliver value to customers, largely through configuration of Value Streams and promulgation of requirements for Capabilities and Enablers. If a company were to explore providing individualized or customized versions of its products, for example, business architects would be involved to conduct a gap analysis of the existing Operating Model and Operational Architecture to develop a set of requirements and a plan to evolve to accomplish the goal.

THE ANATOMY OF A DIGITAL BUSINESS

In the *Context* chapter, I made reference and included a link to a good overview article from Red Hat, a prominent, open-source company that sells cloud-related products and services. Red Hat was recently acquired by IBM.[2] Here is another link to the article if you did not have a look at it earlier.[3]

Digital Transformation is the process of integrating digital technologies into all areas of your products and operations in order to achieve maximum agility and efficiency and to allow better interaction among you, your customers, workforce and external stakeholders. As with so many things that relate to managing companies, digital transformation is the proverbial elephant that appears to be something different to everyone that looks at it (blindness not required).

In straightforward terms—digital transformation is implementing the elements of the anatomy presented in this section while adapting your EA and Operating Model to become a digital business. Given the concerns driving the need to transform, this generalized model is intended to enable you to maximize your competitiveness, agility and sustainability.

The diagram, below, is a generic architectural schematic model for a digital company:

The major components of this architecture include:

---

2 https://www.redhat.com/en/about/press-releases/ibm-closes-landmark-acquisition-red-hat-34-billion-defines-open-hybrid-cloud-future

3 https://enterprisersproject.com/what-is-digital-transformation

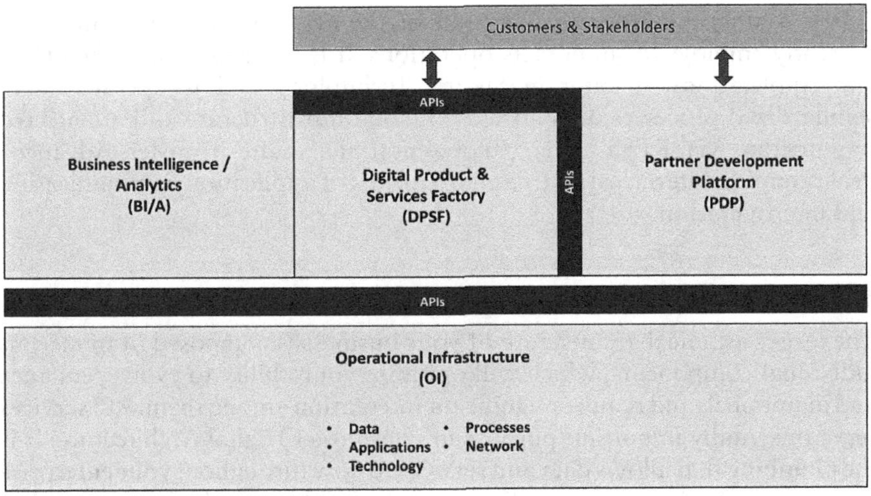

Figure 4.4 Anatomy of a digital company.

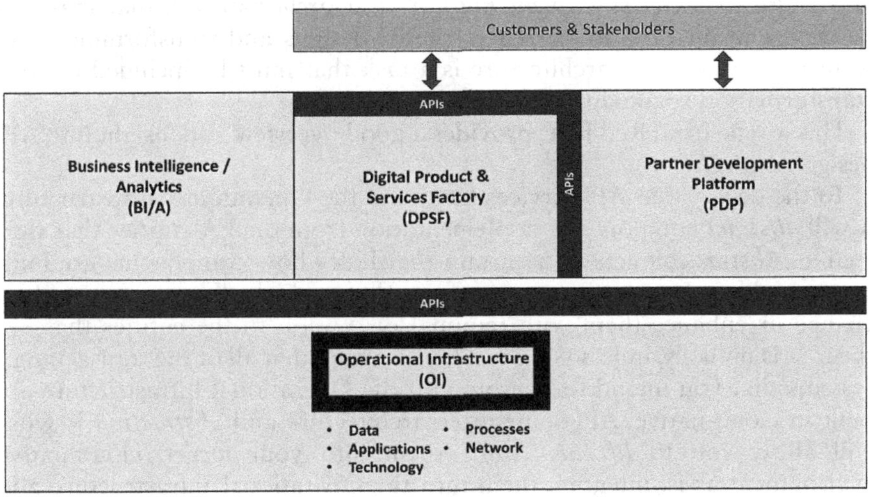

Figure 4.5 Operational infrastructure and API services.

Operational infrastructure and API services

Operational infrastructure

This foundational layer of your infrastructure supports the shared administrative transactional systems, your communication networks and so on. The data that resides in this layer and the services it delivers are exposed to the layers above it via APIs and it is almost certainly cloud based.

It is mainly a rationalized version of the systems that your enterprise currently employs to support its operations. It is comprised of Shared Data and Applications, is built in Shared Technology and is operated with standardized processes. It is hosted on cloud infrastructure and architected to integrate via REST APIs (Representational State Transfer Advanced Programming Interfaces) as a standard means of application communication and interoperation.

API services

The target technical architecture of your business is composed of numerous individual components, which will optimize your ability to evolve, enhance and maintain it, and requires significant integration among them. API services serve this vitally important purpose in your target Digital Architecture. It is the plumbing that allows data and services to flow throughout your enterprise and the standards it employs eliminate a lot of the complexity that used to be required to make systems interoperate. There are certain considerations in systems' designs that are required to make them API-compatible, such as *stateful or stateless implementation*[4] and *orchestration*[5], that may not be a part of all of your current systems' designs and transforming them to fit into your target architecture is a task that must be included in your transformation roadmap.

This article from Red Hat[6] provides a good overview and insight into API design issues.

To the degree that API services front-end the Operational Infrastructure, it will *abstract* components' implementation from the EA entities that they enable. *Abstraction* acts as a curtain that hides how components are built from anything that obtains services from them, which allows you to add to, change or enhance them with minimal disruption to the entities that use them. It is unlikely, unless you are a true startup, that all of the transactional systems that you intend to migrate into the Operational Infrastructure are built in cloud-native, API-compatible architecture and *abstraction* is what will allow you to *lift and shift*[7] them into your target, cloud-native environment as-is, integrate them into the Operational Infrastructure and modify them later to be compatible with your target technical architecture.

All that a developer needs to know about how to integrate with a service via an API can be documented and published in a straightforward guide, such as this one from Netflix,[8] and the API allows developers to modify or add functions to the service (within limits) with minimal disruption to

4 https://searchapparchitecture.techtarget.com/tip/The-key-differences-between-stateless-and-stateful-microservices
5 https://www.redhat.com/en/topics/automation/what-is-orchestration
6 https://www.redhat.com/en/topics/api/what-is-api-design
7 https://aws.amazon.com/products/storage/lift-and-shift/
8 https://netflix.github.io/genie/docs/4.0.0-SNAPSHOT/rest/

anyone that may be using it. Now, endpoints (the underlying systems and services to which APIs provide connectivity) must be designed to work in the paradigm that APIs support in order for you to expose them through it. Your existing systems may not meet these requirements yet, but there are strategies for addressing that.

In 2002, Amazon CEO Jeff Bezos dictated that all integration across services at the company would be implemented via APIs.[9] Employing APIs as a standard integration approach, as Amazon does, ensures that architecture and services may be enhanced or evolved with reduced potential for creating technical debt.

Martin Fowler, an eminent technical architect and software strategist defined what has become known as the strangler fig pattern,[10] which describes an approach to migrate older systems behind an abstracting API interface so that they can be rebuilt a piece at a time when it is most convenient and feasible to do so. This allows a larger architectural transformation to progress without holding it hostage to the need to rebuild legacy systems.

Digital products and services factory

The Digital Product and Services Factory is utilized by integrated teams of product managers and solution developers, who work iteratively and incrementally. This is not a complete departure from what has

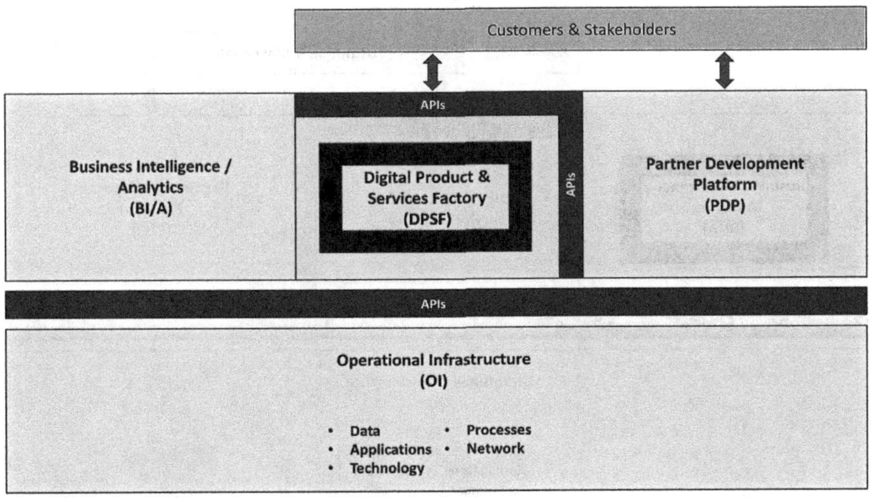

Figure 4.6 Digital products and services factory.

---

[9] https://medium.com/slingr/what-year-did-bezos-issue-the-api-mandate-at-amazon-57f546994ca2

[10] https://martinfowler.com/bliki/StranglerFigApplication.html

been employed to build application systems, heretofore, but now it is employed 'on steroids.' More traditional processes and techniques may be employed to build and manage the operational infrastructure layer, but Agile and DevOps development processes and alternative governance models are required for this one. The priorities for this element of your architecture are speed and quality and automation is applied liberally to achieve them.

The technology, data stores and processes it employs are specifically designed for this purpose. It relies on the Operational Infrastructure foundation for some data and services but has its own enablement under the control of digital product owners, who manage the enterprise's digital offerings. Your ability to build and enhance applications and services on the Digital Product and Services Factory enables you to implement and evolve them rapidly, powered by Agile techniques and DevOps tools. This article[11] speaks to the accelerating integration of business model evolution and agile, DevOps techniques into what's now called BizDevOps.

Business intelligence and analytics

Digital companies are data driven. The ability to assimilate and act on intelligence extracted from data is critical to competitiveness and may be integrated in near real time into products and services that your company delivers—for example, creating individual loan or insurance coverage offers while customers are online.

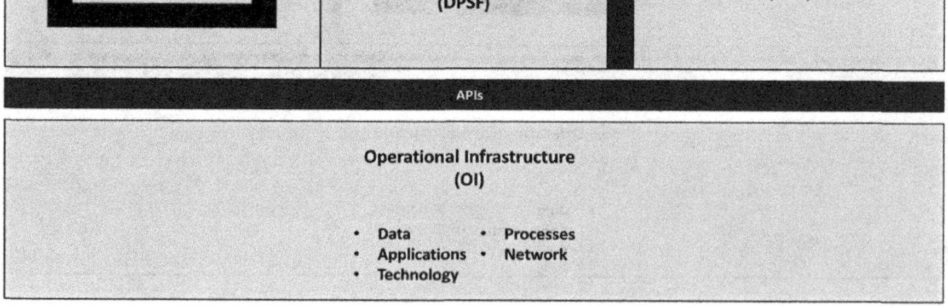

Figure 4.7 Business intelligence and analytics.

[11] https://searchitoperations.techtarget.com/news/252501109/Spurred-by-pandemic-BizDevOps-becomes-a-reality

The ultimate point of Digital Transformation is to identify digital offerings that customers will pay for and deliver them. In this regard, your digital product managers must develop insights and knowledge about what their customers want and need. This may involve a variety of approaches, including customer panels, market research and machine learning on clickstreams or behavioral data. Your ability to consolidate data from the Digital Product and Services Factory, the transactional systems on your Operational Infrastructure and external sources is critical to developing and exploiting customer insights.

Partner development platform

The digital company must be able to partner on the fly with other digital companies, stakeholders and suppliers. As the company's ability to deliver digital offerings matures, new opportunities to deliver them jointly with partners will emerge. The external Development Platform provides access to services from the Digital Products and Services Factory platform and Operational Infrastructure that will allow third parties to partner with your company and extend what you can offer. This element of the architecture exposes well-defined and documented services via APIs to partners to allow access to value-added services and enable rapid evolution of collaborative products and services.

Distributed governance model

Hierarchical, 'command and control' organization models are antithetical to success in a digital company, mainly because they impede decision-making that supports incremental development and evolution of products and

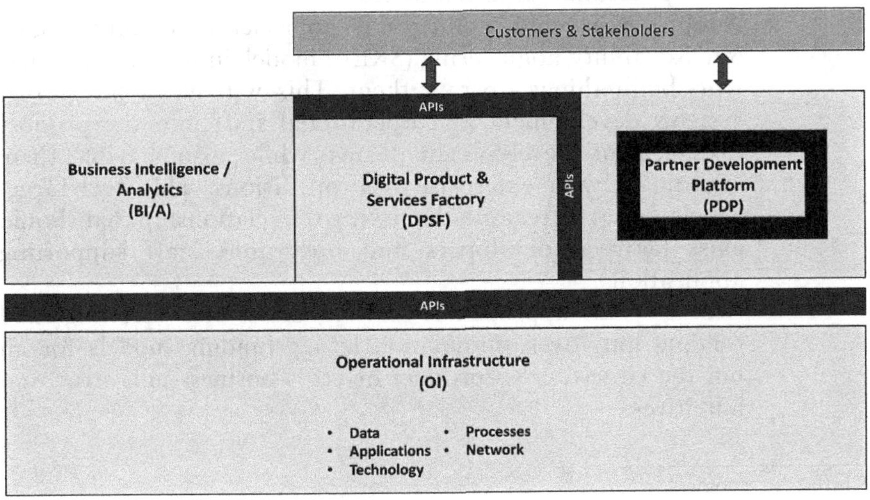

Figure 4.8 Partner development platform.

services. Value-stream management (see Mik Kersten) and Agile/DevOps techniques must be paired to be competitive today.

Integrating Product Management and Technologists into a cohesive team is one thing required to accelerate the ability to deliver new services at speed. The other is to empower the team to make its own investment decisions (within limits) and adopt governance practices that differ substantially from traditional Project Management practices. In much the same way that periodic governance processes, such as quarterly updates or annual budgeting and project funding, impede decision-making, so can the need to work within a traditional Project Management framework.

In the process of transforming your business around the pillars, above, you will need to:

- Adopt a componentized architecture. Given the importance of agility and plasticity, your businesses must be designed around components (capabilities, organizational groups, internal services and enablers) that are ***highly cohesive*** and ***loosely coupled***, i.e., are well-focused and minimally interdependent. Your organization structures and processes must become more fluid—rigid structures will impede agility.
- Evolve from what used to be 'projects,' budgeted largely as capital expenses (Capex), into transformation initiatives that accrue within business units' operating budgets (Opex). You must become willing and able to experiment in a cost- and time-efficient manner, informed by customer wants and needs to develop successful digital offerings. You must move away from traditional project management practices to achieve this. Changes you will have to make include:
    - Adopt iterative delivery approaches including Agile SDLCs and DevOps technology and practices.
    - Adopt a 'you build it you run it' approach based on Google's Site Reliability Engineering (SRE)[12] model, in which developers who build things operate them. This will mean integrating systems development and operational staff into the product management development teams while also having them coordinate with enterprise ICT operations. This TechTarget article[13] does a great job describing the relationship that should exist between developers and operations staff supporting applications.
    - Evolve your approaches and processes for defining and funding initiatives, eliminating legacy funding models for all but the largest, cross-product or cross-business-unit structural initiatives.

---

12 https://sre.google/

13 https://searchitoperations.techtarget.com/tip/What-is-SRE-in-DevOps-and-how-do-they-work-together

  - Adopt a governance model in which authority for investing in digital products' definition, development, delivery and management is delegated to your business units.
  - Make experimental Proof of Concept (PoC) initiatives the point of entry to most large-scale transformation initiatives and learning to manage them as a portfolio.
  - Increase your willingness to terminate initiatives and write off investments in experiments as a cost of being an innovative business without blaming the people behind them.
  - Become increasingly willing to learn from successes and failures and disseminate the knowledge across the organization.
  - Adopt processes that help to avoid creating Technical Debt, which results from designing things to meet short-term needs in ways that create constraints on reusability or the ability to evolve downstream. Distributed application implementation not governed by a centralized architecture team is a common source of it. In siloed environments, potentially reusable components are not reused or solutions that could have been generalized for reuse, aren't. If you manage processes that can create Technical Debt consciously you can balance the benefits of speed against the downstream costs that it can create. Unmanaged Technical Debt is wasteful and anti-agile, so your approach to managing it will have to change in a way that reflects a balance between the costs and benefits.

    Building or evolving digital products will place more of a premium on speed and less on preventing technical debt. Since the apps supporting digital products are likely to be shorter-lived than traditional apps, there should be less concern about technical debt; however, building reusable, generalized components where you are able to will increase aggregate speed and decrease aggregate risk in the long run.
- Get value from reusable components, which depends on your facilitating their being shared and reused. You will need to identify individuals with the responsibility to promote reusability and build knowledge bases, processes and supporting infrastructure to enable your digital product teams to find and share them. This means that you will have to apply Knowledge Management (KM) disciplines to creating, maintaining and managing catalogs of reusable components that product management teams can consult before they undertake potentially redundant systems development.
- Adopt cloud architecture, which can alleviate concerns about capacity and performance limitations but managing costs will require new experience and expertise.
- Extract and preserve value from the information and data you will generate in the course of your operations. You will have to apply considerable creativity, effort and resources to acquiring managing,

preserving and protecting it. You will have to integrate data concerns into almost every digital product decision.

- Maintain data quality, which is crucially important as erroneous or poor-quality data can impair operational system functions and diminish the value of data science activity. You will need to institute processes and staffing to monitor and manage data quality.
- Establish and grow your KM function, which will assume greater and greater importance. Data collected from daily operations, web applications and IoT sensors can pile up at a furious rate. If you do not know what you have, you will never be able to use it effectively. If you cannot steer product developers toward appropriate reusable components, redundant ones will be developed. If you cannot recognize and access informative past experiences, you will repeat them. You need to develop a knowledge base and research interface to ensure that knowledge is found and exploited, not discarded.
- Develop and maintain controlled vocabularies (Taxonomies, Master Data Management[14] (MDM) and so on) to help manage Enterprise Architectures while minimizing debt, such as technical debt. Creating and maintaining these is critical to your KM programs.
- Account for and manage new or transformed risks that arise from the process of transitioning to and operating your organization, as modeled herein. As you travel down the path toward becoming a digital business, managing risks will increasingly depend upon organizational competencies, process effectiveness and efficiency that can differ from what you currently have. Approaches to strategy, operational management and execution capabilities will have to be realigned, as well.

DIGITAL TRANSFORMATION MEANS TRANSFORMING YOUR ENTERPRISE ARCHITECTURE

In the previous section, we covered the major components of your digital business at an enterprise-wide level. They can also be viewed, to be sure, as entities in an EA model. Understanding the relationship between the elements of the anatomy and your Enterprise and Business Architectures will go a long way toward your understanding the underlying logic behind the recommendations I've made about your evolving your business. We also introduced an EA model, which can be applied to a business of any size, including yours, and considering how a digital transformation can impact it will help to illuminate that.

Here is where Digital Transformation will impact on your Enterprise and Business Architecture:

[14] https://en.wikipedia.org/wiki/Master_data_management

- Products and Services
  You will be increasingly challenged to compete with others that have bundled digital services with their traditional products, as GE and Caterpillar have, or simply created new digital services, as many new fintech startups have. Here is a list of 49 new financial services companies that are challenging established industry players[15] in areas in which they previously had predominant positions. This article[16] from StartUs Insights lists a number of specific areas in which startups are disrupting the industry and this article[17] from justcoded.com further characterizes the impacts. Needless to say, finance is hardly the only industry experiencing such changes.
- Capabilities
  Obviously, you don't have a choice about whether to compete with digitally capable competitors. If you will not or cannot deliver the type of user experiences or products and services customers expect, your business will fall behind. There is a diverse set of expertise, experience and skills underlying your ability to deliver them and it is quite likely that you do not have all of them or have not integrated them to achieve maximum synergy from them, if you do.
  Some of the capabilities emblematic of a digitally transformed company include:
  - The ability to provide individualized products and services to each customer
  - Rich user experience functionality that provides such services as personalization, AI-driven product and service recommendation and intelligent contact functions
  - AI-driven marketing and targeting, updated in near real time
  - Robotic Process Automation (RPA) that is integrated into your operational architecture
  - Better exploitation of information and knowledge
- Enablers
  Here's where the rubber meets the road. The Capabilities you will need to compete, are dependent on a number of Enablers:
  - People
  - Value-stream, Product Management-driven product and service delivery skills
    - Distributed authority and accountability structures
    - Technical Architecture Management skills
    - Data Architecture and Governance skills
    - Agile/DevOps delivery skills

[15] https://builtin.com/fintech/fintech-companies-startups-to-know
[16] https://www.startus-insights.com/innovators-guide/disrupting-financial-services-breakdown-startup-driven-innovation-fintech/
[17] https://justcoded.com/blog/the-impact-of-fintech-on-banks-and-financial-services/

    - Job and job-role flexibility—ability to work in automation-augmented processes and willingness to transition as the enterprise evolves
    - Commitment to life-long learning
    - Ability to manage a work force that is composed of employees, contractors and automated functions, which may be geographically dispersed
- Technology
  - Analytics and AI
    - RPA
    - Cloud-native infrastructure, API-enabled
    - Cloud-native application architectures
    - Agile/DevOps, SRE
    - Internet of Things (IoT)
- Processes
  - Manual, robotically-augmented, completely automated
  - Flexibility to reconfigure rapidly, including peoples' job roles and application of automation
  - Application of AI to decision-making
- Information
  - Ability to manage increasingly large amounts of data
  - Maintain a flexible architecture to facilitate exploiting it—e.g., automated feature extraction for ML model building
  - Active KM to enhance the value of the data you manage, making it easier for users to identify and access what will be useful to them.
- Physical Assets
  - Facilities, equipment, etc.

A PREVIEW OF THE TRANSFORMATION JOURNEY

Obviously, digital transformation is all encompassing, affecting almost all of your company's Capabilities and Enablers. Doing it successfully will require careful planning and execution and where it starts is collecting the information you need to plan properly.

Below, is the path you should prepare to travel:

As-is EA and BA models

The place to start is to create an as-is Enterprise and Business Architecture model of your company in sufficient detail to plan your transformation and then maintain it as a guidepost for managing the company going forward. This speaks to the need for it to be as lightweight as possible and I believe that the limited entities in this model's palette will facilitate this. If maintaining the currency of the model is onerous to the point that you don't keep up with it you will severely undermine its value and it will not be available to inform your risk management processes and that will impair your business agility.

The model, as described, above, has a four-layer structure, in which some entities support or are dependent on others that enable the hierarchy:

Model Layer	*Relevant Concerns*	*EA/BA Model Elements*
Business Strategy	To whom do you expect to be selling and what is the value proposition that you will offer? Who are the major competitors that you will have to account for and what is their value proposition?	**Market Segments, Product and Service characteristics**
Business Model	What specifically will you offer and to whom will it be targeted?	**Products and Services targeted to specific Market Segments**
Operating Model	How will you structure your company to produce and deliver the value that you will offer?	**Value Streams, Capabilities**
Operational Architecture	How will you structure and equip yourself to create the value?	**Capabilities, Enablers**

This model should be constructed top-down. Strategy should inform the Business Model, which should determine the Operating Model and so on. Corporate or administrative functions and capabilities that are largely transparent to customers should be included in the Operating Model and Operational Architecture layers.

As you may imagine, given the speed at which things evolve, your as-is model will not be completely accurate for long. This is only to be expected. Given the ongoing importance of the model, it is imperative that you identify a group and assign it the responsibility for maintaining the model and establish processes across the enterprise that ensure that this group captures the necessary information in a timely fashion. As transformative initiatives and product evolution takes place, the model should be kept in sync. Beyond the responsible EA group, this will require contributions from architects of various stripes and members of your KM team.

There's a foundational philosophical element here—**you should plan and execute change through the lens of how it impacts your EA**. If you adopt this thinking, you will look at every initiative you consider with an eye toward understanding:

- Who else in the business might be impacted by what you intend to do,
- Who else might be interested in and benefit from it,

- Whether there is something that already exists that you can reuse or that can give you a head start on whatever it is you are intending to implement,
- How you might execute it in such a manner that it can be generalized to make it reusable and
- Where there are dependencies that might create risks.

To-be EA and BA models

The forward-looking EA and BA models must incorporate the major components of your digital business anatomy into them. So, in addition to inventorying and documenting the elements of your current business and any in-progress or already approved initiatives, you will also have to accommodate the implementation of your new digital business building blocks in preparation for mapping out how you will transition or consolidate existing digital capabilities. Obviously, the journey from as-is to to-be will be a long and potentially meandering one. Therefore, it may well make sense to articulate some transitional state models, as well.

Gap analysis and implementation initiatives

When a sufficiently comprehensive as-is model is in place, you will perform a gap analysis to identify what you need to do to transform toward your targeted to-be state. This is unquestionably going to be a substantial and complicated list. Here, again, your EA framework can form a useful basis for articulating and structuring the work to be done:

- **Strategy, Markets and Segments, Competitors**
  Articulating your understanding of the markets in which you compete, how they might change, how you expect them to and what your competition looks like and is capable of doing will drive your strategy and influence the priorities of your planning efforts.
- **Products and Services**
  Given your view of your markets and your strategy, you will construct a portfolio of your existing Products and Services, identifying how you might evolve them and new candidate Products and Services for experimentation and development.
- **Value Streams**
  As your portfolio of existing and prospective Products and Services comes into focus, you will need to identify the elements of your Operating Model that will be applied to their development, production and delivery. This will inform organizational changes you may require, allocation of resources and investment.

- **Capabilities**
  The Product and Service portfolio will define needs for Capabilities that you will require. This may dictate revision or enhancement of existing ones as well as implementation of new ones.
- **Enablers**
  Finally, the portfolio of Capabilities that you have planned for your to-be model will be dependent on a variety of Enablers—staff, technology, processes, assets, information. Enhancing or implementing Enablers is a bedrock feature of your transformation plan.

Execution competency and capability gaps

Your gap analysis will result in a portfolio of initiatives. At this point, you should evaluate how prepared you actually are to execute them. A highly diverse set of skills and experience will be required and it is unlikely that you have everything and everyone you need on board. This Red Hat article[18] presents a list of what they view as the critical IT staffing needs for a company undertaking Digital Transformation. It is indicative of just how wide and diverse the set of disciplines required to succeed is.

This is the point at which you will need to take stock and start to evaluate how you will equip yourself with the people, expertise, processes and technology you will need to execute your transformation. You will also need to plan how you will govern, manage and control it.

Roadmap and execution plan

You should now have a lengthy portfolio of initiatives, probably years worth, and you will need to create an executable plan from it. The competing and conflicting priorities and interdependencies will be dizzying but breaking the initiatives down and creating workplans for them has to be done to create a master roadmap and program for the transformation. It will contain initiatives as diverse as cloud migration, DevOps adoption, Capability consolidation, restructuring the Product Management function within your business units, initiation of a product incubator and inception of an integrated strategy and transformation governance process.

Oh yes, your risk management process will need to be revamped, as well.

When you have completed your plan, it will probably need to go before your executive management and your board for approval. The numbers, the timeframe and scope will be daunting. Expect a lengthy process of presentation, explanation, retrenchment and, hopefully, approval to proceed.

---

[18] https://enterprisersproject.com/article/2020/12/digital-transformation-teams-2021-9-key-roles?page=0%2C0

RISK MANAGEMENT AND THE CONTROLLED TRANSFORMATION JOURNEY

A simplistic and unfortunately oft-applied approach to risk management is "think of everything that could go wrong, try to prevent it but plan for what you will do if it happens." This is, needless to say, not going to cut it if you're running an organization undergoing change, as everyone is today. Assessing strategic risks—making vs. not making market-facing changes, for instance—can be very different than managing operational risks more focused on BAU than competitive positioning. Also, the increasing impermanence of enterprise elements—organization structures, systems, processes, etc.—changes the cost-benefit calculus of interventions you may already have in place. If something will be superseded in a brief time, what you're willing to do to ensure its sustainability now may be quite different than it might have been a few years ago.

I make the case for AERM based largely on two factors—(a) digital transformation is necessary for your sustainability and (b) risks will change at least at the rate that your business changes.

Colonel John Boyd coined the term **O.O.D.A. Loop**, in the 1950s. Colonel Boyd, known as the "Fighter Pilot who changed the Art of War", was an F-86 pilot and commander of a fighter group during the latter part of the Korean War. The OODA loop (observe, orient, decide, act) describes how a pilot reacts to events while flying combat missions but it is equally applicable to many other decision-making situations, such as running your business. The application of this model to strategy and business management is discussed in this article[19] by George Stalk and Sam Stewart of the Boston Consulting Group.

Elements of AERM address each of the steps:

- **Observe:** Identifying event indicators you will monitor focuses your attention to enable rapid recognition. Thinking through a model of what's important before a change in your business 'goes live' helps reduce noise once it does.
- **Orient:** Highlighting characteristics that differentiate indicators and events from each other allows you to filter out noise and make sense of what you're seeing more quickly than you otherwise could.
- **Decide:** Working within an established framework, with specified parameters, articulated assumptions and pre-determined actions, reduces decision latency.
- **Act:** Having a pre-determined action gets you moving faster than you would if you had to Orient and Decide from scratch under the pressure of exigent circumstances

[19] https://www.bcg.com/en-us/publications/2019/tempo-art-of-disruption

Bottom line—you're changing your business to be more agile (I hope) and you need to adapt your ERM practices to shorten the OODA loop. In order to do that, you will need to have already conducted a risk assessment, which in a substantial business can take months that you will not have, *before* a threat presents itself. You will need a model of your enterprise that accurately represents the relationship of elements of the enterprise in order to perform iterative ERM updates as needed. EA, BA and other models are intrinsic to how I suggest your AERM should work.

In the following sections, I will present some details on the disciplines and techniques that you should apply to create the AERM framework that will enable you to implement and maintain the currency of the short OODA loop that you will need to sustain your enterprise.

The first one is quantitative analysis—statistics. If you're going to create cost-effective treatments for risks, you have to be able to assess them quantitatively. I don't think it's a requisite for risk managers to be quantitative heavyweights but understanding things like Expected Value, Variance and Distributions is necessary to develop cost-effective strategies for dealing with risks. Bayesian Networks and Inference are also meaningful, and you should understand how it applies but you can probably live without understanding how to employ and operate them.

Second, are EA and BA. These disciplines are employed to create models of your company that highlight interrelationships and dependencies so that you can account for them in creating your AERM framework from risk assessment to determining risk strategies to selecting treatments.

Third, is business process mining and management-decision process mapping. This is often performed as a component of EA but it is worth calling out due to the importance of tying AERM to decision processes and that can't happen if they're not identified and well-understood.

Finally, there are a number of disciplines associated with planning, executing and monitoring the progress of the controlled transformation you will be undertaking, whether it's just your AERM capabilities or your enterprise on a broader basis. After you have designed your AERM capabilities, you will have to transform to enable them and there are a number of disciplines that will serve to make your transformation successful.

HAVEN'T I ALREADY DONE SOME OF THIS?

Good news! It's likely that you have already implemented some components of your digital architecture as you executed initiatives in the course of some of your recent business activities.

Do you have a website? Do you sell over the web? Do your web-enabled capabilities integrate with third-party services? Are you an affiliate of other web sellers? Do you have an affiliate program, yourself? Have you moved some or all of your operational infrastructure to the cloud? Are you doing

Agile/DevOps development? Are you employing AI? Have you implemented Business Process Automation or Robotic Process Automation?

If you answered yes to a number of these, then you are at least ankle-deep in the sea of digital transformation.

This can be both a blessing and a curse. If you are like many large companies to which I have been exposed, relevant capabilities may have been implemented by early adopters in various business units and exist in inconsistent and incompatible forms throughout your enterprise. They may have been implemented in technology that has matured quite a bit or even been superseded since it was first deployed. You, therefore, may have some in-house knowledge, experience, expertise and skilled staff, but it's likely that your digital capabilities are neither cohesive nor optimally leverageable. Now, in addition to transforming your organization and operational processes, you may also have to accommodate or transform components of your digital architecture that already exist. You will have to change the tires on your car while you're driving it on the highway.

To the degree that standardization that facilitates velocity is an important goal of your Digital Transformation effort, a plethora of tribes, each with their own version of things, will create resistance to change just when you will need to change the most. Prepare to exercise your diplomatic skills as you may have to undo almost as much as you will have to do in order to move forward.

On an optimistic note, if you can standardize your processes and the technologies that enable them it will position you to react to events much more quickly than you could if you had to analyze situations with no reference points and then design and execute solutions for dealing with them, ad hoc. While there will be pain in consolidating disparate cloud implementations on a common platform (or committing and gearing up to operate on a hybrid cloud solution), the speed with which you will be able to implement new solutions on a cloud platform you know well should more than compensate for the short-term pain that you will experience in transition.

AERM AND THE DIGITAL ENTERPRISE

The AERM approach is built around the EA model, which should inform and guide your transformation efforts. An example of how this works is contained in *Case Study 1*, in the following section. The case demonstrates how the EA model can be used to discover dependencies among Capabilities and Enablers and use this information to inform the selection of alternatives for treating risks.

The outcome of the case is our identifying an approach to mitigate a one in 400 risk of business disruption to reduce it to a one in one million, or so, by acquiring some assets and restructuring part of the business' supply chain. The EA model made it easier to identify other Enablers that represent potential risks to the business, alerting us to the need to analyze and treat them, as well.

The visual representation of the EA model, implemented in a graph database, contributes to this, but there is no particular requirement that you employ any specific technology to house your EA model data.

Working in this way, companies focus on risk generators, not just guessing about how to avoid negative avoiding outcomes. Clearly, it is preferable to avoid a negative result than it is to mitigate it after the fact. It facilitates developing insight as to what is driving operational risks within your company and contributes to your intuition about underlying sources of risk among your suppliers, customers, partners and other stakeholders. Case study 1 is also an example of that. The structure of the supply chain alerted us to the need to determine the probability of either of two input providers failing, which was out of our control, but which was still a risk for which we needed to plan.

Earlier, we gave an example of a shipping company that could have a shipment delayed by a cyclone. The recipient has an option to insure against delays, which would come at the cost of the premium determined by underwriters' assessment of the probability and impact of such an event. There are undoubtedly numerous other sources of risk to shipping, such as ice bergs or pirates, which could also be perils for which we might choose to acquire coverage. Insuring against these perils has incremental costs, and either can be included or excluded from the policy. Your risk appetite and risk tolerance will determine how much risk you will immunize your company from by purchasing insurance and how much you will retain by either accepting a deductible or simply not insuring it.

So, what makes this '*agile*?' If you are evaluating a prospective initiative and its incremental impact to your Capabilities and Enablers, you will be led naturally to investigate changes that create or modify risks. Then, you will be able to identify related entities with dependencies that create correlated risks. Thus armed, you will be much better prepared to deal with your evolving risks comprehensively and at speed. Similarly, if you are planning to modify an entity in a way that changes its risk profile, you will be able to identify everywhere the entity may have been redeployed and all interdependencies that might propagate the revised risks within your company.

KM is another element of the AERM approach that can help to accelerate the RM process. To the degree that effective KM helps you to identify existing experience, approaches, Capabilities and Enablers for potential reuse, you are more likely to redeploy something you already have, be it a business process, a piece of software or a supplier relationship, and this will come with known risk characteristics that you will have already assessed and for which you may have already developed treatments.

It should be noted that most of this is not completely novel. Early in the book, I noted that you probably already know how to do this. If you've been in operation for a while, you can probably identify some large fraction of the risks inherent in your operations or even changes you may be contemplating. What AERM adds to your RM capabilities is the ability to identify related and correlated risks much more reliably and rapidly than you might have otherwise and apply the knowledge and experience you will accumulate more reliably and comprehensively. Also, by doing this systematically and with automated support, you will make it easier for less experienced or knowledgeable staff to benefit from your enhanced RM capability.

If you are headed toward or even in the middle of a Digital Transformation, your company and your EA model will be in a constant state of flux. If you do not implement agile enablement for ERM, then you will certainly be taking risks of which you are unaware or for which you are unprepared. Anything less than a continuous process will simply not enable you to keep up.

CHAPTER SUMMARY

Key concepts addressed in this chapter include:

- Why you *do* need Digital Transformation.
- The Anatomy of Your Company—its Enterprise and Business Architecture. Capabilities and Enablers, organized into Value Streams that deliver Products and Services to your Markets.
- The Anatomy of a Digital Business—the architectural components that you need to enable you to compete in the digital marketplace.
- Digital Transformation requires that you augment and integrate your as-is EA/BA with the digital business Capabilities and Enablers you will need: the Operational Infrastructure, API Services, the Digital Products and Services Factory, a Partner Development Platform, Business Intelligence and Analytics capabilities and a Distributed Governance Model.
- Your transformation journey starts with a plan and that should center around an as-is and a to-be EA model, from which you will conduct a gap analysis to identify, prioritize and sequence initiatives.
- Risk Management in the course of transformation is critical.
    - You're probably not starting from zero, but you will need to enhance and expand your capabilities considerably.
    - How establishing the EA model is a foundation for managing your evolution will enable AERM in your digital enterprise.

CASE STUDY 1: A STREET-LEVEL STARTUP—INTRODUCING EA AND BA TO AGILE ERM

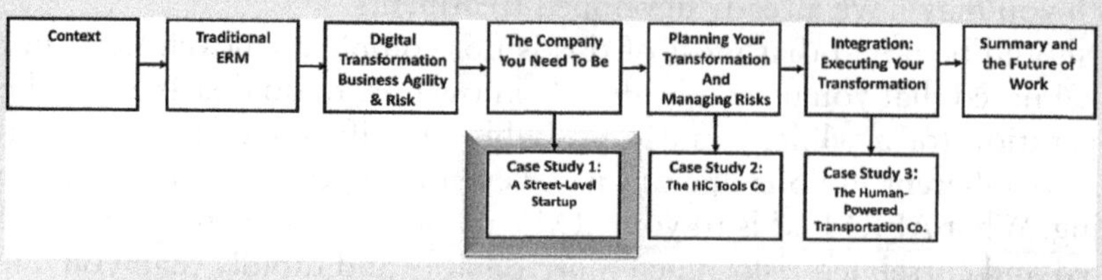

A BI-LEVEL MODEL FOR EARLY-STAGE AND ESTABLISHED BUSINESSES

In the *Context* chapter, we introduced a target model for digital businesses to evolve toward—a portfolio model that incorporates an incubator of experimental products and businesses in the process of maturation. The goal is to have a stream of prospective new products or even whole businesses to roll out, evolve and mature. This same approach can and should also be applied to evolving established products or services as they come under attack from competitors. As a result, we foresee companies ultimately operating in the manner of both established businesses and startups. Therefore, this case study will be applicable to both early-stage entrepreneurs and established companies, alike.

We will emulate elements of Eric Ries' approach in the Lean Startup.[20] In our approach, we will:

- Work within a development and launch plan that minimizes investment required, reduces time to market and maximizes the opportunity to acquire information that will guide the product's evolution
- Develop a product concept and solidify it as quickly as possible, focusing on what's necessary to progress it along the path to either launch or cancellation
- Expose the product to as many potential customers as possible to enable us to determine whether it is something that they would be willing to pay for and identify how it might be modified to become so, if it is not
- Evolve the product iteratively, honing it until it is ready to transition into a Minimum Viable Product (MVP)[21]
- Launch, test, evolve, repeat

This case will introduce the application of Enterprise and Business Architecture and risk-based thinking and decision-making to inform the process of starting a business.

THE CASE: A STREET CART

Suppose we note that food carts are proliferating in a downtown area in which many people work. We see long lines at them at lunchtime and think that an upscale offering of sausages made from exotic meats could be successful—a premium product at a premium price. How do we go about putting a cart on the street to sell our products?

---

20 http://theleanstartup.com/
21 https://en.wikipedia.org/wiki/Minimum_viable_product

What is required to meet the goal?

- Startup funding
- Marketing—pricing targets, sales volume estimates, advertising and publicity
- Sausage, bread, drinks, condiments, paper goods, etc. Suppliers for each item.
- Location
- Licenses, health department certificates
- Cart, someplace to store the cart when not in use and a way to transport it to where it will operate
- Staffing

How do we implement our initiative? How do we prioritize and stage the effort? Here are just some of the concerns:

- What is the best way for us to understand the market we're targeting? What geographic boundaries should we set for ourselves? How should we estimate the total number of potential customers?
- How can we develop the recipes for the sausages we will sell? How can we have sample batches made? How should we expose them to people and see how they respond to them?
- What's required to obtain a license and health department clearances? Do we need the cart first?
- Can we reserve a location? Do we need to a location to obtain a license, or vice-versa?
- How can we determine our cost of goods? Can we get accurate quotes without making purchase commitments?
- How much do we think we can charge for our sausages? What sales volume can we expect?
- Who will staff the cart? Can we do it if we cannot hire someone? Should we spend some amount of time running the cart ourselves before hiring someone else to do it?
- What functions and features does the cart need? Where can we have it built? How much will we need to spend? What is the cost/benefit of additional features? Is there an alternative to purchasing it?
- What are the logistics and cost to store and transport the cart?
- We should try to get funded as late in our process as we can. The more that is known, the less likely we are to borrow money for something that is infeasible or to borrow the wrong amount.

This is quite a list, and it's probably not even exhaustive. Furthermore, the questions we have and the tasks we must accomplish seem to be circular and interconnected. There are also subordinate goals to consider. We want to minimize the time and costs involved with merely evaluating our opportunity and we want to avoid giving our idea away to anyone who could run with it and beat us to market.

PRE-MVP RISK MANAGEMENT—EXPERIMENTAL AND DEVELOPMENTAL PHASES

There are a number of risks that must be addressed between the germ of the idea we have and the launch of our cart. There are two phases or steps in this scope of our venture—Experimentation and Development. There may well be overlapping tasks between these phases. For instance, it will be impossible to truly test product viability unless we have completed some product development.

Experimentation

Experimentation consists of the research, analysis and problem solving necessary to determine whether it's even worth obtaining funding or investing our own time and capital in pursuing this business. No investor or lender will consider participating in our business without the information that is gathered in this phase of the project, and we should not consider investing ourself unless we can answer the same questions that outside participants would ask if we pursued it with them.

This phase is strongly focused on risk mitigation. In it we will attempt to identify and educate ourselves on what we don't currently know and identify the challenges we will face if we decide to go forward. We will prioritize obtaining information and identifying hurdles that could preclude our success to minimize the possibility that we will do fruitless work or spend on things that will not change the outcome if our venture idea is not viable.

Finally, we will plan for the Development phase so that we can meet similar objectives—minimize time, effort and expenses while evolving our product offering to maximize our potential for success.

The following tasks are undertaken in the Experimentation phase. At the conclusion of this phase, a go/no go decision will be made to determine whether to continue to work toward an MVP launch:

- **Market Assessment**
  This is among the most important among our risks. If there is too much competition or the population to which our point of sale will be accessible is insufficient, we cannot get our business off the ground. Our products might be well-liked, but we need to be sure that we can

achieve adequate sales volume to stay in business or we will undoubtedly lose whatever upfront investment we have made.
  - Importance: Critical
  - Approach: Direct observation and counting foot traffic during designated hours in the area we have mapped out as our target territory. We can employ two to four workers to do this for a three-to-four-hour period for a number of days and base estimates on an aggregation of the data. We will also produce a census of the competitors in our market and estimate how many customers are served by a representative sample of them in the same three to four hours.
  - Cost to execute: 64 to 80 man-hours, roughly $800
  - Dependency: none
- **Product Development**
  This is one of the areas where the rubber meets the road. People may be intrigued by the idea of rattlesnake sausages but how do they really taste? We probably need to develop recipes for three different sausages for product viability testing but five or six by the time our MVP launches so that we can offer a different variety from our cart every day.
  - Importance: highly important
  - Approach: identify two or three butchers in the area that carry exotic meats and are willing to work with us to develop our products.
  - Cost to execute: $TBD
  - Dependency: none
- **Product Viability**—customer testing and marketing planning
  This is among the more important among our risks; however, it is something that we will have a chance to fix if we are not as successful with our initial incarnation as we would like to be. Consider a trial and repeat sales model: potential customers may be intrigued by the idea of what you're offering and, hopefully, will be attracted to come back and purchase again in the future. If we can present several choices at the time customers first try our sausages, then they may be interested and willing to come back and try new ones at a later time. If they are not overwhelmed with the first one they try, this may allow us to sidestep a complete rejection.
  - Importance: important
  - Approach: provide samples of up to three different recipes during the three- to four-hour period. Get responses to a three-question survey from each customer that samples the product.
  - Cost to execute: cost of goods—$TBD; 64 to 80 man-hours, roughly $800
  - Dependency: initial product development and sample production run
- **Resolving licensing and legal concerns**
  While we cannot get to our MVP launch without the required licenses and Health Department inspection certificates, our city clearly has processes

for this. In this regard, we will simply need to do the research necessary to identify what the requirements are then incorporate them in our pre-MVP execution plan, remaining mindful of any lead time or prerequisites.

- Importance: moderate
- Approach: look for information on the municipal website or visit the relevant departments, if necessary.
- Cost to execute: nominal
- Dependency: none

- **Obtaining a location**

  This is equal in importance to the licensing and certificate requirements. If the city assigns locations, we will need to know how we can acquire one and, if not, we will need to factor this into our operating plans. If during our market assessment we see the same carts in the same places every day, we can probably assume the reserved locations are enforced by the city.
  - Importance: moderate
  - Approach: Look for information on the municipal website or visit the relevant departments, if necessary.
  - Cost to execute: nominal
  - Dependency: none
- **Cart Acquisition**

  We will need to evaluate options for acquiring a cart. First, we will need to establish our requirements for it. What features and functions will we need? Second, we need to look at options that minimize the commitment required. Do we have an option to rent one until we have established that our business is sustainable? Can we piggyback on another vendor's cart for a while?
  - Importance: highly important
  - Approach: Connect with cart vendors and follow their recommendations. Obtain estimates, as appropriate. Often, licensees lease out licenses, locations and carts, just as taxi owners rent their medallions and cabs to other drivers. This option, if it exists, should be evaluated.
  - Cost to execute: nominal
  - Dependency: none
- **Cart Operations Requirements Planning**

  Finally, we need to understand exactly what day-to-day operation of the cart will entail. If we don't identify everything that will be required, we run the risk of putting ourselves out of business when it was wholly avoidable.
  - Importance: highly important
  - Approach: Conducting a process similar to an enterprise risk assessment can help to consolidate the information necessary to perform this task.
  - Cost to execute: nominal
  - Dependency: all of the previous tasks in this phase.

Development

Development consists of the tasks required to actually prepare for launch once a decision to proceed has been made. This phase is also strongly focused on risk mitigation and here is where we first come face-to-face with AERM and see how it is integrated with business management and planning and operations.

AN ENTERPRISE AND BUSINESS ARCHITECTURE MODEL OF THE BUSINESS

The diagram below depicts an EA model of our food cart business, implemented as a Neo4j labeled property graph database:

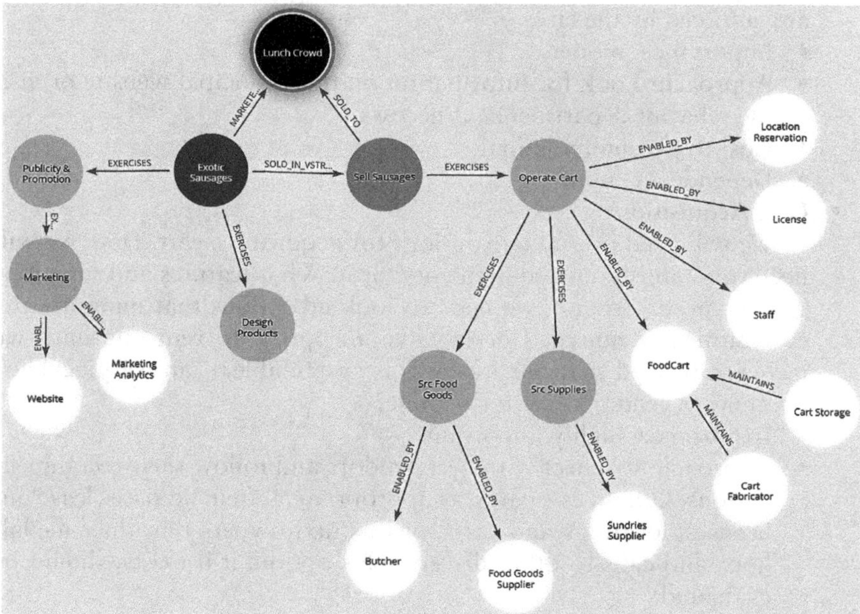

Figure CS1.1 EA graph of the cart business.

What the model depicts is the anatomy of our prospective operation. It shows us what is interconnected and what is interdependent. There are, for the moment, four layers of the model:

- The Market to which we're selling and the Products that we are selling into it
- The Value Stream through which we're delivering value (our products) to this market

- The Capabilities (what it is we can do or make happen) that are exercised in operating the value stream
- The Enablers that are required to exercise the Capabilities

These layers correspond to an EA and BA framework:

- Strategy (what we're selling and to whom: Products and Services to Market Segments mapping)
- Business Model (what we're selling: Products and Services)
- Operating Model (how we're designed to produce what we sell: Value Streams and Capabilities)
- Operational Architecture (how we've implemented the design: Capabilities to Enablers mapping)

This being a simple model, there are no cases of shared dependency or interconnection. Imagine what this graph would look like if we had two carts, which sold both overlapping and separate products, to say nothing of what a model from a large corporation would look like. Implementing a model like this in a graph database will facilitate its use for numerous purposes, however.

Applying the EA model to manage risk: elementary AERM

Having this model in place can guide the entire Development phase and the risk management process. How?

You will notice that each Capability depends on subordinate Capabilities and/or Enablers. Take, for example, the Operate Cart Capability. It is dependent on numerous other elements of our model. One of them is the Capability Src Food Goods, which is dependent on the enablers food goods supplier and butcher. If either of these enablers fails, then Operate Cart fails, and we are unable to go out and earn money until it is addressed. We have identified a risk to be analyzed, treated and managed.

Let's say that we get food supplies delivered each morning before we take the cart out. Each of these Enablers has some probability of failure. The food goods supplier might fail to deliver our required supplies with a probability of .001 or about 1 day in 1,000, and the butcher might fail to deliver with a probability of .0025 or about 1 day in 400. If *either* event occurs, we're out of business for the day. If either occurs and lasts for more than a single day, then we will be out of business for longer.

Here's a subset of the EA model with a new Enabler added for the Src Food Goods Capability—Refrigerated Storage. It is highlighted in the graph, below:

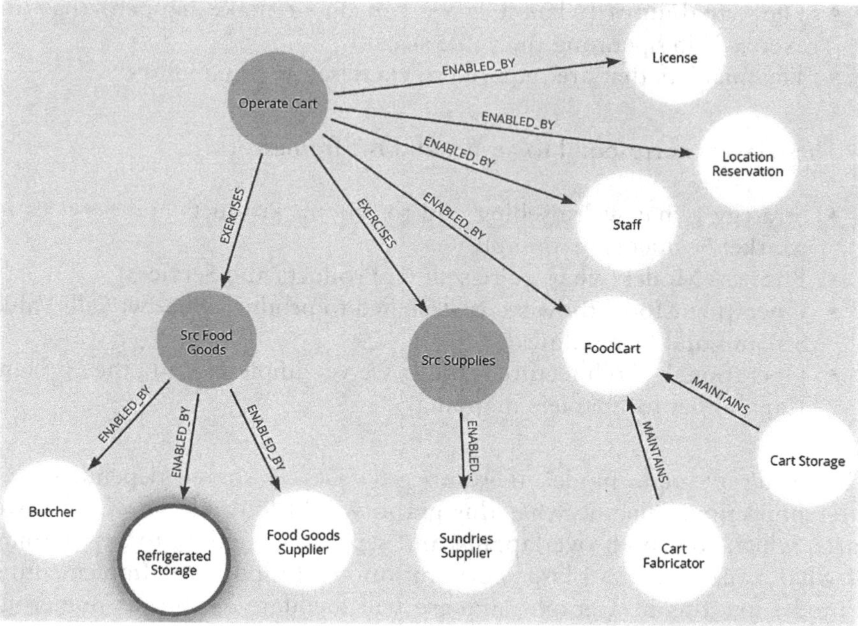

Refrigerated Storage can be used to buffer the supply chain that supplies edible goods to our business. Given our estimates for the lost profits per day of an outage and the likelihood of source failure from *either* of our two providers, we can assess whether the cost for Refrigerated Storage makes sense. If so, this risk is one that we will *mitigate* by reducing the impact of an occurrence. We can't eliminate the impact forever—fresh food will only last for so long, even when it is refrigerated—but we can evaluate the probability of an outage of a number of days for either Enabler and act accordingly. Part of our mitigation treatment plan will include enacting a sourcing business process in which we purchase food in a pattern that ensures that we maintain an inventory of one or two days of supply in Refrigerated Storage and replenish it at prescribed intervals.

Note now that the failure model of provisioning for our cart will change. Before Refrigerated Storage, we would lose one or more days sales if either or both providers failed. Now, we will lose sales only if either or both suppliers fail ***and*** our Refrigerated Storage fails. If Refrigerated Storage fails but the suppliers do not, we can still operate the cart. This reduces the probability that we will be out of business substantially—the probability of a failure that prevents us from operating is the probability of a supplier failure times the probability of a Refrigerated Storage failure—so, maybe something like one in a million.

In this model, risks flow *up*. Risks associated with an Enabler that has an ENABLED_BY relationship with or a subordinate Capability (one that is EXERCISED_BY a parent) are potential sources of failure for the parent entity. The representation in the model of entities that exercise or are enabled by a number of subordinate entities makes it easy to identify *and* and *or* relationships and statistically model them. For instance, we can see that our ability to operate the business can be curtailed if the cart is unavailable *or* our location is unavailable *or* our license is expired *or* our staff member is not present *or* any of a number of other things. We can estimate the impact of a failure at the parent level and then we can create statistical models of these things and track their interplay, correlation and so on.

This is a good example of what AERM is predicated on. If you build and maintain a sufficiently detailed EA and BA model, you should have ready access to all you need to identify connections, dependencies and interrelationships that create or magnify risks. It can help you perform a comprehensive risk assessment on a snapshot of your enterprise, and it can guide the process of identifying what will be impacted by changes in your company before or as you make them and help you keep your RM efforts in sync with your evolving business. Many EA models are way more detailed than what is required to enable AERM. The high-level EA model on which this is based is designed to minimize the work needed to maintain it to what is absolutely necessary to realize the value from it.

As you will see, there are other management models and disciplines that play similar roles in AERM processes. For the purpose of this case study, the EA/BA model is a sufficient example.

In the next chapter, we will discuss planning for the transformation and a substantial number of other disciplines, people and processes will come into play.

CASE 1 SUMMARY

This case study is predicated on and introduces a few concepts:

- Businesses will have to adopt management practices of both startups or early-stage ventures and established enterprises. The disciplines surrounding product or service development and evolution may well be appropriate for a Lean Startup approach.
- Maturing a startup business from an idea to an MVP should proceed in two phases—Experimentation and Development. This is a risk-based approach. Experimentation is intended to surface anything intractable that will prevent any chance of a venture's success and will set the stage for the work that will take place in the Development phase.
- An Enterprise and Business Architecture model of your prospective venture will provide invaluable benefits, especially to RM. The scaled-down, yet still comprehensive versions that AERM employs are designed to be workable, especially when their maintenance is embedded in the evolutionary and transformative processes in your business.

Chapter 5

Planning the transformation journey and managing its risks

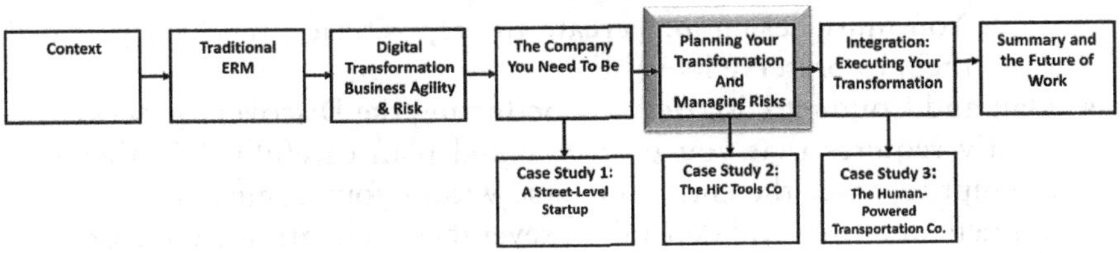

COVERED IN THIS CHAPTER

- **Change vs. Transformation**—Change and transformation are two different things. Change is often executed within a small, defined domain with little concern for its impacts outside of the 'blast radius.' Transformation is a thoughtful transition from one defined state to another, one in which correlated and interconnected impacts are taken into consideration. We advocate that you plan for transformation, not just change.
- **Risk Management, the Enterprise and the Controlled Transformation Journey**—There are three layers of risk that you must manage—Strategic risk, Operational Risk and Transformation Risk. Much of Transformation Risk is project risk—risk that is more often viewed in terms of project completion within scope, time and cost parameters than it is in terms of achievement of business goals—which disappears when the transformation is completed; however, the scope of a Digital Transformation is so large and the execution time so lengthy that its risks must be managed differently from those of an individual initiative. You should view the act of transformation itself as a Capability to be developed and not a project to be completed. Exercising the Capability involves initiatives, which do have project risks attached

DOI: 10.1201/9781003188605-6

that expire when they are completed, though their outcomes may certainly come with risks attached to them.

- **Scope and Manage Transformation**—the transformation process will likely be long and complicated and will involve numerous mutually dependent initiatives that you will have to sequence thoughtfully. Setting the scope and planning carefully is crucial to your eventual success. These steps are your path:
- **Transformation Governance**—It's critical that a senior executive have clear responsibility for managing the transformation. Diffusion of authority and governing responsibility can doom it.
- **Establish Model Infrastructure, Taxonomy and Pattern Library**—You are about to collect and analyze a large amount of information and data. You must design and create the repositories in which you will store them to preserve its value.
- **Plan and Conduct Discovery**—Conducting the Discovery process efficiently requires that you prioritize and plan carefully. Whether you attempt to cover the entire universe within your company or work a segment at a time will depend on several considerations. Wide or deep is a choice that can have significant implications for the success of your transformation.
- **Compile As-Is Model**—The starting Enterprise Architecture (EA) for your transformation must be documented comprehensively. EA and Business Architecture (BA) will be the framework within which individual initiatives and their attendant risks will be defined and managed.
- **Compile To-Be Model**—The target EA will define what your company will look like when the transformation is complete. Your target will be consistent with the *Anatomy of a digital business* presented in *The company your need to be.*
- **Conduct Gap analysis**—Employing before and after EA models will facilitate your deriving what you will have to do to transform your current Capabilities and Enablers to those consistent with your target EA.
- **Create a Portfolio**—When you have an inventory of initiatives from your gap analysis, you will create a portfolio from which you can manage them.
- **Transformation Strategy Formulation and Roadmapping**—You need to identify and prioritize your transformation goals, articulate your risk appetite and tolerance and build an overall roadmap for your transformation. This will inform the program plan that you will need to control and manage its execution.
- **Portfolio Analysis and Program Definition**—With all this information in place, you can build your transformation plan. The mutual dependencies that are likely to exist between your to-be Capabilities

and Enablers will make this a complicated process. You should be prepared to execute agilely and flexibly as much will change while you're at it.

There is a case study of a company going through this process in the chapter that follows.

CHANGE VS. TRANSFORMATION

Rob Llewellyn of CXO Transform[1] views *Transformation* as evolving your organization to do new things, while *Change* is doing old things in new ways. *Transformation*, according to him, always results in a new or updated Business Model. This is an eminently sensible and defensible view. After all, why bother to expose your company to the risks and expend the time, money and energy to evolve only to continue to do what you have been, especially when it's rapidly losing validity?

I substantially agree with Rob's view, but I will use the terms *Change* and *Transformation* in a different way. We will look at *Change* and *Transformation* in the context of executing an evolutionary process. Rob's approach is a little more about *what* you should do and mine is a little more about *how*. These two usages may overlap but are not in conflict with each other.

While modifying a building is usually a significant and lengthy undertaking, evolving your enterprise should take place as an ongoing series of iterations, even if the end goal is a substantial transformation. In this regard, I differentiate *change* and *transformation*. *Change* is, well, change. Companies often just react to threats, needs or opportunities by *changing*, ad hoc. *Technical Debt* is caused by compromised design from rushed implementation that induces excessive effort or costs when it becomes necessary to modify, maintain or enhance what you've built later. *Change* may relieve immediate pressures but leave Technical Debt in its wake. *Transformation* is an intentional, choreographed process by which your enterprise's architecture is transitioned to a new state. *Transformation* is performed mindfully, with consideration for the interrelationships of elements of the architecture and the intent to balance benefits, costs, and risks and to minimize negative side effects, such as Technical Debt. Ultimately, *transformation* reduces your short- and long-term risks, while the same cannot be said about *change*.

Enterprise and Business Architecture models are intrinsic to executing *Transformation* in a planned and controlled fashion. Identifying all the elements that will be created or modified and understanding their relationships and dependences is key to executing efficiently and to managing the risks inherent in the process.

1 https://cxotransform.com/p/courses

RISK MANAGEMENT AND THE TRANSFORMATIONAL DIGITAL ENTERPRISE

Three layers of risk

Enterprises embody three layers of risks, each of which has unique characteristics. The diagram below reflects the relationship among the various components and indicates associated goals, which can be threatened by risks inherent to them:

In this model, exogenous information is coming inbound from the marketplace and is interpreted by the product management to create a set of Product or Service specifications. These inform requirements for Capabilities and Enablers. Transformation initiatives are initiated to create or modify them so that the prescribed Products and Services can be delivered.

In treating risks associated with transformation, you will have to understand the differences among them and adopt strategies geared to mitigate each of them.

- **Strategic Risks**
  Strategic risks are those associated with your company's market position, competitiveness and profitability; overall—these are the goals of ownership. These are risks relating to things not within your company's control. You can do your best to create marketable products, but you cannot make customers buy them. You can achieve a desirable market share, but you cannot prevent others from coming along with a new product or service that will out-compete yours. This article from the Harvard Business Review[2] provides a good perspective on

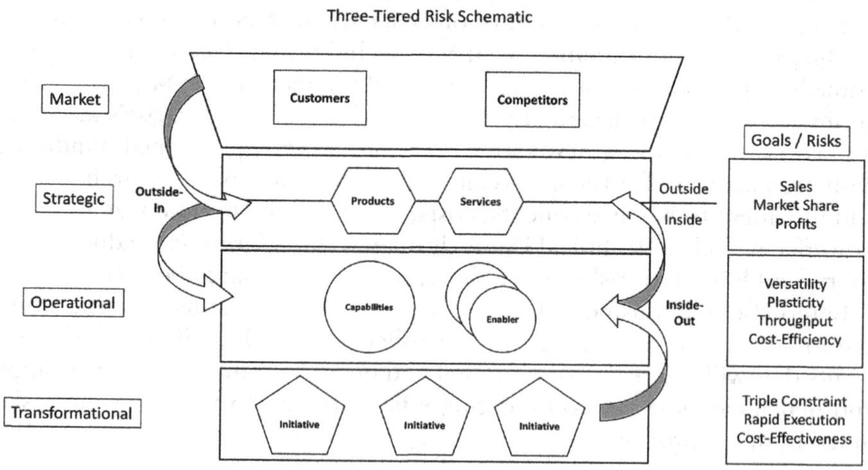

Figure 5.1 The three tiers of risk.

[2] https://hbr.org/2021/05/how-to-calculate-risk-based-on-where-your-profits-come-from

managing enterprise-level strategic risks, which recommends focusing on things that can attack the areas of your business where the most profits are generated.

The interface between these risks and your operational risks is where your outside-in and inside-out strategic imperatives collide. Your ability to manage strategic risks is tightly bound to the Capabilities and Enablers that make your company what it is and managing the risks associated with them, combined with your ability to identify and produce salable offerings, is what will allow you to manage them.

- **Operational Risks**
Operational risks are those associated with your Business-As-Usual operations. These relate less to WHAT you are doing than HOW you're doing it. The goals for your Capabilities and Enablers are versatility and plasticity (see this article from the Caminao blog[3]), throughput and cost-efficiency.

Versatility and plasticity express highly desirable traits as viewed from either side of the interface between strategic and operational concerns. Versatile Capabilities can be modified or reconfigured to respond to changing needs without being rebuilt, which facilitates rapid response to opportunities or threats. Plastic Capabilities can be re-architected without interrupting delivery of services predicated on them. These two powerful concepts capture important aspects of the essence of how business agility can be enabled and realized. Versatility enables adaptation without reconstruction, speeding delivery of enhanced or evolved services. Plasticity enables architectural transformation with minimal disruption, allowing evolution of infrastructure and expanded enablement for new services.

It's relatively quick and easy, though clearly quite important, to come up with a new product idea or a thought about how to respond to an external challenge, but it requires effort, time and money to validate and deliver on the idea. Strategic opportunities may be transient and ephemeral, so business agility is crucial to competing. As we've discussed, such agility can only result from your developing or evolving Capabilities rapidly when you need to and speed exacerbates risks, risks that Agile Enterprise Risk Management (AERM) is intended to help you identify so you can manage them.

The flow of requirements coming from your market-facing decision makers comes outside-in. Your response is inside-out and takes the form of developing new Capabilities or Enablers to deliver on their vision. Just as you may evolve and transform to respond to external stimuli, you may also envision new or improved Capabilities or Enablers that make it possible for you to create and deliver innovative

3 https://caminao.blog/2015/06/22/agile-architectures/

offerings that can clearly contribute to new Products or Services that bring substantial rewards.

- **Transformational Risks**
  The goal of transformation is to deliver change, mostly in the form of new or evolved Capabilities or Enablers, and do it reliably, rapidly and cost-effectively. Transformation is delivered via initiatives and risks of not meeting initiative goals flow upward in the form of sub-optimal business agility and, ultimately, impaired competitiveness.

  One thing that differentiates transformation risks from those in the layers above it is that they are transient to the degree that the initiatives to which they are attached are. Once work stops on an initiative, regardless of whether it succeeded or failed, risks that were associated with its execution are extinguished. Conversely, risks associated with the Capabilities and Enablers that the initiative was intended to create or modify will persist as long as they are in use. You may evade the risks of failing to meet scope, time and budget constraints by taking shortcuts in execution (or ignoring new information which might necessitate pivoting) but, as Benjamin Franklin said,

  > The bitterness of poor quality will remain long after the sweetness of low price is forgotten

  Finally, it is important to understand that your ability to transform is a capability, itself, one that you will exercise repeatedly and on which your business agility will hinge. As you execute your digital transformation, you must build and mature your ability to transform at the same time.

To summarize the above, you must

- focus your transformational and risk management efforts on the **Strategic** Products and Services and customer segments that produce (or have the potential to produce) most of your profits and also developing the transformation muscles you will need to maintain your competitiveness,
- manage **Operational** risks associated with sub-optimal Capabilities and Enablers—those insufficiently versatile and plastic as well as those that under-perform and those that impede your business agility and
- control **Transformational** risks that can impair your ability to add to, evolve and enhance your operational EA.

Managing risks in conjunction with transformation

With this framework understanding of risks, how should you approach the digital transformation and adoption of AERM that you are preparing to undertake?

At the Enterprise and **Strategic** levels:

- Articulate your strategy, focused on the Products and Services that are or will be most important. Since the EA models that will define the starting and end points of your transformation are hierarchical, this will serve as the guidepost to prioritize your transformation planning.
- Ensure sufficient executive level buy-in and establish senior-level leadership with hands-on responsibility for success. Digital Transformation must be a business-driven imperative even though many aspects of it are technical.
- When a plan has been established, ensure that executive and business sponsors take ownership of non-technical risks. Obviously, a business executive won't be comfortable overseeing the risk of integrating the elements of your CI/CD pipeline, but he or she should be willing to oversee the organizational restructuring that creates the technical side of the integrated product management team.
- Identify, articulate and include program goals that will contribute to development and growth of your transformation capabilities. While the program you will define now will have a designated end point, it will, in fact, never really end. You are aiming to create an organization capable of rapid evolution and this will mean never really reaching any static end state.

At the **Operational** level:

- Your EA model is lens through which you will view and monitor the state and transitional progress of your company. It is the linchpin of your transformation and AERM. Since much of the detailed program planning can't proceed until you have it in place, you should prioritize establishing it as early as possible.
- Begin to map risks that you know about to the Capabilities and Enablers to which they attach. You might currently have them defined at higher or the highest levels, e.g., business outcomes rather than elements of your Operational Infrastructure (OI), but you will need to dig deeper to prepare for AERM.
- AERM drills down onto how risk is propagated upward from sources to entities higher up in the EA model, for instance how a Product's sales might suffer from a plant outage resulting from various causes. One of the things you should remain cognizant of is how changes or transitions at lower levels can impact risks at higher levels. You will probably be executing a large number of such transitions over the course of your transformation.

In the context of your **Transformation**:
One of the risks of any large program is political. You need funding and resources that other people in your company would like to have committed to their needs. You will probably require that other people in your company divert from work they're doing to do work you need them to do and you're going to need people to accept significant changes in roles or processes. Your ability to mitigate political risk, and one that is crucial to your ultimate success, is your ability to communicate and gain acceptance for what you're proposing.

To the degree possible, people will be more willing to accept your program plan if they feel they've had a hand in creating it. You will need to do more than simply create a plan you believe will work and present it as a fait accompli. In his book, *Unconscious Branding*,[4] author Douglas Van Praet says that **if you want someone else to completely believe in your idea, you must make them believe that it was their own idea all along.**

This is sage advice; however, in the case of a substantial organizational transformation, there's a catch—you must be able to maintain control of the process and steer away from the unfeasible and the inadvisable. You will also have to deal with everyone's desire to be either first, to get benefits immediately, or last, to watch everyone else and make sure the transformation is going to work before committing to doing it in their domain. While much of this is internal salesmanship, evading land mines will require that you have a thorough grasp of technical and architectural issues, some of which might be new to you at the time you begin. You need a team of experts that cover the areas in which you will be working, and you may be best off to bring them in from outside the company. After all, if the company had a cadre of such experts on board, you would probably not be doing what you're doing.

From the standpoint of technology, here are some strategies to help mitigate the risks of your program:

- Examine alternative execution and delivery options for each element of your program.
  - What will create value if partially delivered?
  - What will create value if delivered standalone?
  - How can you work around mutual dependencies?
- Consider what is visible and tangible to business users—elements of the Digital Products and Services Factory (DPSF) are front-and-center; elements of the OI and APIs, are more behind the scenes.

[4] www.amazon.com/dp/0230341799?asc_campaign=commerce-pra&asc_source=browser&tag=undefined

- Transformation creates its own risks and impacts others.
  - Create an orchestrated state-to-state migration model: transform, don't just change.
  - Use the EA model to see how interim states of relevant entities may impact risks, for how long and at what intensity.
- Begin experimenting with what you understand how to do least.
- Continuously monitor and evaluate your assumptions regarding how things will integrate and work together. Remember, assumptions are potent sources of risk.
- Monitor early-stage execution closely to identify where assumptions may not be holding up and you may not be meeting expectations. Make course corrections immediately.
- Identify what is hardest to do and plan to do it either first or last.

Now, it's easy to fall into a trap of your own making and this must be avoided at all costs—you believe that transformation, or at least the part of it you're selling right now, will require a certain quota of time, resources and budget and should produce a laundry list of benefits. When a company bridles at making the investment, it's not unusual for less-experienced project owners or managers to nervously bargain away time and resources, often out of the contingency budget, to gain acceptance and regret it later. As aviators say, ***"never take off on your backup systems."*** In short, don't do it. You're going to hit unforeseen impediments and need plenty of forbearance as you navigate the transformation and the longer you can put that need off, the more likely you will be to have delivered some value that will get you some slack when you need it.

So, look for opportunities for low-hanging fruit and quick wins. Initiatives that provide fuzzy indications of progress and don't produce tangible deliverables that stakeholders can see until very close to their scheduled completion are inherently risky and it's hard to blame stakeholders for viewing them guardedly. With that in mind, it's important for you to establish realistic expectations and meet or exceed them. Under-promise and over-deliver, especially early on.

The scope of what's required for digital transformation is so large and the mutual dependencies so numerous that not only do you have to navigate the hairball, but you will have to do it for many cases involving technology or business processes or teams with which (or with whom) you are unfamiliar. You need to be mindful that applying technology with which you are unfamiliar to business processes that are new to you with a team with whom you haven't worked is a pretty sure path to failure. As you compile the initiative portfolio from which you will produce your transformation program, you must identify these situations and develop strategies for dealing with them and the risks they represent.

SCOPING AND PLANNING THE TRANSFORMATION JOURNEY

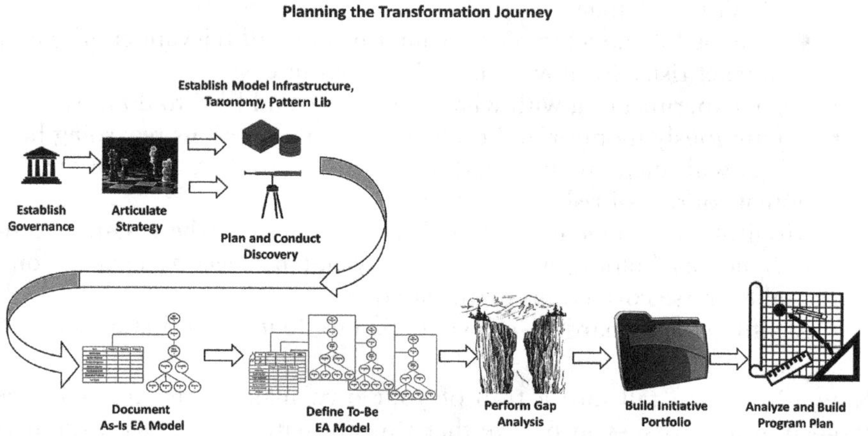

The transformation planning process is depicted in the diagram, above. At the highest level, it includes:

- Establish who's governing the transformation and who will assume to-be operational responsibilities as elements of the transformation are implemented,
- Articulate your transformation strategy and identify your Critical Success Factors (CSFs) for it,
- Establish your model infrastructure (the repositories where you will maintain your metadata), the Taxonomy and the Pattern Library,
- Plan for and conduct Discovery,
- Compile an as-is EA/BA model,
  - Map known risks to (assumedly from your existing risk register) the lowest levels of the model that you can,
- Create a to-be EA/BA model,
- Perform gap analysis and populate the transformation initiative portfolio,
- Analyze the portfolio to rationalize it, prioritize individual initiatives, identify and evaluate risks,
- Build the master transformation program plan,
- Obtain approval, funding and resources required and
- Execute your program.

In this section, we will explore the process, identifying situational alternatives along the way.

There is a lot of material in this chapter, and I have included a case study: ***HiCTools—developing a transformation portfolio and program plan*** to illustrate the techniques covered in it.

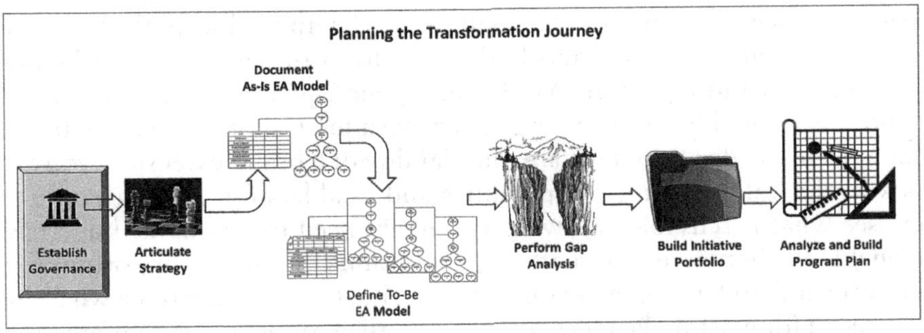

Establish who's governing during the transformation and after

Before anything else, establishing roles, responsibilities and decision-making authority is critical. Navigating from your starting point to a position to compile the EA/BA Model will involve considerable time and effort and will produce an artifact that you will need to maintain and update with data representing activities and business decisions taking place all over your company from the moment it is instantiated. Unless there is a commitment to staffing and processes that will allow the RM group to tap into, extract and maintain the information in the AERM EA/BA repository, its value will dissipate rapidly and the benefits of AERM will forever elude you. If your company cannot make this commitment, then you might as well not start down the path at all.

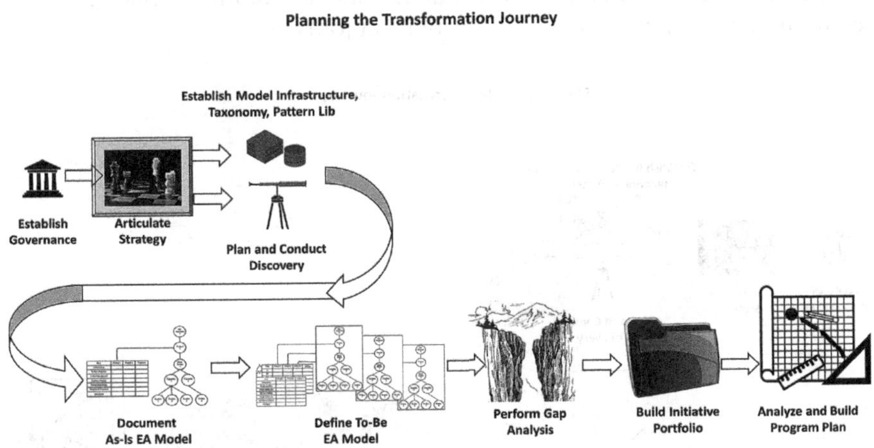

Articulate your strategy

Your EA model and your AERM processes must reflect your business strategy. As we've discussed previously, strategy can be viewed outside-in and inside-out. Scenario and SWOT analysis can be applied in both directions (outside-in and inside-out) and both can inform the process of evaluating your Business and Operating Models and your Operational Architecture to identify what will have to change to achieve a tactical or strategic goal. For example, if you decide to evaluate the viability of a brand extension, you can look at the Value Streams, Capabilities and Enablers for existing Products and see what is reusable and what you might need to modify or build new to enable the initiative. Alternatively, if you think you see an opportunity to innovate and update some of your Capabilities, then you can trace what this may mean for existing Products that rely on them or new ones that might be enabled by them, which could make you more competitive.

Ultimately, your articulated strategy will help you determine the importance of and priorities among Markets you either do or don't serve and Products and Services that you either do or don't sell and where you are or aren't competitive. With this knowledge, you can evaluate where gaps exist in your company's anatomy that you need to address. This article from TechNexus[5] discusses four different aspects of digital transformation strategy.

Priority for changes where there are significant Opportunities or Threats and risks attached to Capabilities and Enablers supporting high-priority Products and Services will increase in importance. Though the mechanisms underlying risks associated with components of your anatomy may not change much, their impact when newly tied to a high-priority Product or Service may increase, magnifying the need to review and revise treatment plans for them.

Gap analysis will be the starting point for constructing your transformation portfolio and strategic gaps will be the starting point for that. This will be an important step in your transformation journey.

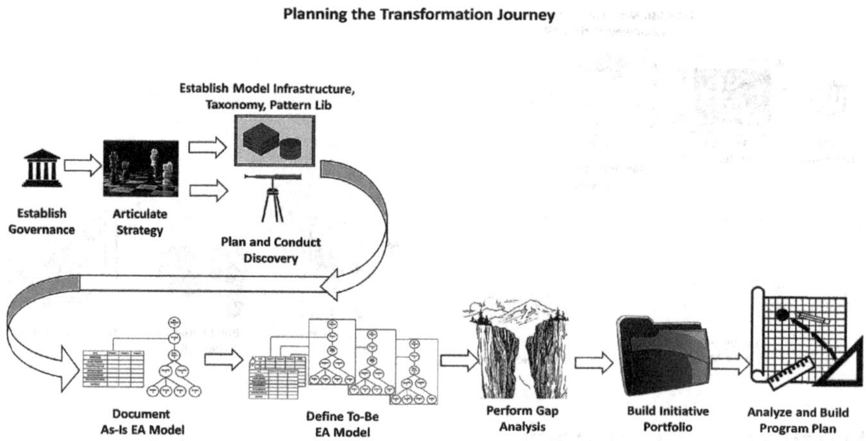

[5] https://www.linkedin.com/pulse/4-types-digital-transformation-andrew-annacone/

Establish your physical model infrastructure—EA/BA models, KM repository, pattern library

It's quite possible that your company has some or all of the required EA information in a tool or a specialized repository that you can augment or extract from to create the model that you will need for transformation planning. It's important to consider the approach you will use carefully. You will want to resist creating a redundant repository unnecessarily when the original is already being maintained by established processes. You will ultimately need to be able to manipulate the data in your model, and this could create conflicts with the people using an existing one and those responsible for maintaining it.

To be clear, you can:

- Establish a new model and repository, if one does not already exist,
- Augment an existing model to include attributes that you will need but which aren't part of the existing data model of the repository or
- Extract data from the existing repository, use it to populate a new one designed for your AERM needs and create a process in which additions or changes in the existing repository are echoed or replicated into the new one periodically.

There are some considerations that should inform your selected approach:

- If you establish a new model or create a separate subset model, you must also plan to keep the model up to date on an ongoing basis. This operational requirement will have to become part of your transformation and must be addressed in the governance plan.
- If you decide to deploy a parallel model, you will have to prevent it diverging from the existing model. Any maintenance process you put in place to extract the data you need will have to be carefully designed and monitored. Periodic audits will be a good idea so that incongruence between models can be identified, rectified and the process that produced it adjusted. There needs to be a single source of truth and that can only mean that one model will be considered the primary or the master.
- In spite of the potential downsides, there may be a good reason to establish a separate model. If the modifications and additions required to the existing model are too difficult to accommodate or would result in something that doesn't work well for one or more of the user sets, that may sway your decision on this issue.
- Make sure that the model infrastructure you have chosen, whether commercial product, home-built solution or even something like a spreadsheet (which I do not recommend), is capable of housing alternate scenarios and versions. It should be capable of housing both your

as-is and to-be models. If you want to be able to revert the model to an earlier state, you will want to make sure that the tools you select to implement it will accommodate this, also. N.B., the ability to manage versioning is quite close to what is needed to maintain alternate prospective scenarios. If you can do one, you can probably do the other.

You will need to consider the representational and visualization capabilities of your modeling tool. You are going to want to accommodate future-state versions of segments of the model that address contemplated initiatives, and perhaps even a number of alternative scenarios so that the impacts of each can be evaluated. Think carefully about how you will use your model and consider whether an existing commercial product makes sense for you. If your company is already using one, you should certainly evaluate whether it will meet your needs and whether you can piggyback on the existing license or, at least, obtain a discount for an additional one. Just make sure that it will work properly with the abbreviated model that we propose and that it provides taxonomy/ontology support that will enforce consistency.

Finally, you might want to employ a graph database, such as the one that I have used (and will continue to) to portray the example EA models in this book. While I like them for this purpose, there may not be many EA tools based on them. Even so, the sorts of data visualizations that are presented here can be emulated by some commercial EA tools, irrespective of the underlying technology that they employ for their repository.

In any event, the goal of this step is to implement your EA model and the processes that will be executed to maintain its currency.

Establish the logical designs of your metadata repositories

Your EA/BA models

The logical designs for your EA and BA models will be determined by how you intend to integrate them into your operational and governance processes, the tools you select, how they will integrate with existing repositories, your taxonomy and the user interface that you intend to provide for the people that will be using them.

Your Taxonomy

Enabling Knowledge Management (KM) is an important objective for your Digital Transformation and for AERM. One thing on which KM relies is a consistent naming and relationship structure among the elements of your company, which will allow you to identify what is related to or dependent on what rapidly and reliably. This is an important facet of your EA model (and all of your metadata) without which you would limit your business agility.

Taxonomy is a backbone element of your KM. Among other things, consistent naming and classification will drive your ability to realize value from your Pattern Library.

Your taxonomy categorizes your understanding of your company, its anatomy and how it fits into the ecosystem in which it operates. It should represent the relationships, mostly as parent-child or class-subclass, among the elements of your model. For instance, your company may have multiple processes and systems that accomplish pretty much the same thing for different business units but do it in a fashion that is different enough that they should be recognized as different things. Invoicing systems for products that are sold and delivered once may not be the same as those that bill periodically for subscription services. However, they are both subtypes of the Enabler class called *Billing Systems*.

> A taxonomy (or taxonomical classification) is a scheme of classification, especially a hierarchical classification, in which things are organized into groups or types.[6]

An ontology extends the knowledge representation of a taxonomy to incorporate a larger picture and a richer set of relationships than the taxonomy alone. Here's an article by Chantal Schweizer[7] that contrasts the two quite nicely.

Now, ontology gets us into metaphysics, quite far afield from where we started. The practical importance of the taxonomy is that it defines classification, terminology and usage that you will apply to your model and all the data in it to ensure that everything is labeled and entities and relationships are represented consistently. As your model grows, nuances that you need to represent may exceed what your taxonomy alone can provide for. Extending the model may then require that you create an ontology to guide the process. At this point, however, we'll leave the subject of ontology for another time and venue.

A taxonomy can go a long way toward enhancing the utility of your EA model by simplifying and accelerating your ability to identify relevant entities when you are contemplating changes in your company. For example, if you will need a payments system for a new business line, you should be able to identify instances of them that already exist in your company so that you can evaluate whether any of them might be reusable to meet your needs. If they are represented in your model with a variety of labels, you could fail to find one that you could have used and therefore end up implementing a redundant one.

6 https://en.wikipedia.org/wiki/Taxonomy

7 https://www.earley.com/blog/what-difference-between-taxonomy-and-ontology-it-matter-complexity

Where are you likely to run into a taxonomy? Well, the Dewey Decimal system[8] is one that can be found at any public library. Or simply look at any corporate or product website or even on any search engine, for that matter. Websites are usually organized hierarchically; content is broken down by presumed areas of user interest and products are assigned into logical categories. Products may appear in multiple categories, but that is something implemented for the website and is not a function of the taxonomy. Ultimately, the organization and classification of information on a site is designed to assist you in finding what you're interested in. The taxonomy that will be applied to the data in your EA/BA model is intended to serve the same purpose.

With respect to classifying and tagging (assigning taxonomic labels to) existing entities, many companies maintain a commercial or home-grown Configuration Management Database (CMDB)[9] that tracks computing assets, what they are, who's using them, where they're located and what recurring expenses are associated with them. The CMDB or its equivalent could be valuable to your discovery process if your company has one. Among other things, it probably has an organization hierarchy embedded in it, which you can use to inform your Discovery process and seed some of your EA model. However, it is likely that there are other systems and repositories that contain similar data and extracting and rationalizing the information in all of them can be an onerous task. Nonetheless, you will want to identify and evaluate the information contained in application repositories that may represent elements of organizational structure and relationships between departments, groups or teams and Enablers. This can help you make your starting taxonomy as comprehensive as possible.

The naming conventions and labels you will apply to the data that will make its way into your model will be easier to manage consistently if you define and assign them prior to entering it into your repository. That said, there's no doubt that your classification scheme will grow and evolve as your discovery progresses and you will need to go back and revise your naming and labeling when classes or subclasses of entities require it. Refactoring[10] is most usually associated with programming but it is also appropriate for restructuring your taxonomy. As you maintain it, you will certainly find needs to restructure it, breaking a category into two new ones, for example, which will necessitate going back into your repository to update the classifications of some of your entries.

Nonetheless, the earlier you establish a preliminary taxonomy, the faster you will achieve consistency that will make your model useful and the easier it will probably be to exploit your repository's capabilities to facilitate refactoring it programmatically, thereafter.

8 https://en.wikipedia.org/wiki/Dewey_Decimal_Classification
9 https://en.wikipedia.org/wiki/Configuration_management_database
10 https://en.wikipedia.org/wiki/Code_refactoring

The relevance to you is this—you will need to tailor the framework of your model to address your specific circumstances. Is your company multinational? Then you may need to add geography to your model. Do you have different brands, as GM does? Then your model may need to be extended to represent that, as well. You should not view the hierarchical model and the entity palette I have employed in the examples presented thus far as a hard constraint, but you should not go wild adding to it, either. The more complicated your model gets; the more effort will be required to keep it up to date. You should add what you need when you need it. As Einstein said:

> Everything should be a simple as possible, but not simpler.

Your Pattern Library

The Pattern Library is a free-form repository of potentially reusable knowledge and tangible assets, which are indexed or tagged to facilitate their discovery and retrieval. These might include technical research, architectural designs, application component requirements documentation, market and consumer research and anything else that might be of value. KM's contribution to the Pattern Library is the taxonomy, which will allow people to search for and identify items of value reliably, and, potentially, a librarian to assist users to search. Assuming that such items will be created on an ongoing basis, KM should have an ongoing role in evaluating and classifying what is going into the Library as it is presented for inclusion. This is a process that should be overseen by the Change Management team,[11] which will be responsible for operations of the transformed enterprise, longer term.

One possibility for implementing your Pattern Library is a data lake.[12] It's worth looking at this Wikipedia article as it addresses a problem with data lakes that could easily insinuate itself into your Pattern Library. It requires a fair amount of discipline to avoid having your Library become a dumping ground for unstructured and unindexed artifacts, which quickly lose their value because no one can find them when they would be relevant.

Initiate and monitor the ongoing governance and management processes of your EA/AERM effort

As the discovery process proceeds, you will be creating foundational assets for your company's transformation process and its ongoing management and governance capabilities. It is imperative that you quality-control the

[11] The change management team is discussed in a later section. It has a transformation program and ongoing operational role.

[12] https://en.wikipedia.org/wiki/Data_lake

data that ends up in the repositories of your management systems and do not allow it to become stale. In the initial step in your transformation, you identified who would be responsible for ensuring that the staffing and business processes required to prevent this are defined and overseen. You must make sure that all of this is operating up to expectations, especially since your company will continue to evolve, even while you are gearing up your capabilities to manage it at speed but have not implemented them in their entirety.

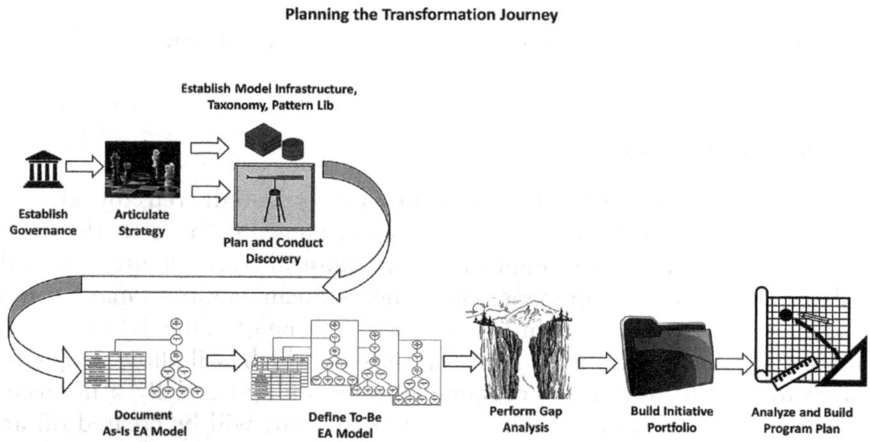

Scope, plan and conduct your discovery effort

Fully-elaborated EA models, as prescribed by The Open Group[13] and John Zachman,[14] are two of many takes on EA. EA is enabled by innumerable commercial tools that vastly exceed the level of detail that you will need for AERM. Part of what makes AERM doable is the constrained level of detail you need to implement it and, therefore, the time and effort required for discovery is far less than what you would anticipate for a complete EA exercise. Nonetheless, comprehensiveness is a necessity and planning is required to achieve it.

Your first step is to determine what is in and what is out of scope. Ideally, your entire company would be in scope but there are many reasons why it might not be. If your domain consists of a business unit that is a part of large conglomerate, you might be limited to what happens 'within its four walls.' You might be conducting your transformation as an experimental exercise in a subset of your company so that the process

[13] https://www.opengroup.org/

[14] https://www.zachman.com/

can be matured before rolling it out to a larger scope. Whatever your scope is defined to be, you will need to:

- Determine how you will partition your domain to allocate your work force to it. If you can work hierarchically in parallel with the model (Market Segment, Product and Service and so on) this can help considerably.
- Identify the subject matter experts (SMEs) who will act as authoritative sources for each segment of your scope, and within each segment, who will represent the components within them, i.e., who understands the systems, processes, assets and all of the other things that make the business work.
- Identify entities outside of your scope, whether within the company or outside of it, that should be evaluated for their relationships and interdependencies with entities within it. You may not cover these at the same level of detail as those within your scope, but you need to know they're out there and understand how they may be connected, how they may create or influence risks and how they may impact or be impacted by changes you might make. Ideally, you will want to represent them in your model.

Prioritize and schedule your discovery tasks

To manage the discovery effort, you will need to create a schedule and staffing plan to conduct interviews and collect data. The order in which you do this can make the process easier or more difficult. You might benefit from meeting with SMEs top-down, so they can roadmap the area they represent for you, or you might focus on what is least familiar to you and work bottom-up so you are as informed as you can be when you meet with SMEs responsible for strategy, marketing and product management, which are likely to be more abstract than the Capabilities and Enablers at the lower levels.

Define and plan to implement a process for checking and resolving omissions and internal consistency issues among the data that you will collect throughout the discovery process. Make sure that you perform this with reasonable frequency as you progress. It is much easier to course-correct if inconsistencies and divergences are caught early than if they are allowed to pile up. A bullet that is an inch off target at 50 yards is ten feet off target at 1,000.

Define how you will format the data and how and when it will make its way into your chosen repository. You might choose to enter pretty raw data into it and employ your tooling to help you identify and address anomalies or you might choose to do this prior to inputting it, ensuring that only vetted data makes it into the repository.

Plan to iterate your discovery process, first to acquire data, then to go back and fill in gaps, then to resolve inconsistencies or misunderstandings and finally to present and obtain concurrence on your model from the SMEs.

Focus on business processes

Plan to allow sufficient time to assess complicated Enablers, such as business processes, especially decision-driven processes.

Business processes are potent sources of risks, especially when they involve decisions and path selection, such as routing a work item to a specific group for processing or exception handling. It is crucial that you identify all decision processes for analysis. Most of them will be obvious but some may not be. Business Process mining[15] involves analyzing data thrown off by transactional processes, whether automated or not, to identify where processes exist within your operations. Commercial tools, such as Celonis[16] and others, can help you identify, document and measure the performance of your processes.

Why is this important? The major reasons are:

- Digital Transformation and improving the performance of your business will undoubtedly lead you to business process re-engineering. If you don't fully understand your processes, you cannot do this effectively.
- You are going to want to apply Business Process Management (BPM) tools in conjunction with the re-engineering process. Automated processes innately incorporate predetermined and/or AI-determined decision criteria, which you will have to risk-manage, monitor and adjust over time.
- Business processes are widely intertwined with Capabilities and Enablers that cross numerous organizational boundaries within your enterprise. Changes to them can create risks and unexpected impacts in surprising places. Your awareness of them is an important element of your RM process.

As you will see, understanding and mapping processes is not trivial and is likely to require that you work with larger groups of people, not just one or two SMEs.

Business process discovery and management decision mapping

Earlier, we discussed strategic, operational and transformation risks. ERM is tied to decision-making, which takes place at each of the levels, with varying frequencies and in myriad places in your enterprise. You make strategic financial and other decisions, such as mergers or acquisitions, at the enterprise or business unit level. These decisions are situation-specific, and

15 https://hbr.org/2019/04/what-process-mining-is-and-why-companies-should-do-it
16 https://www.celonis.com/

they must account for structural and operational risks both pre- and post-transaction. Operational decisions are more closely tied to business as usual (BAU) processes and events. These are often controlled by policies and may be embedded in processes as business rules.

For example, deciding whether to acquire another company should be informed, among other things, by what it will do to your risk profile. Determining that is one of many things you accomplish in the course of *due diligence*. A bank's credit and lending standards are usually embedded as business rules or scoring models in a system that supports loan approvals and by policies requiring escalating senior approval based on the size of the requested loan. This ensures that someone with more seniority, experience and accountability reviews loans when their scale might present a substantial exposure to loss for the bank.

While acquisition decisions don't come along every day, loan applications do. Acquisitions are likely a semi-structured process; loan processing is highly structured. It's important to note that risks aggregate upward. If a bank is acquiring another, one of the things that would impact the value of the acquired bank is how well it manages its loan risks and what the quality of its loan portfolio is. Ultimately, how you do little things can have a big impact on the overall value of your company.

When decision-making is structured, it is much easier to identify when, where and how risk controls should be employed. So, performing ERM properly requires that you identify all decision processes and mitigate risks associated with them. In ISO's 31000 (2018) standard, it advises that ERM be aligned with decision-making processes.[17]

Understanding how a company operates is crucial to designing its architecture and formulating and applying risk controls. Processes are designed to increase the probability of meeting desired performance targets (throughput, error minimization, etc.) and to achieve predictability. They may vary from fully manual to fully automated and both types have their own set of concerns and considerations.

Manual decision processes are often higher-level and associated with governance and strategic decision-making, such as undertaking significant transformations or making acquisitions. In smaller businesses, though, many decision processes that might be automated in larger businesses are not. Decision criteria in manual processes may be less formalized than automated processes because it is not necessary or worth the effort to formalize and encode them.

Automated processes are often applied to handle events that occur more frequently, have higher throughput volumes and are more standardized, such as order management. Business Process Automation (BPA) and Robotic Process Automation (RPA) incorporate embedded decision logic that implements policies or business rules, which should be evaluated regularly for

[17] https://www.iso.org/obp/ui/#iso:std:iso:31000:ed-2:v1:en

effectiveness and appropriateness. Many companies implement decision engines and embedded rule repositories that support multiple applications throughout the company. This ensures consistent application of rules across processes and creates a single source of logic that is easy to update and propagate to wherever they are employed.

Regardless of type, every decision process must be identified and assessed for risks. Manual processes can be discovered through interviews or by reviewing company training or process manuals. Automated processes can be discovered by conducting a systems inventory and evaluating the functions supported. Process mining software helps to discover implicit business processes by reading system logs and analyzing interactions and sequences of transactions among them.

Example: an order management process

The order-to-cash process, diagrammed below, is a simple order management process with two decision points that relate to customer credit:

This swim lane diagram shows the actors and the steps that are executed from the time an order is received until it is either canceled or shipped, invoiced and collected. Each lane in the diagram contains actions and decisions made by a single department and the process flows from left to right. The process depicted contains the following actions and decisions:

- An order is received by sales and is referred to the credit department
- The credit department determines whether the order is within the customer's pre-approved credit limit:
- The credit department checks to see whether the order is from an existing customer or not
  - If this is a new customer, the credit department establishes a credit profile and sets a credit limit
  - Otherwise, it uses the customer's established credit limit
- It checks to see whether the order amount is within the pre-approved limit
  - If it is, the credit department approves the order and forwards it to fulfillment for processing
  - If it is not, the credit department forwards it to an executive officer (EO) for exception review
- When an order is referred, the Executive Officer (EO) conducts an exception review
  - If the EO approves it, the order is forwarded to fulfillment
  - If the EO rejects it, the order is canceled, and sales is notified so it can contact the customer
- When fulfillment receives an order it packages and ships it and notifies the A/R department that the order has shipped
- When the A/R department receives notification of a shipped order, it sends an invoice and collects the payment.

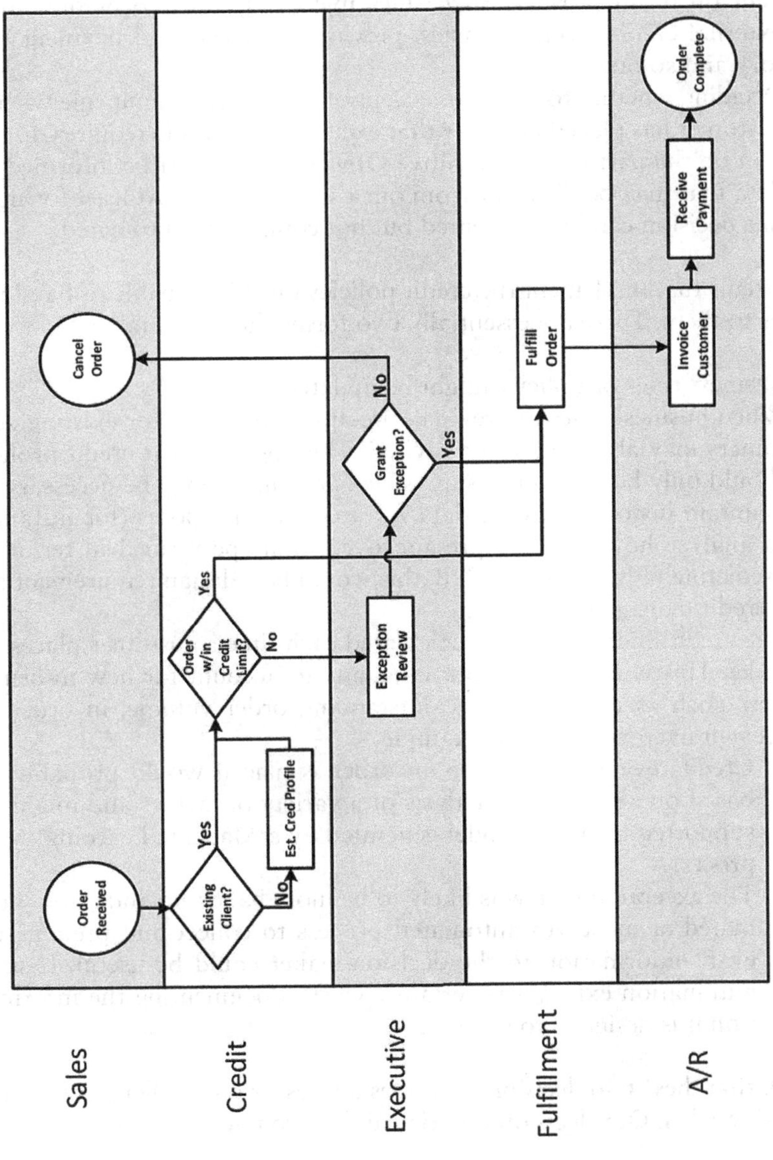

Figure 5.2 An order-to-cash process.

This is a pretty straightforward flow that has two decision processes embedded in it:

- Establishing a credit limit is a policy-based decision process, dependent on business rules. Such rules might rely on information from external credit rating agencies, previous purchase and payment history and so on.
- Deciding whether to make an exception to the credit limit rule when a customer has placed an order that exceeds it. This rule requires discretion on the part of the Executive Officer, which must be informed by data that may be different from one case to another. At least for now, this decision can be augmented but not completely automated.

The systems that implement the credit policies must be capable of handling changes to them. There are essentially two forms this might take:

- Business rules or policies might be updated periodically.
  When business rules are revised, pre-approved limits for existing customers may also need to be revised. This suggests that credit profiles should only be valid until superseded and that it may be necessary to maintain historical profile data for analytical purposes (for instance, to analyze how well the pre-approved limits performed in terms of predicting failures to pay). NB, this would be a design requirement for a credit management system.
- The credit limit might be recalculated each time a customer places an order. This would allow your company to account for new information, such as the customer's outstanding order volume, in order to prevent overexposure, for example.
  - Credit review at the time an order is placed would probably be based on algorithmic analysis of a variety of factors and might be supported by an AI model generated by a Machine Learning (ML) process.
  - The exception review is likely to be more hands-on and semi-automated at most. An automated process to collect and present relevant information to the decision-maker could be useful. If such automation exists, it is certainly worth documenting the information it is designed to present.

The risk that these two decision processes address is the challenge of identifying **bad credits.** Our decision criteria can lead to two possible errors:

- *Approving* an order from a customer who will not ultimately pay or will not pay in a timely fashion (predicting the Customer ***IS NOT*** a bad credit.) This is a ***false negative***—mis-identifying a bad credit as a good one.

- *Rejecting* an order from a customer who would have paid in full and on time (predicting the Customer ***IS*** a bad credit.) This is a ***false positive***—mis-identifying a good credit as a bad one.

There are contingent considerations and risks, as well. If your company habitually approves orders for customers who are bad credit risks, it may impact its financial position or increase its overall risk profile. We might expect to see the percentage of receivables that are written off to exceed industry averages, among other things. On the other hand, if your company rejects an order from a customer or prospect, they may cease doing business with you, cutting off a potential stream of future revenue. Statistical models should be applied to minimize the loss of being wrong about a given customer order and the company's risk appetite and risk tolerance should inform the policies that are applied to credit screening.

So, business processes are designed, either implicitly or explicitly, in consideration of risk concerns and assumptions and incorporate decision processes that must be reviewed to identify and understand how they accommodate and control for risk. It is imperative that you discover and assess each process, identify the embedded decision processes that determine its outcomes and analyze and treat the risks they contain.

Inventory and document management and governance processes

Governance is one of the six pillars that you will build to become a digital company and governance processes are one of the things you will have to transform as part of your program.

To ensure that nothing falls through the cracks, it is imperative that you identify and document all of the governance processes that your company currently has and ensure that they will have a specified 'landing place' in your to-be architecture.

To the degree that they are processes, your governance practices can be modeled on the basis of ***inputs, processing and outputs***. For example, your traditional ERM practice might involve:

- Selecting a defined subset of the company or business to evaluate,
- Gathering information about the risks inherent in the selected domain,
- Performing a risk assessment—identifying relevant risks for scrutiny,
- Analyzing each identified risk,
- Producing a treatment plan for each of the risks and
- Producing outputs:
  - An updated risk register,
  - Activity and status reporting (what areas were covered, what major risks were addressed, etc.)

    - Guidance to operational management or other governance areas to publicize new or updated standards and policies or to make them aware of changes to the landscape of which they should be aware.
- Taking action to treat risks, e.g., purchasing insurance or diversifying sources for critical production inputs.

Using the ***input, processing, output*** framework, you should then find answers to the following questions:

- How and when is any particular subset of the company selected for a risk assessment?
- Is there an event that triggers the process or is it periodic?
- What information is required as input to the process?
- What approach(es) or algorithm(s) is (are) executed to evaluate input and produce output?
- What form does the output take?
- Who receives the output and to what use is it put?
- Ultimately, what action is taken, based on the output?

Any or all of these things can change as a result of the transformation, and you must be sure that you map the as-is process to a to-be state as part of your transformation program plan. With respect to digital transformation, as we've discussed it to this point:

- Decentralization and distribution of responsibilities and decision-making authority can disconnect your governance processes from some of the inputs on which they are based now. You will need to ensure that any such disconnection is addressed in your program plan.
- The inputs generated by new or revised processes may be substantially different than what now exists. If this is the case, you will need to modify your governance process to account for that.
- Your to-be governance processes may have to accommodate substantially different goals than your current ones do. Different inputs, algorithms and metrics may all be required. The processing part of your practices may have to be revised.
- Given the other changes that may be required of your practices, new outputs may be appropriate. New reports, new dashboards and new metrics may be needed.

Execute discovery

Now you should be prepared to execute your Discovery process, collect and validate the data and populate your metadata—the EA model and Pattern Library, tagged and qualified by your Taxonomy. It's almost a certainty that you will have multiple teams operating in parallel and there are some concerns:

- Data quality, comprehensiveness and consistency are very important. Keeping your taxonomy development in sync with (preferably, ahead of) your collection and analysis is crucial to achieving this. If your taxonomy effort falls behind, then you may be better served to avoid entering raw data into your repository so that it can be classified and tagged first.
- It is advisable to have a QA team reviewing data and documenting questions for each of the working groups to resolve as it comes in. Members of the taxonomy team could be valuable members of this one and it may enhance their work on the taxonomy, as well.
- You will need to monitor execution closely as the process begins. No matter how much you go over what to expect, teams will struggle at the outset.
- At the beginning of the process, it will be a good idea to hold regular internal review meetings to allow the teams to decompress, raise procedural issues and resolve them. As discovery progresses, this will become less important, and the frequency of status and progress meetings can be reduced.
- You should assume that your teams will ramp up their productivity as they become accustomed to the discovery process. Don't become overly concerned if they fall behind schedule early but take action if they do not begin to catch up as the process progresses.

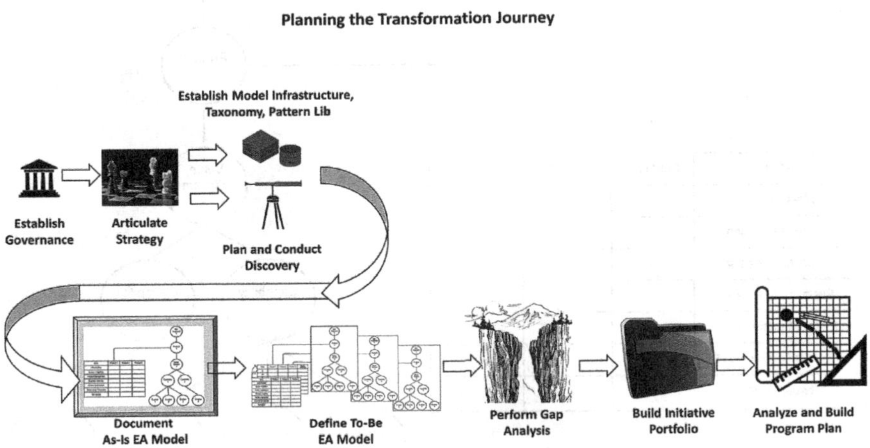

Compile the as-is EA/BA model

Earlier, we presented two sample EA models, embodied in labeled property graph databases. In the chapter *The company you need to be*, we presented a generic model for a business unit in a multi-line company and in *Case study 1*, we presented a to-be model of a prospective startup.
The work products that are the goals of this activity are:

- a comprehensive model that reflects your articulated strategy and covers relevant Markets and Segments, Products and Services, Value Streams, Capabilities and Enablers and
- A collection of the artifacts from which you have extracted the data for your EA/BA models, which will be inserted into the Pattern Library.

The path to achieve this is one of several steps:

Populate your as-is model

The diagram, below, presents a conceptual schematic of what you will be doing in building your as-is EA map. Each of the Products or Services is mapped to a hierarchy of the Value Streams, Capabilities and Enablers that are dedicated to producing them. These should be represented in the boxes of the column in which the Product or Services is represented; however, this

As-Is	Product 1	Product 2	Product 3
Infrastructure			
System Integration			
Product Management			
Business Analytics			
Partner Enablement			
Governance Processes			
Non-Digital			

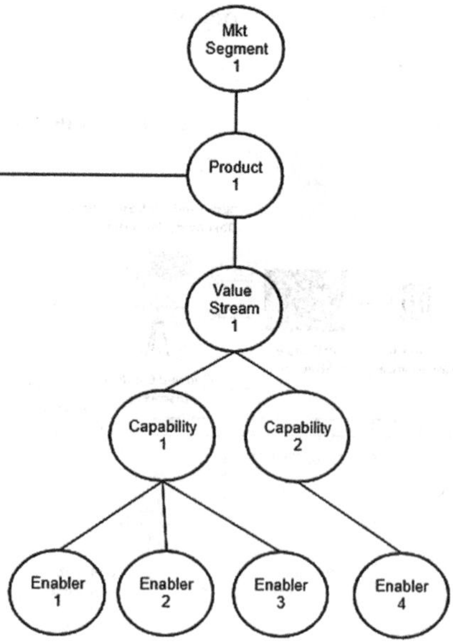

Figure 5.3 As-is mapping approach.

would be too busy to represent here. And, of course, you should not forget to map your non-digital entities, such as your physical plants, equipment and manufacturing teams and record dependencies among them.

Some of them employ common Capabilities and Enablers; some have unique ones. Although it would be too busy to show, Capabilities and Enablers map onto the current rows that represent entities that are analogous to those that comprise the digital business framework. For instance, some Enabler applications run on the existing corporate infrastructure, others may have been implemented and operate on division-owned hardware or on a contracted public cloud infrastructure.

Map known risks to your as-is model

If you have been practicing ERM in the traditional manner, you probably have a risk register[18] but what is in it could vary substantially from what would be optimal to have as a starting point for AERM.

Negative outcomes emanating from risk events normally result from a chain of dependencies. For example:

- If there is a power outage in the area where our plant is, then
  - Our production backlog will build up and orders will be fulfilled late
  - Our delivery pipeline will empty
  - Our sales outlets will stock out
  - Our competitors' products may pick up some of the sales we would have made
  - Some of our outlets may stop carrying our products and, ultimately
    - We may lose sales outlets and/or customers
    - We may lose sales volume, overall
    - We may lose profits

Your risk register may represent this as a single risk, say 'plant outage for n days.' This is inadequate detail for AERM and for managing risks, in general. Certainly, it doesn't help much in determining what steps you might take to mitigate the risk if there are several possible scenarios at play. The options you have for dealing with a power outage may be of little or no use if a tornado damages the plant such that it cannot be operated, power or no.

At least, however, if you have a risk register, you have a starting point for using the information to establish some critical elements of your as-is model. You will need to map what you can see in the register to the entities in the as-is EA model so that you can see where changes resulting from your digital transformation will require that you evaluate morphed or new risks.

[18] https://en.wikipedia.org/wiki/Risk_register

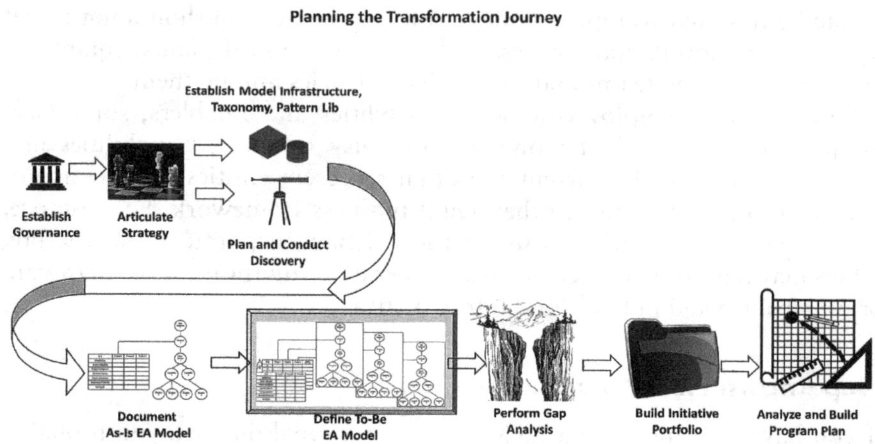

Establish your preliminary to-be model

When you selected your model infrastructure, you determined that it was capable of housing alternate scenarios and versions—your as-is and to-be models, as well as, perhaps, alternate scenarios you might be contemplating. You will need to map elements of the two models together as you chart your transformation. In some places, your to-be model will contain things that don't currently exist and in others, you will be migrating and consolidating current Capabilities and Enablers into new forms and possibly into new Value Streams. You should be able to enrich your EA model with additional data elements, such as priorities and initiative project assignments, which will ultimately be used to visualize sequencing and dependencies. (Models built on NoSQL databases, such as graph DBs or document DBs, can be easier to work with in this regard.) Finally, be sure your taxonomy muscles are working. You will have to update and enhance it and reapply it to account for classes and subclasses of entities that don't exist as you run into the need for them.

Precepts underlying to-be design decisions

Now, you must envision what your to-be digital enterprise will look like. As you contemplate this, here are some guiding precepts to keep in mind:

- The key goals of your transformation are:
  - Strategy Enablement—structuring your company to deliver on your strategy and to facilitate your making changes as evolving circumstances create the need to,
  - Efficiency—the ability to make cost-effective use of the resources you consume,

- Being data-driven—make use of the data you acquire or collect to help identify customer needs and preferences, trends, emerging changes in your markets or environment,
- Effective collaboration and process execution—the ability to integrate people and automation to evolve and accelerate your business processes,
- Product development experimentation—creating a Lean Startup mindset and enabling it with the same capabilities as you apply to product management and
- Business agility—the ability to react rapidly to opportunities and threats, which is your ultimate goal.

Your **strategy** is based on numerous assumptions and consideration of multiple prospective scenarios. Based on your articulation of it, you should be aiming to develop and evolve Capabilities and Enablers that will contribute to your ability to create and exercise competitive advantage and pivot rapidly when you must. Being data-driven and achieving business agility both contribute to your being able to recognize opportunities and threats and act on the knowledge.

Efficiency results largely from design. If you implement a componentized design, you can clone and replicate pieces of the company that can begin work on a problem or opportunity quickly and progress rapidly. Employing reusable components—teams, automation, processes, knowledge and assets will waste less time and achieve more predictable results. You will accomplish this by:

- rationalizing and minimizing oversight and governance processes,
- localizing staff and resources to where decision-making is occurring, for instance, in product management teams,
- employing standardized, reusable technology solutions,
- adopting rapid delivery (Agile, DevOps, CI/CD) practices,
- building a team of experts in each of the pillars who will consult to your development teams to guide them toward consistent design, implementation and execution approaches and
- implementing KM that facilitates people identifying resources they can reuse, minimizing redundancy.

Data-Driven companies recognize changes to which they need to react and opportunities that they can exploit more quickly. As we've discussed earlier, Business Intelligence and Analytics (BI/A) increases performance in each of the steps in the OODA Loop—improving and accelerating pattern recognition, facilitating sense-making, creating a framework for selecting from actions that have already been considered and, therefore, hastening decision execution.

Collaboration and Process Execution are improved by both design and automation. Collaboration tools that support work from anywhere, such as Microsoft Teams,[19] Slack[20] or Confluence,[21] BPM tools and KM enablers are the main contributors you will employ for this purpose.

Product Development Experimentation is an offshoot of product management practices and distributed authority. The skills and knowledge necessary to experiment with, develop and exploit new ideas is common to both the people working in product development and product management. Locating an incubation environment in each Division or product group will allow you to apply your market and product knowledge most effectively.

Business Agility ultimately results from all of these things, and we will suggest that you remain cognizant of them as you design and implement of each of the pillars of the digital business anatomy, which is the framework within which your to-be company should be designed.

Strategy is expressed in terms of WHAT you will provide to WHOM. WHAT requires a HOW—how you will structure your company to deliver the value that WHAT represents. HOW also encompasses the Capabilities that are exercised to produce and deliver value and the Enablers that are required to make them work. Looking at your company top-down from WHOM to HOW is where this process starts. We will look at your existing and prospective Product and Service portfolio as the domain within which your to-be EA model will be defined.

So, compile a list of the Products and Services that you currently provide, identify substantial enhancements or changes that you envision for any of them and then add any that you already plan to offer. You should also include internal administrative services as a part of this list.

Then, beginning top-down for each Product or Service, re-imagine the Value Streams, Capabilities and Enablers as they will exist in your target state. So, for example, a Product managed by a business unit's Product Management team currently supported with a Web app built and hosted by the corporate IT team may look largely unchanged in the to-be model but the Capabilities and Enablers behind it may be vastly different. The corporate transactional systems that enable your sales and billing should migrate toward becoming a service provided on your target OI. Your Product Management teams should transform to employ value-stream management practices, DevOps and CI/CD executed by dedicated technologists. Your customer-facing web interfaces should be transitioned to be supported by DevOps and SRE Ops teams. You should be engaging in experimentation and employing BI and AI to identify opportunities for making your products more competitive.

19 https://teamsdemo.office.com
20 https://slack.com/
21 https://www.atlassian.com/software/confluence

Do you have some of this stuff in place? Great! But . . . how many different versions of these Enablers do you have across your Enterprise? In the many years that I have been involved in IT, I have yet to see any large enterprise that does not have thousands of application systems and redundancies, including even accounting and ERP systems costing $Millions in licensing and annual operating costs.

Ultimately, you need to look at the common elements—Capabilities and Enablers—that are applied across your Product and Service portfolio and recast them as they should appear in your target EA. Your starting point for that will be the existing Products or Services, which will be all over the place with respect to the type of Value-driven management approach supported by the technologies and processes that you're targeting. There are several teams employing DevOps, with different tooling and varying processes. There may be others that are barely operating a web presence, much less web app-enabled services. So, while you would like to adopt a standardized set of practices, processes, tooling and organizational structures, you have multiple existing versions of them and you will need to decide whether to standardize on just one, or a couple or jettison them all and start anew.

The hairball you create from this will grow throughout your planning process. Digital Transformation is a complicated business.

The to-be model framework

The framework to use for describing to-be are the pillars of the digital enterprise identified in the chapter *The anatomy of a digital business*:

- Operational Infrastructure
- API Services
- Digital Products and Services Factory
- Business Intelligence and Analytics
- Partner Development Platform
- Distributed Governance Model

Each of these provides targeted capabilities from a business and operational standpoint. What you will do is map your current EA entities, Product by Product, top down, onto the framework to enable you to identify gaps between what you have and what you will need to reach an 'idealized' state. Grouping related Capabilities across your Product portfolio will allow you to assess the state of each and identify opportunities to re-envision organization structures, consolidate tooling and standardize processes as well as cases in which it may be best to just allow things to continue as they currently are for some time.

For instance, not every product management team will look exactly the same and use the same tooling. The intent is for each team to employ a common philosophy and approach and to reuse tooling and internal services to the degree possible. Many of your administrative or transactional systems are probably not cloud-ready or architected to be API-compatible. You will need to figure out how to accommodate them as you migrate toward the OI that you would like to have. Your nascent data science Capabilities may not have the staffing or capacity to provide services everywhere that could benefit from them. You will have to identify where the most favorable cost-benefit tradeoffs are and prioritize building out solutions to enable them.

Your goal in establishing the To-Be EA Model is to identify where you must evolve your existing Capabilities and Enablers to move toward becoming the *Company You Need to Be*. Subsequently, you will analyze the set of transformation requirements to create a program that you can execute.

You will evaluate and apply your EA elements against the framework elements as follows:

Operational Infrastructure (OI)

- Cloud-based (almost certainly), cloud-native architectures
- Standardized, shared technology, architecture, networks, services
- Integration via API gateway
- API-compatible services

Your operations group probably has something of a schizophrenic role within your company. It is tasked with overseeing your infrastructure—your servers, networks, aspects of data security, your major administrative applications, such as your ERP and accounting systems, SaaS services—and at the same time, the operation of your custom-built applications.

Migration to a cloud-based infrastructure has numerous benefits and some challenges. Cloud-based infrastructures provide elasticity, service redundancy, ease of reconfiguration and easy access to any number of vendor-supplied services. Employing them, however, requires knowledge, experience and constant vigilance on costs. All in all, cloud infrastructure is something you will need.

Almost any cloud-based third-party service that you employ will be API-compatible and you will need any of the systems that you migrate to the cloud to be API-compatible, as well. This involves architecting for statelessness,[22] among other things, and might necessitate that some of your existing systems be revised.

It is not mandatory that you re-architect all of the systems before you migrate them. '*Lift and Shift*' is a strategy in which you simply move an application and all its associated data from your data center to a cloud provider's. It's described in this blog post.[23] You can then access it in the same

22 https://searchapparchitecture.techtarget.com/tip/The-key-differences-between-stateless-and-stateful-microservices

23 https://blog.turbonomic.com/lift-shift-vs-optimized-cloud-migration-strategy

way that you have been but, in the long run, this will create an operational burden that you should eliminate if and when you can.

The hand-off between your developers and your operations group to prepare them to operate and support custom-built applications is almost always fraught. Developers want to offload responsibility for a system so that they can move on to the next development project. Operations strives mightily to obtain the maximum documentation and handoff orientation for any system they will be on the line to support. In the to-be state of your digital business, you will remove much of the burden of managing custom-built applications (those that are specific to selected Products or Services, anyway) by allocating much of this responsibility to the product teams that built them as part of Site Reliability Engineering.

API services (API)

- Managed cohesively
- Coordinated with OI evolution and new feature and function releases

As we discussed earlier, APIs provide tremendous flexibility for the management of your software base. Cloud-native architectures incorporate many different sizes and scopes of software, from microservices[24] (see this article describing examples of very large companies that rely on this architectural style) and containers (here's a good overview from cio.com[25]) to entire application systems that you 'lifted and shifted,' or migrated onto dedicated servers.

This Red Hat article,[26] to which I referred earlier, is an excellent overview. Your API infrastructure will:

- Enable software delivery and deployment processes and allow you to control transition between the versions of the software and services you present to various parties both inside and outside your company. This will facilitate your DevOps processes and your market-facing testing.
- Enable you to monetize services that you want to sell,
- Facilitate security management,
- Be an important element of the Partner Development Platform (PDP).

API services will invariably become an important component of your to-be architecture, so it makes sense to prioritize their implementation.

24 https://blog.dreamfactory.com/microservices-examples/
25 https://www.cio.com/article/2924995/what-are-containers-and-why-do-you-need-them.html
26 https://www.redhat.com/en/topics/api/what-is-api-management

Digital Products and Services Factory (DPSF)

- Value-driven Product Management approach with integrated product management and technical team
- DevOps development paradigm, highly automated testing capabilities
- Site Reliability Engineering (SRE) operational support, including data repositories as necessary
- Business Analytics capabilities

The DPSF incorporates philosophical, organizational, technological, process and governance changes and is a crucial element of the rationale for your digital transformation. Migrating your product management function to work consistently with the DPSF as we've described is what will enable you to define, implement, deliver, operate, support and evolve digital products and services rapidly.

Business Intelligence and Analytics (BI/A)

- BI/A will probably be hosted across your OI and DPSF with most data engineering done on the OI and models deployed out to DSPF as needed
- It will reside behind your API gateway to provide services in a consistent manner
- Real-time AI delivered as a service through the API gateway

Your BI/A capabilities will become an indispensable element of your digital business, especially to your product managers. If you are employing AI or ML now, it's possible that you will not change how you're it doing so much but you may well find that it will become much more heavily used. As you expand the portfolio of digital Products and Services, you will begin to accumulate much more data and might move toward providing real-time services, such as providing product recommendations to customers while they're in purchasing cycles on your web sites or building apps fed by IoT-based services.

There are essentially two forms in which you will apply AI. These are differentiated by whether the circumstances in which they will be employed are static and discrete or dynamic and continuous. This article[27] provides a brief overview of these and other environments in which AI might be applied. In some cases, you will want to deploy a decision model whose parameters are determined by an offline estimation process. In other cases, you will want to determine the next action your application should take in the course of an interaction that is in process. The former of these two might be hosted on your OI, with only the model exposed to be called upon by your

[27] https://www.geeksforgeeks.org/types-of-environments-in-ai/

customer-facing applications. In this case, the data engineering and model estimation would take place 'behind the scenes,' and the model itself is all that your applications would see. The latter might be hosted on the operational side of your DPSF and take the form of a service that your application would call when a decision based on current-state information was required, such as adjusting the path of a process being executed in real time.

Given this, you should anticipate how your BI/A and data engineering requirements will grow over time and architect to accommodate them.

Partner Development Platform (PDP)

- Delivered as a value-added service integrated via APIs
- Dedicated product management/technology teams to develop and support partner services

The PDP is the interface through which you will provide collaborative services with external partners. This will be the connecting point for them to offer products and services to your customers or for you to deliver value-added products and services to theirs. All such products and services will be accommodated through secure APIs in both directions.

Distributed governance model

- Investment autonomy for executives with P&L responsibility for one or more Products or Services
- Product evolution autonomy for product management teams

The governance model required for a digital enterprise departs from the traditional command-and-control model that is common in many companies. In the traditional model, initiatives are proposed, reviewed by a level of management dictated by the size of the requested investment and then approved, or not. Such reviews may take place periodically, commonly during the annual budgeting cycle, and from that point approved initiatives often take on a life of their own in which they proceed on the planned path, even after it has become clear that the goals on which on which they were predicated are unattainable or no longer desirable. 'Use it or lose it' thinking often causes waste on projects that stop making sense even before they are completed.

In the distributed model, executives and product managers are empowered to make investment decisions, within limits, about the products for which they are responsible. This allows them to conduct limited duration experiments in marketing approaches or products, product features or functions to evolve their products to be more competitive. In the section ***A company as a portfolio of businesses***, we discussed the business development portfolio—a group of experimental and developmental business ideas that are assigned to small teams and given limited resources and a short leash to see whether they can be turned into viable businesses. Distributed governance and the product management disciplines and approaches are applied to these nascent businesses, as well.

Define to-be governance and management processes

Given the documentation of your management and governance practices that should have been created during your discovery process, you will now map them to what they will need to look like in your to-be state. You can apply the ***input, process, output*** framework to do that. Then you will perform a gap analysis on your management and governance processes in conjunction with everything else that you will be evaluating to identify required initiatives to incorporate into your transformation portfolio.

At this point in the transformation process, however, you have some additional considerations—governing the transformation itself and managing interim governance states that may persist for some time as the program is executed.

We have identified that Product Management autonomy that enables rapid business model evolution is a major goal of your digital transformation. It brings with it substantial changes and new requirements for governance, for instance:

- What investment limits should be enforced for divisions and PMs?
- What, if any, division or product management processes should be mandated?
- How should corporate or executive management monitor division and Products or Services performance and risks?
- What shared services should the company provide to divisions and what should they be allowed to acquire and use at their own discretion?
- Should the corporation charge back divisions for shared services and on what basis?
- How should compliance be monitored?

So, in addition to transforming your as-is management and governance processes, you should identify whether you need additional or entirely new ones. One thing that may be new to your company, for example, is the degree to which you must reflect changes to your business in your EA model and have those changes trigger a risk management assessment, among other things. I recommend that you ensure that any event that creates a change that should be reflected in the EA model trigger a process that gives the EA and KM teams a chance to review it and communicate it to relevant parties, such as governance groups throughout the company. Further, I recommend that this be anchored to the Change Management team, which we will discuss later.

All changes you plan to execute in your program should be incorporated into the gap analysis you will perform in the following step and incorporated into your transformation portfolio.

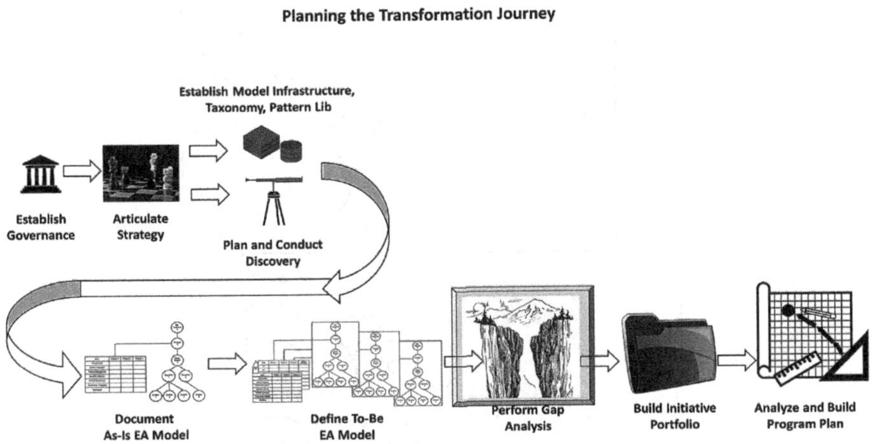

Map as-is to to-be and conduct gap analysis

The to-be EA model is structured in the same way as the as-is model, with a few differences. Instead of mapping onto generic business capabilities, you will now map onto the ones described as digital business elements. Instead of your existing infrastructure, for example, you will now map onto your target OI.

The diagram, below, is similar to the as-is map created in the previous section. It portrays the conceptual process of mapping existing, enhanced, modified and new Products, Services, Value Streams, Capabilities and Enablers onto the digital business framework.

New or modified EA entities represent candidates for your initial transformation initiative portfolio. It should be, pretty much, as simple as that but, as has been credited to several people, including Albert Einstein, Richard Feynman and Yogi Berra:

> In theory, theory and practice are the same. In practice, they are not.[28]

During this process you will undoubtedly identify elements, like Enablers, that perform what appear to be either the same or analogous functions. It is extremely important that you are exploring nuances that differentiate them and employing your taxonomy to ensure that everything you record is

[28] https://quoteinvestigator.com/2018/04/14/theory/

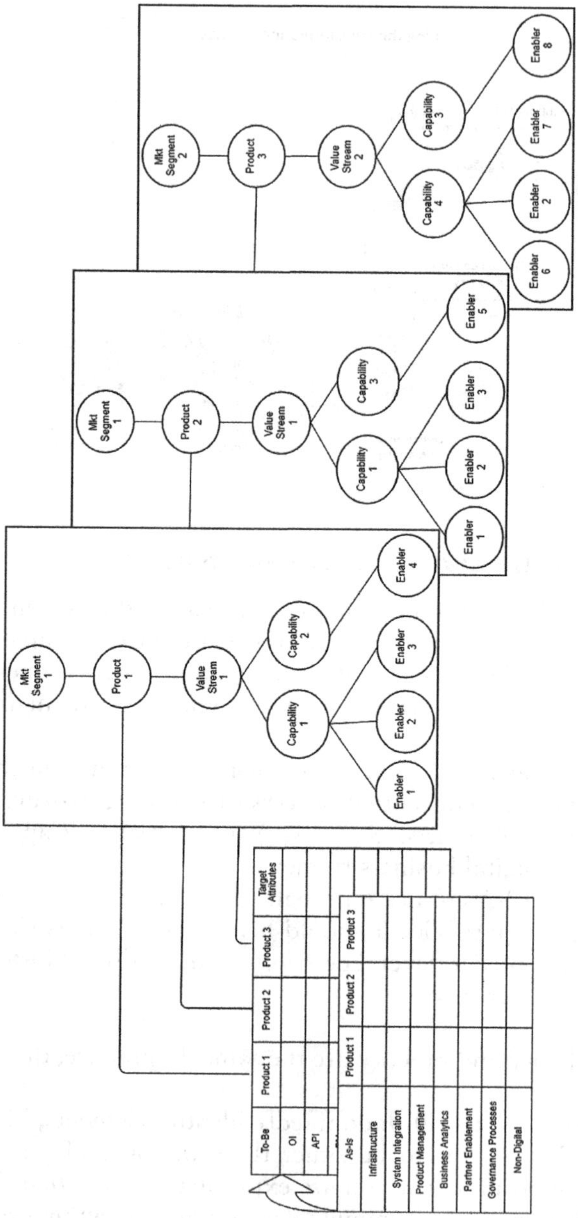

Figure 5.4 To-be mapping approach.

classified and tagged appropriately. That way, you will know whether two systems that appear to be doing the same thing in two different places are functionally equivalent, or not.

At this point, your to-be EA data should be two-dimensional. Horizontally, you will have an inventory of all your Products and Services, perhaps including all of the current and modified versions of them, and all of your prospective Products and Services. Vertically, you will have each of the major pillars of your digital business. In each cell of the model, you will have identified the Value Streams, Capabilities and Enablers that constitute the current state of your company's EA with respect to the pillar.

Let's say you look across all your product hierarchies and note that there is a plethora of different product management approaches, practices, organization designs, technology and so on. You may look at them all and want to standardize but that may not be the best path forward for everyone. Your product management teams are coming to the process with differing levels of knowledge and experience and varying levels of readiness and willingness to change. You can't simply embark on learning and doing simultaneously, or you are likely to create a sub-optimal architecture for your company that might have been avoided if you had done some experimentation, made more-informed design decisions and planned more intelligently. Knowledge gaps must be identified so that addressing them can be included in your program plan.

The information that you will provide as input to the next step in the process is now in a very raw state and hardly ready for program design and portfolio management. This is OK, as long as the inventory that comes out of this step is as comprehensive as it can be.

AERM's EA-driven approach to managing the risks of transformation

Being in transition complicates the challenge of managing business risks substantially. Existing risks may be obviated because they are attached to elements of the business that are being retired while new risks are coming online. In addition, you will need to pay attention to risks associated with the program you are executing, many of which may be transient.

AERM is focused on identifying and understanding ***causes*** or ***sources*** of risk, not just identifying and quantifying potentially negative outcomes to be avoided. This works well on operations over which your company has control. You can restructure processes that aren't working properly, for instance, but you don't have the latitude to do that in a supplier's company. Understanding the underlying causes of why the supplier might fail to deliver, as in *Case study 1*, can be useful information but it will only give you insight as to what you might expect and prompt you to prepare to treat symptoms when you can't prevent or cure the disease.

Strategic goals are generally something over which your company doesn't have direct control. Your strategy may dictate that you grow your market share in one of your divisions but all you can do is put your products out there and hope that they sell. Obviously, you will do everything you can to see that they do well, but in the end, it is the market that will determine whether you achieve your goals, or not.

Several pillars of the digital business are ultimately intended to address strategic issues:

- BI/A should help you to make better decisions, more quickly.
- Value-driven, integrated product management capabilities will allow you to evolve your products incrementally and more rapidly.
- Distributed governance should provide product managers the freedom to experiment without the drag and overhead of unnecessary administrative oversight.

So, you're going through the transformation to remake your approach to managing your business, you need to put the pillars in place to do that and risks will accrue where you don't have them. If we apply the EA-driven lens in this context, we can identify required to-be Capabilities and Enablers but trying to tie risks associated with them with corporate-level business results will be tricky, at best.

Mainly, what you can control is the program intended to implement them, which very much resembles traditional project risk management. However, traditional project risk management tends to focus more on the 'triple constraint'[29] of scope, time and cost. By traditional standards, projects are considered 'successful' if they deliver the original specified product, on time and within budget. That will not be adequate for digital transformation initiatives. Your goal for them is to enable change, not just get them implemented.

How, then, should you apply AERM-thinking to designing your digital transformation program? You should look at the to-be EA entities and interdependencies associated with each of the pillars and use that to inform your staging. When you do this, you can identify Capabilities and Enablers that are critical to the pillar and assess anything that might impede their implementation. An Enabler that is the foundation of a hierarchy that depends on it deserves scrutiny and risk mitigation efforts. You can't build a CI/CD capability without the right tooling and even if you do put a software pipeline in place you won't be able to iterate rapidly unless you have a team that can execute agile development. Not getting foundational elements like this right is a major risk to the goals you have for your transformation.

[29] https://en.wikipedia.org/wiki/Project_management_triangle

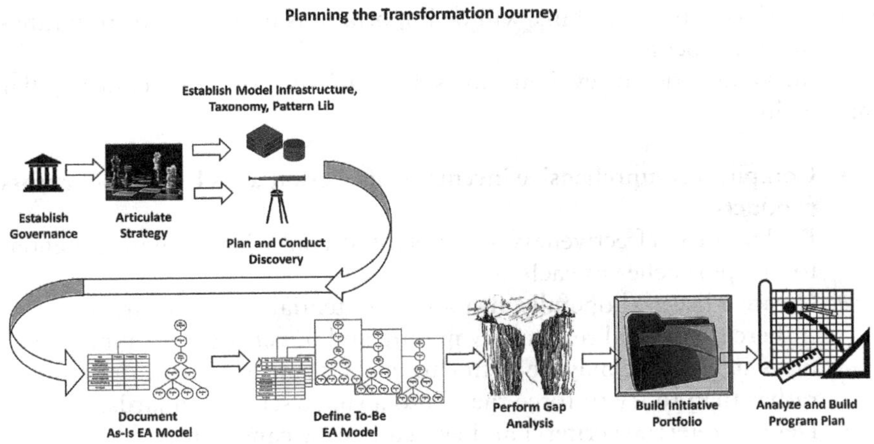

Distill transformation initiatives and populate portfolio

At this point, you will know, for example, that you have multiple approaches to product management, supported by different organization structures, application systems and processes. Similarly, you might have multiple BI/A operations, some embedded in product groups and some supported by a corporate team. You need to take a systematic approach to identify initiatives that will allow you to migrate all of these disparate entities to be consistent with your target digital enterprise model.

Here's the approach I recommend:

First, establish tactical and strategic goals for your business:

- Which existing Products or Services are most important?
- Which prospective ones are?
- What are your most compelling opportunities and threats? What do you have to do to prepare to deal with them?
- What strengths can you build on and what weaknesses do you need to address? Think about Capabilities and Enablers, here.

Doing this will position you to establish a prioritized list of what's most important. Capabilities and Enablers associated with anchor Products or Services might not be ones that you want to transition first. You might want to implement and mature new forms of them on less critical Products and Services, which will hopefully minimize the collateral damage of stumbles and missteps as you get up to speed and make the transition of your more important Products more straightforward. Alternatively, if existing Capabilities and Enablers for anchor Products and Services end up being consistent with your selected to-be architecture, you might weigh this as part of your evaluation criteria. Regardless, it is critical that you establish a framework of what you think will be important as input to your program's construction process.

Then, systematically evaluate as-is for each Product or Service /pillar intersection:

- **Compile a comprehensive inventory of relevant as-is EA entities across products.**
  Evaluate the effectiveness and potential conformance with potential to-be approaches of each.
- Create a list of (hopefully, just a few) potential to-be scenarios.
  If there are several reasonably mature and possibly conforming operations in place, it may be better to allow them to remain operational rather than to try to force them into a single set of standards.
- Define preference criteria and evaluate to-be candidates.
  Consider which of them will produce the best performance, might be easier to transition to, might be least costly, might require less training, might be easier to staff.
- Select 1 to 3 to-be candidates.
  Based on your analysis, select one or more target candidates as your target architecture.
- Develop a high-level transition plan for each existing entity to one of the to-be candidates.
  How will you execute the transition? What dependencies are there? What interdependencies between initiatives do you need to plan for? How long will the initiatives take and how much will they cost? How do they relate to strategic and product development goals?
- Evaluate dependencies and risks, develop risk management plan for transitions.
  Now that you have a list of 'projects,' identify dependencies and risks for which your program plan must account.
- Sequence transitions.
  Based on your prioritization and analysis of dependencies and risks, sequence and schedule your program. Undoubtedly, it will consist of many parallel work streams, with dependencies that will need to be managed closely.
- Incorporate in Program Portfolio.
  Your individual initiatives, or programs consisting of related sets of them, should now be populated in whatever you are using for Project Portfolio Management (PPM) so that you can take control of your transformation process.

Internal corporate and administrative services should be treated just the same as Products and Services you sell to external customers. You should create EA models that identify and document Capabilities and Enablers that support them and consider how to migrate them into the digital company architecture you are building. Many of these functions embody business processes that can be enhanced by digital technology and can be compelling candidates for transformation.

Other than that, the customers for your corporate or administrative functions are internal, you should follow almost the same process as described, above, to identify potential transformation initiatives, evaluate them and add them to your PPM repository.

For each internal, corporate or administration service or function:

- Identify services it provides and to whom
- Identify services and Enablers it uses
- Identify preference criteria
- Identify to-be candidate re-implementation alternatives
- Select 1 to 3 preferred candidates
- Identify dependencies and risks, develop risk management plan for transition
- Sequence transition steps
- Incorporate in Program Portfolio

Finally, you cannot develop a program plan for your transformation without identifying and assessing required competencies. You will need to identify major knowledge or competency gaps and plan to address them in at least these areas:

- Cloud migration and management
- Cloud-native application architecture
- API design and management
- Value-driven Product Management
- Web app and UX design
- Agile SDLC
- DevOps
- Automated testing
- CI/CD
- System Reliability Engineering, Operations
- Business Process Management—process mining, BPA, RPA, DPA
- Product development, Lean Startup approach, incubator operation and management
- BI, AI, ML, data science, data engineering ops
- Governance re-design for distributed management

Initiatives to re-skill existing staff or to bring in new staff with required skills and knowledge must also be added to your PPM repository.

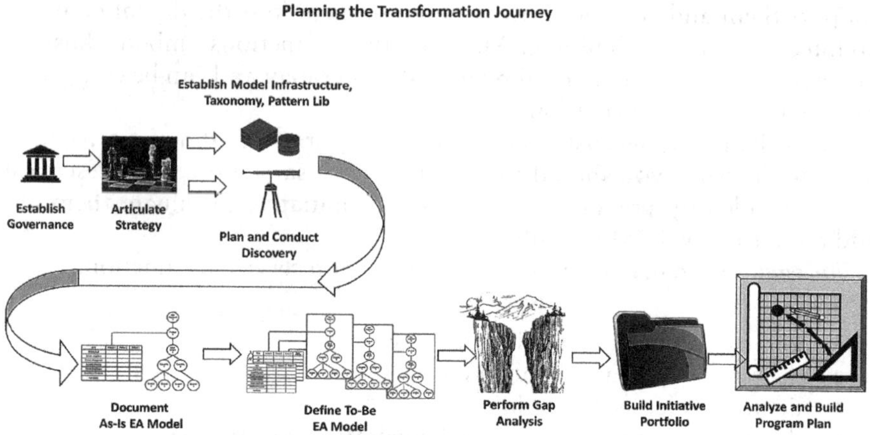

Analyze the portfolio and develop your transformation program

Now it's time to begin to address the hairball we discussed earlier. You simply can't do everything first, regardless of how many resources and how much money your company is willing to dedicate to a massive, parallel execution. You can do a lot in parallel but dependencies between initiatives to build out the to-be architecture of the pillars will require that you must sequence a lot of your work. And, getting to the to-be state that you defined at the outset will take long enough that when you get there, what's desirable then will not look so much like what you started with.

Establish concrete business goals

First, establish concrete business goals and progress metrics you will use to assess how you are doing with your transformation. You will use metrics associated with these to assess and report on your progress. This article from McKinsey[30] addresses how CEOs should assess their transformation progress. While the article is couched in something of a retrospective context, it's worth considering. If you internalize how you are going to determine whether you are succeeding, it will inform how you approach your transformation.

Among other goals, you might consider:

- Decreasing time to deliver new or revised Products or Services
- Introducing a targeted number of new Products or Services

[30] https://www.mckinsey.com/business-functions/mckinsey-digital/our-insights/how-do-you-measure-success-in-digital-five-metrics-for-ceos

- Reducing execution time and staffing requirements for various processes
- Implementing a business incubator in each division and populating it with a targeted number of experimental businesses
- Increasing your company's customer retention
- Improving your company's image and brand equity, evidenced by, say, a Net Promoter Score[31]
- Improving customers' user experience and service
- Developing a targeted number of digital business partnerships

You should articulate and document your goals, which will inform how you monitor the progress of your digital transformation program.

Establish priorities to sequence your transformation

Then, establish priorities for your transformation. One very important subject that is mentioned in many articles on transformation priorities and progress is that of *width vs. depth*—should you try to establish the enterprise pillars and foundations of your digital company and then build on them or should you target specific businesses or products and focus on creating digital value from them? There's a good case to be made for depth:

- It will allow you to see how all the elements of your digital technology stack integrate. For example, you might learn something about how your chosen application delivery environment could be best served by specific aspects of your API design, which will allow you to apply it going forward.
- It will give you the best chance to validate your digital approaches early so you can course correct when it will be least disruptive to your transformation.
- It will give you early returns on your investments.
- It will help to focus your program on business goals more than on technical ones.

You need to keep in mind that the goals of digital transformation are not technical. No one cares if you become expert at cloud migration or CI/CD application delivery or ML. Your customers care if you can deliver innovative products and services rapidly and at good prices. Your employees care if your digital business processes and collaboration approaches and tools eliminate unnecessary overhead that takes time from their doing what they are there to do.

Earlier, I mentioned Jeanne Ross and her book, *Designed for Digital*. In it, she observed that you cannot work toward all of the pillars at the same

31 https://en.wikipedia.org/wiki/Net_Promoter

time, and she presented examples of companies making progress, each working in a different order. However, she observed that you will need to make some progress on each of them, even the ones that you have deprioritized, to address dependencies among the pillars. Your company's strategic priorities, existing skills and expertise and readiness and willingness to change, among many other considerations, must inform how you stage your plan.

I don't have a recipe that you can follow to organize your digital transformation effort. What I do have is some observations and recommendations that you may find helpful:

- Let your strategy dictate your priorities. It will do you no good to transform your organization, processes and technology if you do not survive to exploit them.
- It's unlikely that it will be a straight path from as-is to to-be. Be open to planning for intermediate states in the process of transition for each of your pillars.
- Transformation and steady-state operations require different skill levels. You will need expert advice to assist you in making architecture, tooling and process design decisions early in your transformation and you may not have the right people on board for these at the outset. You should plan to bring in seasoned experts to help you define and execute your transformation. You should also plan to upgrade your skill base to be ready to adapt to and operate your transformed company while you are in transit.
- Most transformations that fail, whether digital or not, fail because of people issues. Get a handle on the organizational issues that will accompany your transformation and develop a strategy and plan to deal with them. Bring in a specialist consultancy to assist you with this.
- KM and Taxonomy are important to creating and maintaining the value of the information you have collected about your organization, on which you will base its target design, and which will anchor AERM. Start this practice as early as you can.
- The cloud will be the foundation for almost all your technological enablement. It's best to learn how to manage cloud migration and operations early in your process.
- Data is and will be one of your most important assets. In all likelihood, you will begin to collect and accumulate it at a faster and faster rate. You will need to develop a Data Architecture practice (if you don't already have one) and data management skills for larger and larger volumes of data. This practice and these skills must incorporate cloud technology because that is the only place that you will find the elasticity to accommodate what will be your growing need for storage and processing horsepower.

- Migrating your existing infrastructure and application base is going to be a large, time-consuming, expensive and risk-laden task. There are many benefits to be gained from transforming to your target OI, but you can employ APIs to make a lot of what you have look and work like what you are planning to transform to. We discussed how APIs abstract how and where things are built from whatever is using them and this is an excellent application of the technology to give yourself time and flexibility.
- BI/A, AI, ML and other advanced disciplines can operate largely asynchronously, and therefore independently, from most of the transactional systems that need to change as you transform for some time. (That is, while they will rely on data produced by transactions, they will not integrate directly or interoperate with the source systems.) This will give you some leeway to allow you to continue with whatever you are already doing for a while; however, you will probably need to ramp your capabilities up not long into your transformation. It's quite possible that if you have been doing BI, you've been doing it in the cloud. If not, this is one thing that might make sense to migrate early. Unless you have been using AI extensively, you probably do not have the data scientists and engineers you will need to do this, so building these capabilities is something for which you should plan.
- If your current business model does not focus on operational partnerships, the PDP can probably wait for a while. Generally speaking, the skills, expertise, technology and processes needed to implement this are much the same as those you will employ for building out for your product management and API management capabilities. If you can wait, you will be better prepared to do this than you are likely to be now, and it will not be competing for your resources with other initiatives early on.
- Your governance practices apply mainly to business processes. Your business processes probably won't change that much early in your transformation, but change will accelerate as you progress. It makes sense to rethink your governance practices early and implement new ones or revised versions in sync with new business processes as you implement them.
- Give serious thought to how you can experiment on a small scale before implementing large changes. For instance, you can pilot DevOps on small projects before moving to BizDevOps. You can try reformulating your Product Management practices on a limited basis before moving all your product management teams over. You can move a subset of your in-house-based application systems operations to the cloud and stabilize your operational processes before migrating your biggest, most important and widely used applications.

The following chapter contains a case study of the HiCTools Company, an enterprise going through the process described in this one.

CHAPTER SUMMARY

Key concepts addressed in this chapter include:

- How to prepare for a Digital Transformation and adoption of AERM.
- How *change* differs from *transformation*.
- The three layers of risk in an enterprise and how to approach managing risk in the context of transformation.
- The lifecycle of the transformation:
    - Establish leadership and governance.
    - Establish scope and create a plan to transform.
    - Establish your metadata model infrastructure
    - Conduct Discovery and populate your as-is EA and BA models
    - Compile to-be EA and BA models
    - Conduct a Gap Analysis to identify the initiatives required to effectuate your transformation.
    - Articulate your transformation goals, your priorities and your risk preferences to inform the transformation strategies that will guide your planning process.
    - Analyze the portfolio of initiatives and create a master program plan for your transformation.

CASE STUDY 2 THE HICTOOLS COMPANY TRANSFORMATION

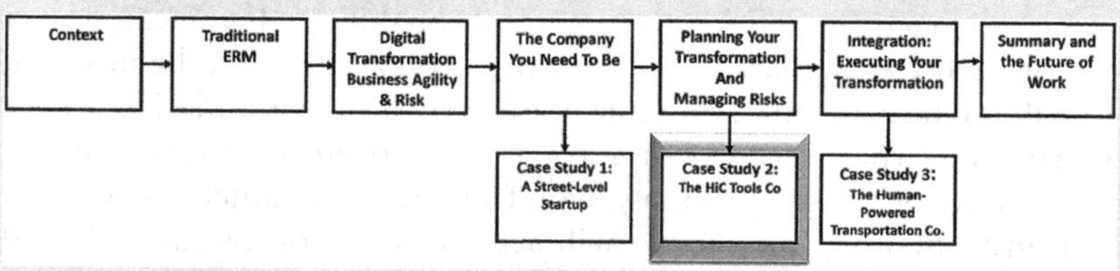

This case study will present an abbreviated example of developing a transformation portfolio, performing a gap analysis and deriving a program plan from it. It will employ the techniques discussed in the preceding chapters.

COMPANY OVERVIEW

HiCTools manufactures, sells and services a variety of tools (originally focused on those built out of high-carbon steel, thus the company's name) and small appliances to Industrial, Commercial and Consumer users. It has some products that are specific to each of these lines of business (Divisions) and others that appear in somewhat different forms across two or all three of them. HiCTools started as an industrial tool supplier and expanded into the commercial and consumer markets to grow the company.

Each of these Divisions are operated semi-autonomously, share some facilities, processes and systems but also have independent ones, as well. HiC would like to standardize and eliminate redundancy in the long run but realizes that it may not be feasible in the near term. It would like to employ BPM tools and collaboration technology to streamline its operations and make itself more agile. It also intends to migrate a lot of its operations onto a public or hybrid cloud, which it can manage centrally.

While it has some web-based services and sites, it has decided that it will need to transform itself into a digital enterprise to remain competitive. It will follow the process defined in this book to guide its transformation. To reiterate from the *Scope and plan the transformation journey* section, the subset addressed in this case study includes:

- Establish who's governing the transformation and who will assume the to-be operational responsibilities
- Compile an as-is EA/BA model
- Create a to-be EA/BA model
- Perform gap analysis and generate a transformation initiative portfolio
- Analyze the portfolio to rationalize it, prioritize and schedule individual initiatives and identify and manage risks

Needless to say, it will not be possible to chase down every nuance and detail in this case but we will cover enough breadth to convey a reasonably full spectrum of the approach, issues and concerns that HiC will need to address in order to make well thought-out decisions about its path forward.

HICTOOLS' STRATEGIC TRANSFORMATION GOALS

Before it embarks on a transformation, HiC must articulate and prioritize what it is trying to achieve by transforming. Within the markets in which it competes, HiC is:

- A solid mid- to upper-tier vendor among industrial tools companies. It has several predominant products and is strongly profitable. The division achieves more than 20% EBITDA.[32]
- A middle-of-the-pack competitor among commercial tool vendors. It competes with larger companies that have more name recognition and larger distribution networks, like DeWalt, Black & Decker and Makita. HiCTools has an EBITDA of 12% in this division.
- An emerging competitor in the consumer tools and small appliance market. The consumer division has an EBITDA of less than 7%.

32 https://en.wikipedia.org/wiki/Earnings_before_interest,_taxes,_depreciation_and_amortization

HiC has goals specific to each of the divisions and for the company, as a whole:

- Add digital services to the products in the Industrial Division to expand its value proposition to customers and deepen its relationship with them.
- Similarly, add digital services to products in the Commercial Division.
- Explore the possibility of creating a tool rental service with or without partnering with commercial/retail outlets, such as home centers.
- Increase its presence, digital offerings and market share in the Consumer Division.
- Evaluate potential acquisition and divestiture opportunities that will allow HiC to reshape the company if it makes sense to.
- Establish a strategy review and valuation process to be applied regularly to each division to determine whether a change in strategy or an acquisition or divestiture is appropriate.
- Expand offerings by partnering across divisions.
- Increase business agility; accelerate responses to opportunities and threats.
- Adopt value-stream product management approach, evolving the product management organizations and practices in each of the divisions.
- Rationalize the corporate infrastructure, migrating to a cloud-based model and adopting APIs as a standard integration strategy.
- Create an incubation program for new products for each of the divisions. Define and reuse a standardized business process for developmental portfolio creation and management.
- Identify and eliminate aging and redundant application systems.
- Adopt standard application development technologies and practices to accelerate delivery, including Agile techniques and DevOps and CI/CD practices, targeting cloud-native architectures.
- Transform governance processes from periodic to continuous. Integrate them more seamlessly and constructively into operational business processes.
- Increase application of BI/A where it is appropriate. Staff and provision the resources required to realize value from it.
- Create improved visibility into division, corporate and project/initiative performance for board and executive management.
- Identify opportunities to apply BPM automation to improve business process performance and make it easier to modify them.
- Implement solution(s) to improve collaboration and make it easier to integrate workers to working remotely.

This is clearly a pretty expansive list, but it is reasonably representative for an average multi-line business of any size. The approach of casting the business' existing EA against the framework of the digital business will provide a useful basis for gap analysis and transformation planning.

TRANSFORMATION RISK CONSIDERATIONS

HiC operates in competitive markets in which the rate of change and the entry of new competitors is accelerating. Risks that it must mitigate while transforming include:

Disruption

One thing HiC does not have is a surfeit of resources. It must be concerned about dropping the ball on BAU while undergoing transformation.

The cost of failure is high

Transformation is a substantial investment, one that HiC cannot afford to get wrong. Beside the fruitless investment that a failed transformation would produce, the failure would also leave the company in a diminished competitive position.

HiC doesn't know what it doesn't know

Because so much of what Digital Transformation requires is new to the company, HiC must find a way to make well-informed decisions about the process. It will undoubtedly need to bring in outside experts, but it will also need to develop in-house expertise along the way. If it fails to do this, HiC runs the risks of poor program design, sub-par execution or failing to properly prepare itself to operate the company that the transformation will create.

Digital transformation requires substantial organizational change

The majority of failed transformations of any sort are thought to tie back to people issues. HiC has never executed a transformation of the scope of this one and must mitigate the risk of upending its organization and impairing its ability to do what it does.

Alignment of expectations

A lot of what will be done in the course of the transformation will not lend itself to simple and rapid progress monitoring. Integrating new organization, process and technology architectures is complicated and takes time and understanding if everything is working as expected may not be possible before most of the work is substantially completed. This creates risks and HiC's transformation management team must develop intuition about how elements of the architecture work together and maintain close contact with the execution teams to keep on top of progress.

AS-IS MODEL

Step one in the transformation planning process is to establish an as-is EA model. We will use the framework of the elements of a digital business to categorize HiC's EA.

Organization and governance

HiC is a pretty typical industrial products company. It is partitioned into three lines of business (divisions)—Industrial, Commercial and Consumer—each headed by an Executive VP who reports to the COO. Product Management in each of the divisions reports to an EVP, who has P&L responsibility for it.

HiC employs periodic governance models—annual budgeting and project funding, quarterly and annual risk management and auditing. Corporate and administrative functions, such as IT, HR, Legal, Finance and Accounting, are each headed by a VP reporting to the CEO or COO.

The EVP for each division has investment discretion for projects up to $2.5 million that require less than a year to implement. Beyond that, review by the CEO, COO and Board are required and bringing new investment proposals to them off schedule (i.e., outside of the annual budgeting cycle) is discouraged.

Generally, divisions are expected to rely upon corporate services, such as IT, unless there is an exceptionally good reason for contracting outside the company to implement projects or to purchase services.

The business lines share some Capabilities and Enablers but each of them has some that are specific to it, largely because the manufacturing, storage and handling requirements are different and because the markets for the products have limited overlap. This has resulted in some redundancy in Capabilities that employ different Enablers—operational teams, processes, systems and facilities.

Product management and customer-facing elements

Each division has autonomy in how product management, marketing and sales is performed.

The **Industrial Division** has a single team that performs marketing, sales and product management, which reports to the division EVP. Industrial has a dedicated product design, prototyping and manufacturing team that is responsible for monitoring the marketplace jointly with the marketing team, designing new and enhanced products and developing and testing them to the point at which they are ready to sell.

The marketing and sales group is also responsible for defining and overseeing implementation of the division's web presence, which consists of a subset of the corporate site, and any services provided through it, such as basic customer support. The web site was built and is maintained by corporate IT, in-house.

The **Commercial Division** is organized similarly to the Industrial Division. It also has marketing, sales and customer interface and product design and manufacturing teams that report to the division's EVP.

In addition, Commercial purchases and re-sells certain products from other vendors, some of which are sold under the vendor's brands and some of which are white-labeled. Procurement of third-party products is the responsibility of a team that works with both the product management and the design and manufacturing teams and reports to the Division's EVP.

One of Commercial's larger customers is Consumer, for whom it manufactures many of the tools that it sells.

Commercial operates an independent web site and a set of web apps, built by an outside consultancy and are hosted on a public cloud. Commercial has been experimenting with and developing a variety of membership services, free thus far, to draw in and engage contractors, who are its target customer base. It is hoping to develop a tool rental program for its higher-end tools in partnership with local hardware and building supply stores. If successful, this could provide a short-term boost in sales as partners would need to acquire an inventory, albeit at discounted prices, and a longer-term revenue stream, which would be split between HiC and the partners.

There are links between the corporate and Commercial's sites but there is almost no actual integration between them.

The **Consumer Division** has a larger product management, marketing, sales and customer interface team. It is split into two groups—one for consumer tools and one for small appliances—each of which report to an SVP that reports to the EVP of the division. Consumer does not manufacture any of its own tools or the appliances it sells; however, it does design some of them and works actively with vendors to evolve and refine the products they buy to fit in with the image it is trying to convey. Consumer's largest single supplier is the Commercial Division, which manufactures many of its products under its direction.

Whereas the other divisions have a fairly narrow set of sales channels, Consumer sells through many retailers and multiple sites and channels on the web. It has an affiliate relationship with Amazon, and about 45% of the Division's sales take place there. The Division operates an extensive web presence and provides a number of web apps, all of which are supported on a public cloud and delivered through various app stores at no cost. Its web presence and the apps were all built and are supported and maintained by an independent contractor.

Consumer may have between 30 and 50 new products in development or in trial at any time and adds about 20 to its catalog each year, while retiring a similar number. The catalog currently has 250 to 300 products and about 550 SKUs.[33]

Consumer is always looking for new ideas for marketing and selling its products and constantly surveils the web for sites and properties with whom it might create co-marketing partnerships. It is also continuously building and expanding its AI capabilities to increase its sales and optimize its business results.

33 https://en.wikipedia.org/wiki/Stock_keeping_unit

Operational Infrastructure, API services

HiC's IT group and its existing applications and infrastructure are quite diverse and rapidly aging. It has moved some archiving and backup workloads to the cloud but operates most of the company's transactional and administrative systems on a heterogeneous set of platforms that employ a variety of integration strategies. A small fraction of the applications and infrastructure are API-compatible, and most would not be easy to modify to accommodate APIs. Some of the existing staff have begun training in web technologies but it is not prepared to support applications in a cloud-native environment on a commercial level.

Industrial, which has low-volume, high-value sales, employs rudimentary, custom-built process automation for its order management and invoicing processes. Nonetheless, they are still largely manual. Commercial employs this same automation but also has a BPA solution to assist its back office with routing fulfillment orders and handling invoicing inquiries. Consumer employs a prototype RPA implementation to automate its order processing and makes use of external vendors' SaaS (Software as a Service) offerings provided on the cloud to manage shipping, fulfillment and customer service.

The existing IT team is not particularly capable in cloud-native application architectures and while it employs Agile-like techniques for in-house application projects it does not employ DevOps and CI/CD processes. At this point, HiCTools is not prepared to operate an infrastructure consistent with a digital enterprise.

Business intelligence/analytics

HiCTools does not, for all intents and purposes, have an enterprise-level BI/A program. Consumer has implemented a prototype program and is building models in a few areas, which the company hopes to expand. While HiC has some data engineers, home-grown data management capabilities and a couple of data scientists, it is still seeking direction.

HiC believes that there are opportunities to employ ML to model and understand customer behavior on its websites, identify product features and functions that resonate with prospective customers and improve cross-selling and up-selling, among other things. However, it is lacking a visionary that can identify opportunities for AI and ML and guide the company through defining a program plan to develop and mature its capabilities.

TO-BE MODEL

Given what is known about HiCTools' business, what should its digital enterprise, future-state model look like? We will employ the digital business anatomy framework again to identify the goals for the to-be anatomy.

Subsequently, we can map the existing anatomy elements against the to-be goals and identify where migration, modification, new implementation, reorganization, process re-engineering and other transformations are needed.

Redesign of the organization, responsibility allocation and governance model

Organizational restructuring will undoubtedly be necessary to transform. It will require significant planning, expertise and oversight. HiC's board would be well served to obtain the assistance of consultants that specialize in organization design and development as they plan and execute their transformation.

Some of the organizational changes that may be required are:

- Reformulating the Product Management function to integrate marketing, product design, technology (in a variety of capacities, including Agile product features development, operation of the DevOps pipeline and CI/CD processes and SRE/operations staffing) and business analytics.
- Initiation of product development teams and business incubators.
- Reallocating assignments within the IT organization to distribute parts of it out to divisions and to create specialist teams for cloud operations, API management and to provide advanced solution, technical and data architecture support.
- Establish a BPM center of excellence if one does not already exist.
- Formalizing a KM function if one does not already exist.
- Formalizing the BI/A function if it has not been already.

For HiC to achieve the business agility it's targeting, responsibility for many decisions must be pushed down to the people that are closest to them and responsible for executing on them. The idea is to eliminate the request-response loop between operating teams and executive management that can add latency to a team's ability to act. For those responsible for Products or Services, such authorities may include:

- Prioritizing or reprioritizing product development initiatives, including systems work to develop and refine features and functions by running customer-facing experiments, when necessary,
- Investing in Product or Service additions, enhancements or modifications,
- Making use of chargeable internal services, such as BI/A work,
- Implementing non-standard solution elements, if necessary,
- Expending resources to refactor elements of Products or Services to avoid or eliminate technical debt,

- Vetting and authorizing budget and resources for experimental Product or Services development,
- Engaging in business process re-engineering and application of BPM, BPA or DPA tools, at a localized level and
- Identifying, negotiating and creating deals with prospective business partners.

Similar authority can be granted to those responsible for shared Capabilities and Enablers. For instance, a facility manager who runs a warehouse or factory should have authority to make changes, within reasonable limits, to improve the performance, reliability or costs of the facility.

Governance at any company takes place at a number of levels. At the corporate level, it focuses on managing:

- The interface between the company and the outside world and the markets in which it operates,
- Corporate administrative functions, such as accounting,
- Enterprise shared services, such as human resources and
- Functional elements—divisions or departments, mainly—of the company and their interactions with each other.

At an operational level, it focuses on ensuring that BAU processes are executed as they are designed to be and that they are producing the results and performance that are intended for them. Typically, this takes the form of internal auditing and regular performance reporting.

To the degree that a goal of Digital Transformation is business agility and increased responsiveness, corporate-level governance process will have to evolve to achieve this in the to-be company. It makes little sense, however, to re-envision corporate governance process until the operational ones are defined. After all, how could we design a process to govern something until we know what we are trying to govern. While this is an important part of the to-be model, it will have to wait until the Operating Model and Operational Architecture are defined.

Product management and the digital products and services factory

Clearly, this is a substantial area to explore. Product Management is heavily dependent on the Digital Products and Services Factory, but also on Capabilities associated with physical product development, as well.

The diagrams, below, show each part of a generic pattern for the to-be Product Development process, which is a subset of the EA attributable to Product Management. The Capabilities and Enablers that are currently employed by each of the divisions are not uniform. What HiC needs to do is determine where the differences are so that it can assess what it does and does not need to transform and identify when it will need to transform the pieces that require it.

The Develop Product Value Stream is executed across these Capabilities, in a combination process that may be executed iteratively and in stage-gated fashion, or in series:

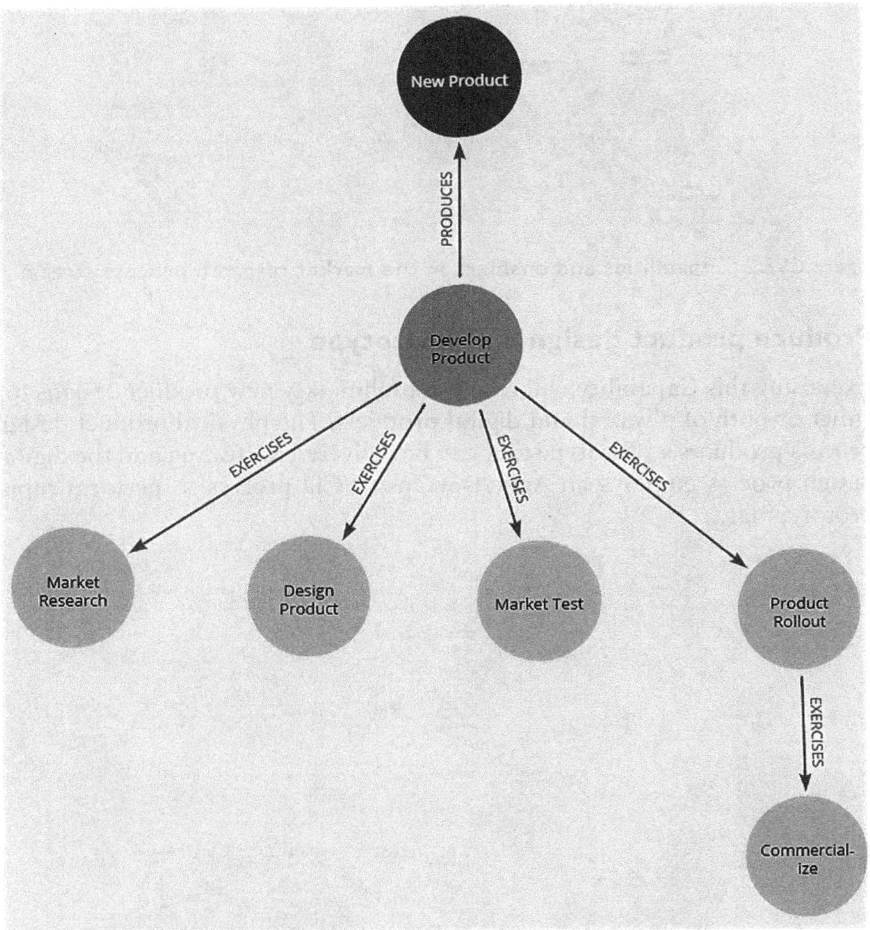

Figure CS2.1 Capabilities in the develop product process stream.

Perform market research

This Capability involves market surveillance by the marketing team with support from the data science and data engineering teams. The information collected and analyzed here will inform the product design process.

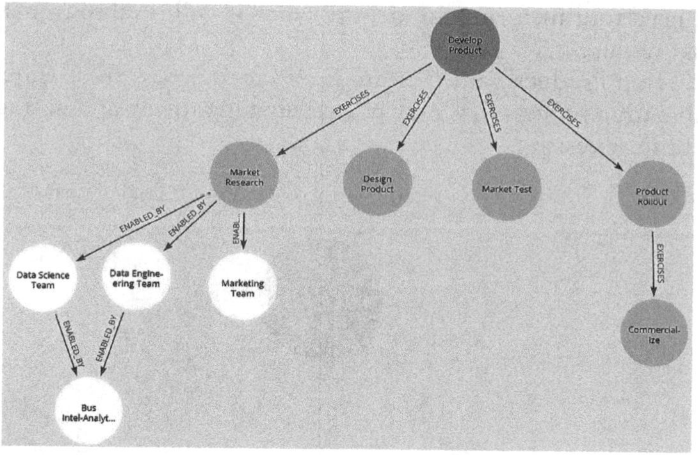

Figure CS2.2 Capabilities and enablers in the market research process stream.

Produce product design and prototype

Exercising this Capability will result in preliminary new product designs for either or both of physical and digital products. The physical product design process produces a prototype that can be delivered for testing and the digital design process employs an Agile/DevOps/CI/CD process to perform rapid prototyping.

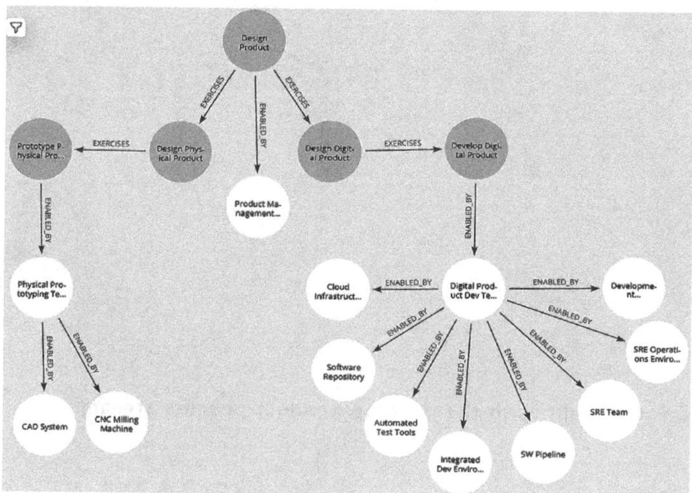

Figure CS2.3 The design product process stream.

Perform market test, exposing product to customers

This Capability encompasses exposing the prototype product(s) to potential customers to obtain feedback from them. This would be likely to initiate an iteration of redesign, prototyping and testing, which is not shown here.

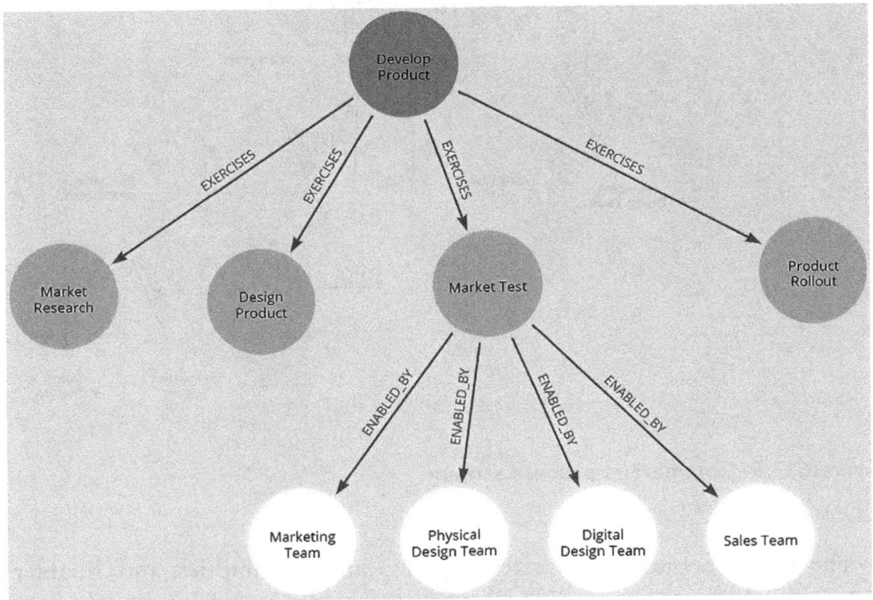

Figure CS2.4 Market test process stream.

Commercialize and roll product out

These Capabilities involve all the activities necessary to prepare a new product for rollout, such as creating packaging, updating the relevant website, preparing the customer support team to support purchasers and corporate support, such as legal review of packaging or content to be included with the product.

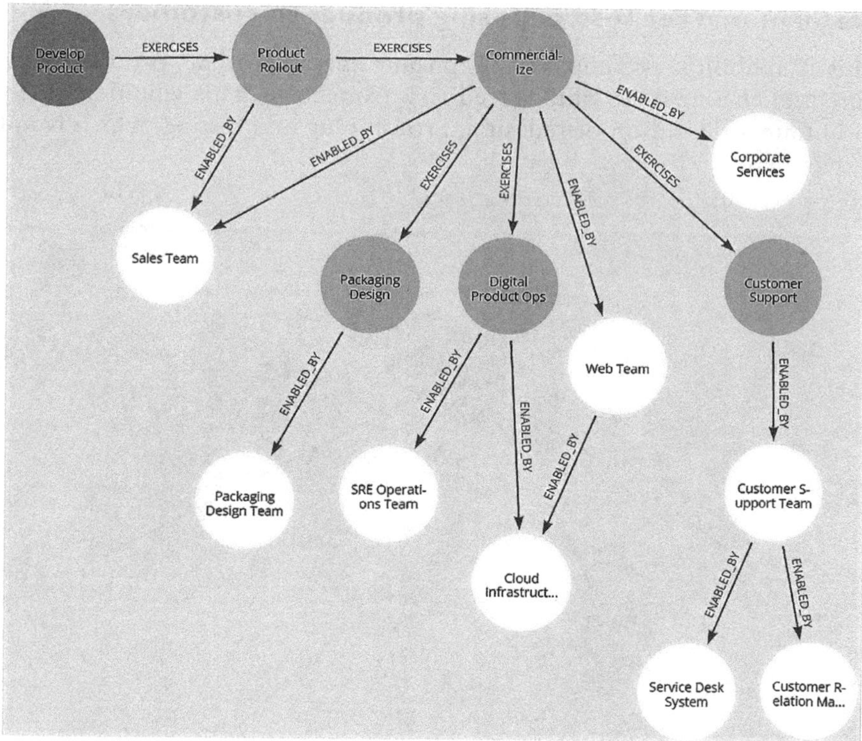

Figure CS2.5 Commercial process stream.

The table, below, summarizes the relevant Capabilities and Enablers across the divisions:

	Industrial	*Commercial*	*Consumer*
Value-Stream Product/Service Management Approach	1	2	2
Existing Digital Products or Services	0	2	2
Rapid Prototyping-Physical Products	2	1	0
Rapid Prototyping-Digital Products or Services	0	0	2
Business Intelligence/Analytics Utilization	0	1	2
Agile/DevOps/Ci/CD/SRE Ops	0	0	1
Developmental Product Portfolio	0	1	3
Digital Partnerships	0	0	1

The value in each cell, from zero to five, indicates the degree to which the capability exists in each division. Zero indicates no capability and five indicates a to-be level.

What's reusable across the divisions?

- Industrial's rapid prototyping tooling and know-how
- Industrial and Commercial's product design and manufacturing skills and processes
- Consumer's development product portfolio management approaches and skills
- Consumer's web presence operational capabilities (largely contracted but could be brought in-house)

Operational Infrastructure, API services

From the standpoint of its IT infrastructure and knowledge, HiC is far from ready to transition to the to-be state. However, what needs to be done is to evaluate how far it can transform the other pillars with the existing infrastructure and plan to transform what it has in the most cost-effective and risk-managed way.

The table, below, summarizes the state of HiC's relevant Capabilities and Enablers at the enterprise level and across the divisions:

	Corporate	*Industrial*	*Commercial*	*Consumer*
Cloud migration	I	0	0	I
Cloud Infrastructure Management	I	0	0	I
Cloud-Native Application Architecture	0	0	0	0
SRE Ops Capabilities	0	0	0	0
API-Compatible Application Architecture	0	0	0	0
API Management Capabilities	I	0	I	I
Hybrid Cloud Infrastructure Operations Processes	I	0	0	I

What can be reused? There is not much, at this point, but:

- HiC has some cloud experience, in the form of the backup and archiving workloads it is currently operating.
- Some of the experience that Consumer has in working with its web-presence vendor and Amazon may be useful.

Business intelligence/analytics

At this point, HiC essentially has no BI/A capability to speak of. It's certainly good that they have been dabbling in it, but they need someone to take a leadership role in developing it for strategic impact. As it happens, more and more of the services that companies like HiC employ will have AI capabilities embedded in them. Customer care apps that have Natural Language Processing (NLP) capabilities in them are a good example. This Medium article[34] elaborates a number of use-cases for AI. Note the two columns at the right in the table toward the bottom of the article. They may be most applicable to HiC.

While making use of such services will enable HiC to keep pace with many of its competitors on a superficial level, it will not impart a significant strategic edge, however.

What's reusable here? If HiC has tooling that it's happy with, that may be a useful starting point.

Partner development platform

HiC has almost no digital partnering relationships, though there may be opportunities for the Commercial and Consumer divisions. These will become clearer as HiC develops plans to implement digital services, of which it currently has none.

The need for the PDP should be subordinate to more pressing issues in HiC's transformation program.

GAP ANALYSIS

Now that we have documented the as-is and to-be states of HiC's digital pillars, Value Streams, Capabilities and Enablers we can identify the initiatives necessary to transition from as-is to to-be. This is a preliminary process that will produce a raw list. In the following step, we will analyze them, prioritize them and create a sequenced program plan.

Gap Analysis is intended to identify WHAT needs to change to reach the specified end state. In the next section, HiC will explore HOW to change, which includes considerations of immediate vs. longer-term benefits, costs, dependencies, sequencing and risk management, among others.

Organization and governance—people issues

Ultimately, HiC will have to address a multitude of organizational and developmental challenges on the path to to-be. It's worth grouping them within the context of the pillars within which changes will occur:

[34] https://medium.com/@Brian.johnson_62680/artificial-intelligence-ai-top-use-cases-and-technologies-used-today-3c22e1a63e78

Operational Infrastructure

- HiC's existing IT organization is pretty traditional. It includes user-facing developers, systems administration, network management and so on. Its revised structure will have to support essentially two operational platforms—the enterprise platform and the SRE operations platform, which will be operated by members of the technical staff that are attached to the Product Management teams. This suggests some changes:
  - Both platforms will be heavily cloud-dependent. Cloud management skills are a must. Beside merely keeping things running, the operations group will need to have the knowledge and skills required to manage cloud services costs, which can get out of hand if not closely controlled.
  - The SRE operations teams embedded in the Product Management groups will require real operational experience. Some of these teams may be seeded with existing IT operations staff.
  - Cloud architectures allow for innumerable options for accommodating any given requirement. Architectural expertise and the ability to define and implement reusable solutions will be a key to creating a cohesive support environment for HiC's user community, including the Product Management technical team members.
  - Multi- or Hybrid Cloud operations management skills. Operating a multi- or hybrid-cloud infrastructure creates a layer of complications across the board but also provides a number of important benefits. HiC may choose to operate across clouds to avoid vendor lock-in, to provide operational redundancy or be forced into it by choosing to use services that are provided by vendors that are available only on a specific cloud, such as Salesforce.[35]
  - Application cloud migration requires some specialized knowledge and experience. IT operations will have to acquire or develop these skills in order to play its role in managing transformation to the to-be OI.
  - BI/A has some requirements that are unique to it—the need for extremely large amounts of data storage and intermittent requirements for massive amounts of computing power, which is why the cloud is an excellent solution. IT operations will require the knowledge required to deal with these issues in providing support to BI/A.

---

[35] Actually, Salesforce announced late last year that it would begin to provide its services on multiple public clouds: https://www.zdnet.com/article/salesforce-revamps-architecture-aims-to-run-its-applications-on-any-public-cloud/

API management

- This is another area in which knowledge and experience will be required to define, implement and manage a centralized/distributed service on which almost all of HiC's other services will rely. HiC will need to develop or acquire this knowledge, especially early in the process of defining the overall architecture for its API infrastructure. This is especially true in light of the role that APIs will probably play in the cloud migration of HiC's application systems.

Product management

This is certainly an area in which organization change will be substantial.

- **Product Managers** will need to be re-oriented to work in a value-stream paradigm, which may be a big change from what they're used to. Staff acquisition and development will be necessary.
- **Marketing** staff and **Digital Product Strategists** may constitute new capabilities for the PM team. These roles should incorporate the ability to work closely with **Data Scientists** from the BI/A team.
- **Digital Product Designers** will have to work within the new paradigm, which may also be a change for them. **Physical Product Designers** will have to adapt to this, as well.
- Each PM team will require technical and engineering resources that HiC does not have now:
  - Agile application developers
  - Testing specialists
  - Software pipeline managers
  - CI/CD release managers
  - SRE operations staff
- Each division will require a **Product Development Team** to be responsible for incubating prospective Products or Services. These multi-disciplinary teams will require a subset of the PM capabilities:
- Hands-on Product Managers
- BI-capable marketing and product strategy staff
- Physical and/or digital product designers and developers, including technical resources to support them

Business intelligence and analytics

- This set of Capabilities and Enablers is now rudimentary and requires development and evolution into an internal service organization. It needs:
  - Someone to set an agenda and lead it.

- Data scientists, who should each be focused on individual divisions and/or products, which, presumably, will have individual nuances for which AI models will need to account, and services, based on scope and immediacy of need.
- Data engineers, who can be managed as a pool and allocated to work on data science operations and projects as they are allocated.

Partnership enablement

- As indicated previously, this pillar may be put off for some time. Nonetheless, it should be treated as an internal service and an external service offering. Therefore, it would be advisable to begin to assemble a Product Management team to develop Partnership services offerings.

Governance

- It is likely that there will be significant changes to governance processes and some of them will result in the need to make organizational changes to various groups. Many of these will be to disperse members out to work more closely with groups and departments who's work will be in transition from project-oriented to Value-Stream or Product-oriented.
- The scope of the digital transformation effort will require executive-level oversight. HiC will need to assign members of its various governance groups to the transformation management team either full- or part-time to keep up with it.

In addition to organizational and governance changes specific to the pillars, there are other areas in which organizational additions or changes will be required:

- **Transformation Management Executive**
  Due to the enterprise-wide scope of the digital transformation effort, a senior executive should be placed in charge to marshal resources and staff and to resolve the inevitable issues that arise. The scope of the knowledge and experience required may well necessitate a new hire for this role.
- **Change Management Team**
  As the transformation program is under way, there will be a lot happening in parallel and orchestration and problem resolution will be critical. Change Management will act as a de facto program and project management office. It will report to the Transformation Management Executive and can be staffed by available project managers who are sufficiently senior and knowledgeable. HiC, however, doesn't have

enough of these resources with the required knowledge to keep what's currently going on going at the same time as it attempts to undertake digital transformation. It will have to acquire external resources and develop internal ones at the same time.

- **Knowledge Management**
  KM is not something that HiC currently does. It will require a small team, led by a specialist who has overseen from-scratch KM projects, is conversant with taxonomy development and is familiar with appropriate tools[36] to perform this function going forward.
- **Enterprise and Business Architecture**
  Enterprise and Business Architecture is also not something that HiC practices on a formal basis. To the extent that AERM is dependent on the availability of an up-to-date EA and BA repository, these are disciplines that it must have. In all likelihood, it will have to acquire and develop the people it needs for this purpose, as well as adopt or acquire appropriate tools to support the function.
- **Business Process Management and Automation**
  One of the major goals of digital transformation is to improve collaboration, increase process throughput and improve accuracy. All of these are goals of BPM, and the discipline is specialized to the degree that it should be supported by a dedicated group. HiC will require someone to lead it that has the requisite skills and experience and familiarity with specialized tools that will be employed under various circumstances.
- **Training and Staff Development**
  A great deal of training and up-skilling will be necessary to develop the staff that HiC will need during and post-transformation. It will be a good idea to create a training team to manage the process of staff education. In aggregate, HiC will need to identify major knowledge or competency gaps and plan to address them in at least these areas:
  - Cloud migration and management
  - Cloud-native application architecture
  - API design and management
  - Value-driven Product Management
  - Web app and UX design
  - Agile SDLC
  - DevOps
  - Automated testing
  - CI/CD
  - System reliability engineering, operations
  - Business process management—process mining, BPA, RPA, DPA

[36] https://www.intechopen.com/books/ontological-analyses-in-science-technology-and-informatics/taxonomy-and-ontology-management-tools-a-general-explanation

- Product development, Lean Startup approach, incubator operation and management
- BI, AI, ML, data science, data engineering ops
- Governance re-design for distributed management

This is a daunting list of organizational development and changes! But, as we've observed previously, digital transformation is a necessary, messy and complicated business.

Capabilities and enablers—technologies, processes and assets

Having outlined the organizational development challenges, HiC must now focus on the Capabilities and Enablers that it must put in place to make the transformation function. Within the framework of the six pillars, these include:

Operational Infrastructure

Ultimately, the OI will be a key set of Capabilities and Enablers that will help HiC to realize business agility. Key characteristics that HiC requires, among other more standard concerns, are:

- **Elasticity**, the ability to grow and shrink capacities to match demand. This includes storage, processing power and network throughput.
- **Flexibility**, the ability to reconfigure elements of the infrastructure with minimal effort and moderated risk to accommodate new ways of supporting existing workloads or implementing new things.
- **Cost Optimization**, the ability to minimize and manage operational costs.
- **Access to Advanced Third-Party Services**, the ability to integrate SaaS products and services easily.

The answer to a lot of these and other considerations is the cloud; however, this does not come without effort on HiC's part. It will have to:

- Conduct a cloud migration for most of its corporate and transactional systems
- Create a cloud infrastructure management team and implement or utilize a variety of monitoring and reporting services that will allow HiC to keep on top of what is happening and what it is spending on cloud services.
- Adopt cloud-native application architectures, wherever possible. Obviously, if the commitment is there, HiC can ordain cloud-native as a go-forward standard. Migrating and transforming existing

applications must be done on a case-by-case basis. There is a progression of approaches for this.[37]

- Lift and Shift—just take an application and re-host it on a dedicated set of resources at a cloud provider, known as Infrastructure as a Service (IaaS). An advantage of doing this is that it can facilitate HiC's employing the strangler fig architectural pattern to integrate existing applications into its evolving OI and replace them a piece at a time at its convenience.
- Partial Re-engineering—decompose and recompose an application, maintaining most of its structure, so that it can make best use of the cloud's available capabilities, such as elasticity, scalability, load balancing and availability management options. This is known as Platform as a Service (PaaS).
- Migrate to a vendor-provided application—simply transition from existing on-premise or hosted application to a third-party service, known as Software as a Service (SaaS).
- Completely re-engineer to cloud-native standards—completely rebuild an application to optimize its use of cloud-based capabilities and services. There are benefits to this, many of which are intermediate- to longer-term in nature. This is the highest-risk option, especially for an organization like HiC that has limited cloud development experience.

- **Implement a subset of the OI to provide SRE Ops capabilities and support**. It's likely that the SRE subset will merely be a set of components and resources carved out of the enterprise OI that Product Management teams' staff will be allowed and enabled to manage and maintain, themselves.
- **Adopt Hybrid Cloud Operational Processes**. (This is optional.) Hybrid (combined on-premise and public clouds) or multi-vendor clouds (deploying elements of the OI to different vendors' clouds) create advantages and disadvantages. They provide resilience to failure and options that help avoid vendor lock-in, but they are more complicated to monitor and manage. To the degree that it may be impossible for most companies to completely avoid multi-vendor cloud adoption, HiC may want to consider adopting a suite of tools that can make this easier to manage.
- **Learn and implement Infrastructure as Code (IaC) capabilities**. IaC is described in this Wikipedia article.[38] It allows a user to build a text file containing specifications for a configuration of cloud-based assets and execute it to instantiate them at will. This is especially useful for

[37] Here's an article from BMC Software that describes IaaS vs Paas vs SaaS: https://www.bmc.com/blogs/saas-vs-paas-vs-iaas-whats-the-difference-and-how-to-choose/

[38] https://en.wikipedia.org/wiki/Infrastructure_as_code

standing up a service, exercising it and then tearing it down, thus executing a workload and then terminating the charges associated with running it, such as might be the case for ML model building.

API management

As we've discussed, API interfaces will ultimately be the glue that holds the OI together and may be a key element of HiC's strategy to migrate its existing and new application systems into a cohesive architecture. HiC must develop API management capabilities and implement tooling in support of them. This Infoworld article[39] provides a list of tools for HiC to investigate. In addition, most cloud vendors provide their own tools, such as AWS' API Gateway[40] that are certainly serviceable; however, in a multi-vendor cloud environment, it may be advisable to employ tooling that can be used from a central location. Red Hat provides such tools.[41]

Product management, digital products and services factory

- **Adopt Value-Stream Digital Product/Service Development Tools**—*BizDevOps*[42] is becoming the term of art in the industry. This requires an integrated tool suite to perform properly. This page from TaskTop[43] and this one from Plutora[44] describe capabilities required. HiC should adopt one of these or a competing tool in conjunction with adopting DevOps agile delivery approaches to help it achieve a velocity of software development and deployment that will make it competitive.
- **Adopt and standardize on a set of Agile Software Development Practices**—There are different Agile System Development Lifecycles (SDLCs) in use today, which are more alike than they are differentiated from one-another. HiC currently employs different Agile SDLCs in different divisions and standardizing on one to use with its DevOps processes would provide it with flexibility to reallocate development staff as needs dictate.
- **Adopt DevOps or BizDevOps tooling**—This includes several components. This article[45] contains a list of an examples of each of them. Components that HiC requires include:
  - Code repository (e.g., GitHub[46])
  - Integrated Development Environment (IDE)[47])

39 https://www.infoworld.com/article/3398484/10-best-api-management-tools.html
40 https://aws.amazon.com/api-gateway/
41 https://www.redhat.com/en/topics/api/why-choose-red-hat-apis
42 https://enterprisersproject.com/article/2019/9/devops-what-is-bizdevops
43 https://www.tasktop.com/value-stream-management/
44 https://www.plutora.com/blog/value-stream-management
45 https://raygun.com/blog/best-devops-tools/
46 https://github.com/
47 https://en.wikipedia.org/wiki/Integrated_development_environment

  - Continuous Testing tools[48])
  - A build tool (e.g., Gradle[49])
  - Deployment management tools (e.g., Jenkins[50] or AWS Code Deploy[51])
  - An IaC tool (e.g., Puppet[52] or Ansible[53])
  - A monitoring tool, of which there are a plethora, that apply to HiC's development environment and its production environment
- **Staff and Adopt System Reliability Engineering (SRE) Operations Processes and Practices**—HiC should add operations Capabilities and Enablers to its Product Management teams who will be responsible for monitoring production applications and responding to issues that arise from their operations. These teams will be tightly integrated with the DevOps testing and deployment management processes, as well as overall cloud management for the subset of the OI environment that is under their control.
- **Migrate Existing Digital Products or Services into the defined DevOps environment**—Standardizing the way software and applications are built is a key to achieving agility. It will benefit HiC to migrate existing software to the common management environment so that it will become more maintainable and easier to enhance.
- **Expand Rapid Design and Prototyping for Physical Products**—HiC currently has some Capabilities and Enablers that support this, mainly in the Industrial Division. It should investigate whether it makes sense to expand on these and move them downstream to make them available on a smaller scale within the Commercial or Consumer Divisions.
- **Business Intelligence/Analytics Integration**—Product Management teams should start looking for opportunities to incorporate AI and ML into their management processes and potentially into their products and services. This will require their becoming customers of BI/A services and integrating members of their marketing and product strategy teams with members of the BI/A team. There may be opportunities for the two teams to operate some of the data management and modeling tools jointly.
- **Build and Operate Developmental Business Lifecycle Processes and Initiate Portfolio Management**—HiC should have each of the divisions consolidate all of the product or service ideas actively being considered or under development and migrate them into a standardized developmental process with an actively managed portfolio. The tools for rapid digital and physical product development and evolution will

[48] https://en.wikipedia.org/wiki/Continuous_testing
[49] https://gradle.org/
[50] https://www.jenkins.io/
[51] https://aws.amazon.com/codedeploy/
[52] https://puppet.com/products/puppet-enterprise/
[53] https://www.ansible.com/

exist but the processes around experimental business development and portfolio management are separate from them.

- **Look for Digital Partnership Opportunities**—While at the outset of its transformation HiC will not be positioned to exploit integrated partnership opportunities at the level it expects to long term, it should begin to envision where such opportunities might be found and what they might look like. Ultimately, HiC should include in the developmental business approach a requirement to consider whether new business ideas could be delivered faster, more economically and more easily by partnering than by undertaking a from-scratch or go-it-alone approach.

Business intelligence and analytics

Enabling BI/A requires two disciplines—Data Engineering and Data Science. HiC must expand and mature its BI/A capabilities by:

- Creating a BI/A team, as described earlier,
- Developing a portfolio of services that the team can deliver in an efficient, economical and repeatable fashion,
- Implement tooling that will enable the development and delivery of services:
  - Databricks[54] is an example of an integrated toolset that supports ML Ops,[55] which is a part of AI operations.
  - AWS[56] has a large suite of similar and related services.

AI/ML tools are evolving quite rapidly. AutoAI[57] is reducing the expertise required to specify and making it easier to implement and deploy AI models. AWS SageMaker[58] is one of many examples of this.

Partner development platform

Developing digital products and services in partnership with an external company is different than developing them in-house. Partnership can take many forms. In some cases, HiC might effectively be a customer, purchasing a service from a partner which it will then provide to a customer of its own. In others, HiC might be providing a service to a customer, who will then package and resell it to the ultimate consumer. Issues relating to where customers originate, who ‘owns’ them and who should have access to their

54 https://databricks.com/
55 https://en.wikipedia.org/wiki/MLOps
56 https://aws.amazon.com/machine-learning/
57 https://en.wikipedia.org/wiki/AutoAI
58 https://aws.amazon.com/sagemaker/

data are all up for negotiation and must be resolved and the ability to work in a manner consistent with the partnership terms must be supported by the platform.

Mutual adoption of an integration approach is required, REST APIs are the standard currently, and cohesive management of application states is necessary. For instance, if one of the partners initiates a transaction that must be completed on the other's service before a user task can proceed, then this must be accounted for. If an error occurs on one side, then the ability to unwind a partially completed transaction in its entirety must be supported. The skills to do this will certainly exist within HiC's development teams, but it is more complicated when trying to perform it across different participants' platforms.

There is also a product/service aspect to this. HiC will want to develop a suite of functions that make it easy for potential partners with all levels of expertise and ability to work with them. It should be easy to partner and consume basic services, as often as possible, without any manual interaction. It should also be possible to work jointly to develop more sophisticated integrations. Perhaps there might be an opportunity for HiC to provide billable professional services for more complicated engineering and solutions.

Finally, there will be a need to track utilization information necessary to allocate revenue, perform billing and manage payments, as necessary.

HiC should treat this as a developmental business and define and implement an experimental version of what it might offer. This would provide an opportunity to exercise its Developmental Business Lifecycle Processes and gain insight into the functional requirements and features of what the PDP should offer.

PORTFOLIO FORMULATION AND PROGRAM DESIGN

Guiding objectives

Overall, the Digital Transformation Program will consist of literally hundreds of individual initiatives. It's not feasible or necessary to delve into even a small minority of them here, but we can present a framework for HiC to employ to inform the construction of its program plan:

- **Keep what's going, going.** The need and desire to transform should not short circuit progress HiC is currently making or potentially impair its current operations.
- **Use what HiC currently has.** It will be possible to enable some Capabilities with existing people, processes, technology and assets. HiC should try to see what it can accomplish with the least change possible, at least in the short term.

- **The world is not going to stop while HiC transforms.** New threats, opportunities and requirements will continue to emerge and will have to be addressed; however, HiC must now look at each potential initiative in a new way. It will have to weigh the benefits of implementing something short of the to-be architecture and refactoring solutions it builds to reach conformance later vs. those of waiting until a to-be-compliant solution is possible. This obviates the need to build and re-build solutions, shouldering the costs and risks that relate to that.
- **Many Capabilities and Enablers can be decomposed and partially implemented.** In many cases, there will be opportunities to implement partial solutions that are to-be-compliant and integrate them into an envisioned solution in its entirety later. By exploiting this option where it exists, HiC might be able to avoid adding to the overall backlog of things to be transformed. For example, Implementing the entire Agile and CI/CD software development Capability is a substantial task but adopting a standard software repository is something that is relatively easy to do. Keeping new software assets in the target repository now will make it easy to integrate in the CI/CD pipeline later.
- **To-Be will change before HiC reaches it.** The lifetime of HiC's digital transformation will be years and it's only to be expected that technology advancements will force it to reconsider and redesign aspects of the to-be company before it's even instantiated. Business Agility is a seminal goal of the digital transformation, and it can only be realized if HiC achieves the ability to pivot and remake itself as circumstances dictate.
- **Agility is the result of planning.** We've discussed Risk Management and the OODA Loop. Program and Project Management focus a great deal on identifying and considering alternative approaches to implementation and how to respond to things that vary from what was assumed. There are innumerable interdependencies among the program initiatives and invariably, things will not progress as planned. The ability to trace dependence among the Capabilities and Enablers that HiC is building will be a key to its ability to respond to variances, regardless of their cause.
- **Focus on value.** This article from McKinsey[59] has insightful observations and recommendations about how to achieve enterprise agility. One important recommendation is to focus on initiatives that tie directly to value realization.

Earlier, we used the term *hairball* to describe how interdependent the initiatives constituting the transformation program would be. Any digital transformation will have numerous mutually dependent initiatives executing

[59] https://www.mckinsey.com/business-functions/organization/our-insights/the-impact-of-agility-how-to-shape-your-organization-to-compete

in parallel, creating a need to plan for intermediate states and start-and-stop progression. Attempting to use common planning tools, such as Gantt Charts,[60] at the overall program level will only result in an unusable mess, though they may make sense for limited-scope, tightly connected initiatives. A tool such as PlanView[61] that integrates initiatives at the enterprise level, is worth investigating.

Consider this—HiC wants to adopt Value-Stream product management, which requires Agile, Ci/CD development practices and processes and SRE operations, which requires tools not currently in use, which requires the OI be in place and all of these require skills and experience HiC doesn't currently have. Thus, HiC will have to not only change the tires on the car while it is driving down the highway, it will also have to pave the highway at the same time.

With the guiding objectives and the complexities of mutually dependent initiatives in mind, these thoughts should inform how HiC might prioritize and plan its transformation.

FOUNDATION AND INITIATION: PRIORITY 1 INITIATIVES

These are mainly foundational to the inception of the transformation program. They involve taking concrete steps to instantiate new or modified teams and produce early-stage deliverables and results.

Create plan to address cultural issues

It's worth repeating, and emphasizing, that ***most transformations, including digital transformations, that fail, fail due to people issues***. This Deloitte and Wall Street Journal article[62] and this Russell Reynolds whitepaper[63] are among hundreds of posts on the subject. It's critical that HiC develop a communication plan to bring its existing staff into alignment, set expectations about how the transformation will proceed and communicate the rationale that informed the plan.

Select transformation leadership

It is critical that HiC assign overall responsibility for the transformation to a suitably senior executive, preferably one that reports to either the CEO or COO and who will have the authority to resolve conflicts among members of the company's divisions. While some CIOs may have this type of

60 https://en.wikipedia.org/wiki/Gantt_chart
61 https://www.planview.com/
62 https://deloitte.wsj.com/cio/2019/07/18/the-role-of-culture-in-digital-transformation/
63 https://www.russellreynolds.com/en/Insights/thought-leadership/Documents/Culture%20as%20Key%20Factor%20in%20Industrial%20Digital%20Transformation.pdf

influence, many technology-enabled business transformations that are overseen by CIOs who don't have the necessary enterprise-wide influence fail to gain the level of cooperation and willingness to change and doom initiatives to insignificance or outright failure. HiC would be well advised to make a careful selection here.

Stand up the change management team (transformation program management office)

HiC should stand up the Change Management Team immediately after selecting the Transformation Leader. Merely putting together the detailed program plan will be a tremendous amount of work and shortchanging the effort because staffing is not in place is a wholly avoidable risk. HiC does not have sufficient Program and Project Management staff with the necessary knowledge and skill sets to do this. It is appropriate to bring in outside resources to build this group, with the intention of transitioning to internal resources as they come up to speed.

One of the things it will make sense to do is to assign this team responsibility for ensuring that relevant data and information is collected, stored and disseminated to where it will be used. Such data includes EA and BA model data, taxonomy updates and master program schedule and progress information.

Define transformation governance processes to be employed

HiC must identify how and how often it will measure progress on the transformation and who will be responsible for performance against each indicator. It will not work to make the Transformation Leader responsible for accomplishing things that are the purview of division or other senior corporate executives. Responsibility and accountability without authority is a path to failure.

Plan for organizational redesign

Managing the evolution of the organization is very much a chicken-and-egg problem. Does HiC try to create the organization as it will need to be in advance of transforming its Capabilities and Enablers or does it transform them first. The answer to this is, of course, "it depends." This article[64] describes seven alternative approaches to effecting organizational change.

As with the Change Management Team, there are mutual dependencies that must be addressed. What can HiC change first among the Capabilities and Enablers it's targeting early in its program? Value-driven priorities must

[64] https://www.cleverism.com/major-approaches-models-of-change-management/

compete with skills-related feasibility gaps to help determine program staging. Timing is another issue to consider. Installing CI/CD capabilities will take a long time and a lot depends on them working well. Tool selection and training in their use in the context of the processes in which they will be used is a precursor to this and it must be accommodated.

Finally, there is the issue of selecting an approach to organizational transformation. Should HiC prototype its organizational changes and give itself the chance to iterate toward an optimal design? Is there one optimal design or might there be a few or even several that will best accommodate its existing staff?

Compile training and upskilling requirements

Earlier, we identified a list of knowledge, experience and skill requirements that HiC will require in the course of its transformation and in support of ongoing operations, thereafter. Staging the program plan will require that HiC plan to bring in outside help where necessary and allocate ramp-up time to bring participants up to speed in areas in which they may not be conversant.

Given the changing nature of jobs and careers and the rapid evolution of technologies, processes and business models, it would be strategic for HiC to plan to maintain a robust training Capability focused on its Capabilities and Enablers.

Plan for transforming the product management function

HiC currently has a range of PM approaches from very traditional (Industrial Division) to something more in line with the target approach (Consumer Division). To the degree that it would like to move all its divisions to incorporating digital products and services into their repertoires, it makes sense to standardize their PM approach, processes and supporting technology.

HiC should articulate and document what the approach will be and how it will be applied and then conduct orientation and training sessions for PM teams. Given staffing and skill gaps at the outset of the program, HiC should plan to make this training something that it can deliver at regular intervals as staff is added or reassigned from other areas of the company.

There are two levels of considerations with respect to PM operations—executive governance and decision-making and BAU operational decision-making. Executive governance will take the form of making investment allocations within a division's product and service portfolio. BAU decisions take place at the product or service level, usually made by hands-on staff. HiC needs to articulate the roles and expectations for corporate executive oversight, division-level oversight and BAU managerial oversight and incorporate it into its governance plans.

Define architectural subject matter expert (SME) team requirements

Achieving HiC's business agility goals will require that it implements a componentized organization structure[65]—that is, one in which independent groups with highly-focused specializations work together to speed delivery of value to customers. One way to facilitate this is to build centers of excellence in several areas to act as internal subject matter experts, communicate standards and best practices and help to maintain libraries and repositories of reusable knowledge and components.

On the technical side, HiC should have specialist groups focused on:

- Cloud Architectures, Cloud Management, Cloud Migration Strategies
- Application development practices and processes relating to CI/CD software delivery and to legacy application operations, maintenance and support
- API Management
- Data Architecture
- Security

HiC does not have all the relevant expertise in-house at this point and will have to bring in outside SMEs to advise and help train HiC's personnel at the outset of the process. Ultimately, it should look to develop the skills and knowledge needed to shoulder this burden on its own at its earliest opportunity.

Stand up the enterprise and business architecture team

Enterprise and Business Architecture are cornerstones of AERM and are intrinsic to the recommended approach to transformation and risk management. Following the recommended process, these groups will have been involved in producing the as-is and to-be models from which the transformation initiative portfolio is derived. Therefore, these teams must already exist. What HiC must do at this point is to integrate them into all transformation processes so that they can capture and maintain all changes that impact the model, and which create or modify sources of risk that the ERM team should address.

Stand up the knowledge management team

Just as EA and BA play an important role in ensuring that AERM delivers the value that is intended, so, too, does KM. The KM function should already exist, given its role in development of the EA and BA models—developing

65 https://cisr.mit.edu/publication/2020_0601_BuildingComponentizedOrganization_RossBeathNelson

the initial taxonomy which ensured that the data collected by the EA and BA teams was be tagged consistently. This ensures that functional and SME teams can identify reusable components consistently. This team should remain in place in perpetuity to advise on usage and to monitor and update the taxonomy as HiC evolves. The team must also be integrated into all operational processes that add to or modify EA or BA model data or any other knowledge repository, such as development and commercialization of new products, revision of major operating processes or, for that matter, any other Capability or Enabler.

Stand up the business process management team

BPM plays a pivotal role in the digitally transformed company. Process automation and re-engineering are critical Capabilities that, when exercised, create efficiency, increase throughput and increase quality. The discipline of BPM encompasses Business Process Automation, commonly known as *Workflow Management*,[66] *Robotic Process Automation*[67] and *Digital Process Automation*.[68]

In the previous section, we recommended that companies focus on processes for primarily two reasons—re-engineering processes is a gateway to efficiency and processes are the sources of many operational risks and evolving the processes that create them can provide relatively low-cost opportunities to mitigate them.

Process Mining[69] is a set of techniques through which processes, some of which may be implicit and the result of nothing more than common practice, are identified. While identifying process Enablers was performed during the as-is discovery and to-be design, in-depth analysis of them was probably not performed unless process SMEs were available. HiC needs to instantiate a BPM team and initiate the task of identifying and analyzing processes throughout the domain of the company that is undergoing transformation. This group will stay in place permanently post-transformation.

Compile a work-in-progress inventory

HiC should also secure or create a WIP inventory of all existing development or transformational initiatives going on. It will need to evaluate whether these should continue as planned or whether their context has changed sufficiently to warrant reconsideration. For all that will continue, the transformation program must account for and accommodate the work required to execute them and their eventual impact.

---

66 https://en.wikipedia.org/wiki/Workflow_management_system
67 https://en.wikipedia.org/wiki/Robotic_process_automation
68 https://www.integrify.com/digital-process-automation/
69 https://en.wikipedia.org/wiki/Process_mining

Create a preliminary master program schedule

The preceding initiatives will result in creating or evolving Enablers, mostly teams with specific knowledge and skills. HiC now needs to identify, prioritize and schedule initiatives to produce specific outcomes with regard to the Capabilities it needs to realize its objectives. Given all the work that will be required to stand up the organization HiC aspires to be, many of the second-level initiatives will have to start while Enablers are in development. For instance, elements of the new Value-Driven Product Management approach may be prototyped, evaluated and iterated prior to the implementation of the entire suite of CI/CD tools and processes.

Creating a high-level schedule is the first concrete step in unwinding the hairball and will require significant project management expertise and involvement from numerous participants. It will be a top-down and bottom-up exercise in which business priorities—what new, modified or enhanced products or services are division executives' and Product Managers' highest priorities—are matched against what new, modified or enhanced Capabilities and Enablers need to be in place to make them happen. Identifying interim states and assessing and mitigating risks will be a major test of the judgment of the people working on it.

Ultimately, giving representatives from all of the teams access to provide input and feedback on the schedule as it evolves is crucial to identifying discontinuities, unaddressed dependencies and avoidable risks, as well as to encourage teams' buy-in to collaborate and be responsible to produce deliverables on a mutually agreeable schedule.

While more detail would certainly be better, there will, of necessity, be some major large placeholders that will need further work. In the next phase, the teams will begin to address these.

PROGRAM EXECUTION: PRIORITY 2 INITIATIVES

This stage builds on all the work done in the foundational stage and represents the point at which the transformation of operational Capabilities and Enablers begins. How many initiatives HiC will take on in parallel is an important strategic decision that will have significant impact on the risks of the transformation. Doing more in parallel incurs an overhead burden of coordination and will create a greater need to go back and refactor some of what is built as architectures and designs mature and evolve during development.

The urgency that HiC perceives with respect to its need to transform must be balanced against its risk appetite and risk tolerance. Risks associated with the transformation include:

- Failing to create the ability to deliver products or services on which it is predicating its future competitiveness, either in a timely manner or at all.

- Spending substantially more time and money in implementation.
- Implementing in such as manner as to preclude efficient options for future initiatives.
- Simply not achieving the business agility that is the overriding goal for the transformation.

Transformation risk management will be addressed in a subsequent section. This section deals more with sequencing. Some of the initiatives that will be executed are continuations of the foundational initiatives, others involve instantiating some of the pillars.

Operationalize change management processes

- Implement BPM and collaboration tools supporting Change Management processes.
- Initiate processes, monitoring and reporting

Produce technical architecture deliverables

Various technological architecture teams were created in the previous phase; in this one, they will perform tool selection and produce standards in several areas that will guide implementation of numerous elements of the pillars. These include:

- Select tooling and processes to enable CI/CD for the DPSF:
  - Code repository
  - Integrated Development Environment
  - Continuous testing tools
  - A build tool
  - Deployment management tools
  - An IaC tool
  - Development and production environment monitoring tools
  - Agile SDLC
- Define SRE approaches and standards, define Support Level Agreements, select tooling and implement monitoring and incident management approaches
- Conduct BPM/BPA/RPA/DPA tooling research and coordinate with the BPM team to select tooling.
- Define Cloud Architecture Standards
- Define API Management Architecture
- Define Cloud Migration Program Plan
- Define Data Architecture Standards
- Establish Centers of Excellence (COEs) and SME roles
- Assist with training content development and delivery

Deliver training

- Develop training curriculum.
- Initiate and deliver training.

Perform EA/BA modeling

- Complete implementing the EA repository and user query and reporting interface.
- Populate models
- Integrate data capture with Change Management processes

Knowledge management and taxonomy creation

- Complete implementing the KM and Taxonomy repositories and user query and reporting interfaces.
- Coordinate with EA/BA modeling and change management teams

Business process mining—process inventory creation

- Complete as-is and to-be process inventory.
- Create process portfolio and conduct analysis of improvement and automation opportunities.
- Select BPM/BPA/RPA/DPA tooling.
- Define prioritized business process evolution program, including scope and goals, schedules, budgets.
- Begin executing approved initiatives.

Digital Products and Services factory

- Establish PM organizations and processes within divisions
- Adopt Value Stream Product Management Processes
  - Define performance measures
  - Adopt Value Stream Management Platform
  - Develop continuous improvement approach
- Adopt Agile SDLC approach
- Develop and execute training and mentoring plan
- Implement and utilize CI/CD, SRE Tools and Processes
- Develop plan to migrate existing Products and Services to Value Stream Management approach and begin execution

Design API architecture and implement API management

- Design API architecture (to reiterate, this article from Red Hat[70] is worth reading)

70 https://www.redhat.com/en/topics/api/what-is-api-design

- Implement API Management architecture
- Migrate applications and services to API-compatible versions
- Build API documentation and on-line interfaces

Operational Infrastructure architecture and migration

- Define cloud architecture standards
    - Design for performance, resiliency, manageability, cost containment, etc.
    - Select management approaches and tooling. (See this article from Red Hat.[71])
    - Build and manage infrastructure automation (Infrastructure as Code (IaC)) scripts
    - Define deployment approaches and processes—what will move onto the cloud and who will control it and how will it be monitored and managed
- Initiate integrated operational monitoring, management and reporting processes
- Define application migration plan
    - Inventory existing systems
    - Perform detailed analysis of functions and services, interfaces supported, data transacted, technology employed
    - Define application-specific migration strategy
    - Add to migration portfolio
    - Perform portfolio analysis and develop program
- Execute migration program

PROGRAM EXECUTION: PRIORITY 3 INITIATIVES

This stage is a continuation of the previous one. It addresses pillars that HiC has not yet initiated.

Produce technical architecture deliverables

- Define BI/A standards
    - Data and data management standards
    - Project isolation procedures
    - Management automation and IaC development
    - Integration with KM
- Define how a subset of DPSF infrastructure will be carved out to support developmental business incubators
- Define architecture standards relating to the PDP

[71] https://www.redhat.com/en/topics/cloud-computing/what-is-cloud-management

Business intelligence/analytics migration and implementation planning

- Establish BI leadership and team
- Develop BI service offerings
- Develop plan to migrate existing BI operations to target infrastructure
- Execute BI program

Developmental business lifecycle implementation

- Establish developmental business incubators—governance, teams, technology support
- Build portfolios
- Implement dedicated infrastructure subset
- Migrate artifacts and data for existing development businesses
- Initiate performance monitoring, management and reporting
- Execute developmental projects

Partner development platform

- Establish partnership enablement team
- Establish enabling platform and infrastructure
- Establish opportunity portfolio
- Define service offerings
- Define implementation program
- Execute program

HOW RISKS ARE REFLECTED IN THE PROGRAM

Given how essential success in its Digital Transformation program is to its future, HiC is intent on balancing speed with avoiding debt. We discussed technical debt earlier. It is the sub-optimality of things that get built in haste and which create a need for excessive investment or impediment to change, downstream. In addition to technical debt, there are other forms, such as organizational debt, that result from similar hasty implementation.

HiC is taking an architect, design, implement approach to try to avoid this. It is planning to evaluate its options carefully and create a versatile and plastic design for what it will become, which it will prepare it to execute before plunging into implementation. It is very cognizant of the difference between Agile and agility and realizes that business agility is the result of architecture and design, not rapid software iteration.

In the first phase of its program HiC will:

- Create a communication plan to address cultural issues. Failure to overcome cultural inertia could doom HiC's transformation program from the outset.

- Appoint or acquire a Chief Digital Transformation officer, an executive who will represent HiC's business interests and who can muster support within the company when it is required.
- Establish a Change Management team and initiate the process of assertively controlling the progress of the program and accumulating the information necessary to identify issues and analyze and report on performance.
- Define and institute transformation governance processes. This will involve division executives in the process early and continuously reinforce their commitment to transformation responsibilities.
- Initiate the organization redesign process, which will reinforce the culture of change HiC is trying to create. It will also inform the process of identifying skill requirements.
- Initiate the process of defining and implementing training and upskilling requirements. By beginning this process early, HiC will position itself to stay ahead of its needs as they develop and evolve.
- Focusing on architecture and design of the DPSF and the pillars on which it is dependent. HiC has identified that Product Management is an area that is intrinsic to its digital success and is one that will require substantial change. Therefore, HiC is dedicating resources and early attention to this area.
- Instantiating several architectural SME teams. Architecture is critical to HiC's success, and it will stand up several teams to collect and analyze the information needs to design the program it will execute. These groups include a variety of technical SMEs, EAs, BAs, KM specialists, and BPM specialists.
- Compiling a detailed WIP inventory. To avoid unnecessary redundancy and avoid working at cross-purposes, HiC will compile a comprehensive Work In Progress inventory and map it to the initiatives it will define for the program.
- Create the framework of a comprehensive program plan. HiC's Change Management Team, which will act as the transformation Program Management Office (PMO), will produce a master program plan and schedule, which will include extensive documentation of risks and assumptions that must be monitored and managed.

In the second phase of the program, HiC will:

- Operationalize the Change Management processes, which include automated progress reporting to the degree possible, to enable it to ensure that required information is collected and processed properly. While this may represent overhead on the program in its initial stages, it will protect against technical and other forms of debt as well as centralize a source of data that will facilitate reporting.
- Produce architectural deliverables that will be required to design and implement Capabilities and Enablers. Spending the time to do this is

another way technical debt will be minimized and also provides for validation of assumptions on which designs and implementation plans were predicated.

- Focus on the Digital Products and Services Factory, API Management Capabilities and OI first. The DPSF is one of the most visible pieces of HiC's transformation and it is most dependent on API Management and the OI. However, it is possible to implement some of it in semi-isolation without compromising its architecture while delivering progress that can be demonstrated to the organization.
- Allow its BI/A capabilities to continue as they have been until it is prepared to provide the resources necessary to migrate them to the to-be state.

In the third phase of the program, HiC will:

- Define BI/A architecture and process standards, which are partially dependent on OI and SRE architectures, and implement the to-be version of them. Holding off until this phase will obviate technical debt.
- Implement support for development business teams. This is likely to involve a subset of PM components and implementing it at this point will help avoid redundancy.
- Define the technical architecture and processes in support of the PDP and stand up a PM team to operate it.

In aggregate, HiC is addressing risks in its program by:

- Paying attention to cultural and organizational issues and challenges.
- Ensuring executive and senior management buy-in and participation.
- Taking an architect, design, implement approach to minimize technical redundancy and waste.
- Standing up the teams and processes necessary to direct and manage the program before jumping into execution.
- Identifying opportunities to implement and begin operating components of the pillars before they are completed, to achieve benefits while remaining consistent with the defined target architecture.
- Staging implementation of components to maximize benefits without overtaxing the organization.

CASE 2 SUMMARY

This case presents an abbreviated version of what an end-to-end digital transformation looks like when it is predicated on the EA- and BA-driven disciplines that we recommend in conjunction with AERM.

HiC's prospective transformation began with an as-is EA model in which its important Capabilities and Enablers were identified and linked to the

Products and Services they support. This essentially allowed HiC to identify what it does and how it does it.

Then, a to-be EA was defined. This was informed by HiC's strategy and mapped onto the six pillars of the Digital Company.

Subsequently, HiC performed a gap analysis between the as-is and to-be architectures to identify the initiatives required to become the company depicted in the to-be model. These initiatives were incorporated into the transformation portfolio repository for analysis.

Then HiC analyzed the initiatives in the portfolio to develop a program plan for implementing them. The plan was defined in three phases:

- In the **Foundational Phase,** HiC will instantiate mostly Enablers—teams, technology and processes required to perform detailed analysis, design and implementation requirements for to-be Capabilities and Enablers. An important objective of this phase is to establish governance processes that will be required throughout the transformation program and into steady-state (to the degree that is possible) to-be operations.
- In the **first Program Execution Phase,** HiC will execute analysis and design initiatives:
  - Technical Architecture
  - Enterprise and Business Architecture
  - Knowledge Management and Taxonomy
  - Business Process Mining

  and execute a number of implementations:

  - Digital Products and Services Factory Enablers
  - Elements of the Operational Infrastructure migration and implementation
  - API Management
- In the **second Program Execution Phase,** HiC will execute additional analysis and design initiatives relating to the remaining pillars and execute on their implementation:
  - Technical Architecture
  - Business Intelligence/Analytics
  - Business Development (incubator) Lifecycle Enablement
  - Partner Development Platform

Chapter 6

Integration

Executing your digital transformation and integrating Agile ERM

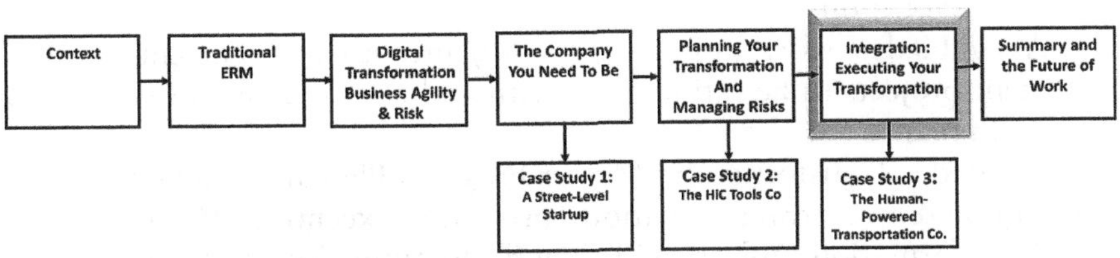

COVERED IN THIS CHAPTER

- **In the starting blocks—where you should be at this point.** You have done a lot of preparatory work to get you to where you now are. You have articulated your business strategy, constructed a prioritized portfolio of transformation initiatives, assembled expert teams, produced numerous work products that you will employ throughout the course of your transformation and thereafter and initiated management processes to monitor and guide your program and ongoing operations.
- **The *disciplines and competences* you will require,** which fall into three areas:
  - Those that enable digital adoption and will persist into ongoing operations when the program is completed,
  - Those required to enable Agile Enterprise Risk Management (AERM) and
  - Those required to execute and manage the transformation process.
- **The business *management and governance processes* you will need** to monitor and manage your transformation and operate your in-transition and to-be company.
- **Implementing the AERM process** and linking it to your ongoing business and management processes.
- **Monitoring and measuring your overall progress,** making course corrections when you need to.

DOI: 10.1201/9781003188605-7

The chapter following this one contains the final case study: The Human-Powered Transportation Company (HPTCo), which illustrates topics from this and earlier chapters.

AB INITIO

At this point, you have clearly already done a fair amount of work. Ideally, you should have:

- Elaborated and documented your strategy to inform the priorities of your execution,
- Assembled a work-in-progress (WIP) inventory of current development projects to be rationalized with and consolidated into your program plan,
- Created a Transformation Master Program Plan and Schedule
- Appointed a transformation program executive (Chief Digital Transformation Officer) with significant authority and the backing of your company's executive management and its board,
- Assembled a Change Management team, which will act in two capacities:
    - Transformation Project Management Organization (PMO) and
    - Operational overseer with responsibility for ensuring compliance with all transformation processes, especially with respect to collecting and preserving data generated by program and operational activities.
- Identified and assigned program leads for the pillars that you have prioritized,
- Identified your governance and management processes and defined the path along which they will evolve to manage your transformation and ultimately be integrated into your ongoing operations,
- Defined an organizational transformation plan, including:
    - Communication plan,
    - Education and training plan,
    - Staff acquisition and augmentation plan and
    - Staff reallocation and reorganization plan.
- Stood up architectural and SME teams:
- Cloud migration and operations management
- Technical solutions (especially for cloud-native applications)
    - Agile Development, CI/CD. DevOps, Site Reliability Engineering (SRE)
    - Business Intelligence and Analytics
    - Enterprise and Business Architecture

    - Knowledge Management, Taxonomy
    - Business Process Management
    - Organizational Design and Development, Change Management
    - Education and Training
- Created initial as-is and to-be enterprise architecture (EA)/business architecture (BA) models and
- Developed an initial taxonomy and implemented the foundation of the Pattern Library.

This may not all be in place immediately upon starting your transformation program. You may have people wearing multiple hats, especially in some of the technical areas and some of your planning and design work may be very preliminary. This is OK, so long as you prioritize efforts to bring them to the level you need them to be to inform and manage your work.

Transformation and operational disciplines

We'll assume that your priorities are similar to those of HiC Tools, i.e., you are going to focus on implementing the OI, API, DPSF and some of the Distributed Governance pillars and leave the formalization of your BI/A and PDP pillars for downstream. Then, as you kick off your transformation initiatives, these are the disciplines you should have in place and functioning:

Disciplines enabling digital transformation

Discipline	*Pillar(s)*	*Who?*
Current Phase:		
Cloud Migration and Operations, Infrastructure Management	Operational Infrastructure (OI)	Operations Team
API Management	API Services (API)	Architecture and Operations Teams
Value-Stream Product Management	Digital Products and Services Factory (DPSF)	Product Management Integrated Teams
Agile, DevOps, CI/CD, SRE	DPSF	Product Management Integrated Teams
Technical and Solution Architecture	OI, API, DPSF	CTO office, Architecture and Operations Teams
Business Process Management	All	BPM Team
Distributed Governance Policies	All	Executive Management, Division Management, Product Management

Discipline	*Pillar(s)*	*Who?*
Subsequent Phase(s):		
Artificial Intelligence, Machine Learning	Business Intelligence / Analytics (BI/A)	Business Intelligence / Analytics Team
Digital Partner Services	Partner Development Platform (PDP)	Product Management Integrated Teams
Developmental Business Incubators	DPSF	Integrated Product Management Teams

Disciplines enabling Agile Enterprise Risk Management

Discipline	*Pillar(s)*	*Who?*
Current Phase:		
Strategy Formulation and Scenario Analysis	All	Executive Management, Division Management, Product Management
Road mapping	All	Executive Management, Division Management, Product Management, CTO, Architecture Management Teams
Enterprise and Business Architecture	All	EA and BA Team
Knowledge Management	All	KM Team
Governance	All	Board, Executive Management, ERM, Compliance, Internal Audit

Disciplines for managing transformation

Discipline	*Pillar(s)*	*Who?*
Current Phase:		
Transformation Management and Governance	All	Chief Digital Transformation Officer (CDTO)
Program and Project Management	All	Change Management Team
Monitoring Transformation Program Outcomes	All	Executive and Division Management, CDTO

MANAGEMENT AND GOVERNANCE PROCESSES FOR TRANSFORMATION AND ONGOING OPERATIONS

Monitoring and management processes for transformation execution

Transformation is not something that will end when the goals identified in your program are achieved and initiatives and activities cease. You will transform your company continuously in the course of its ongoing operation as you keep pace with the evolving environment in which you operate. While you will delegate authority to invest in initiatives, you must be able to ensure that the work your teams are doing is consistent with your strategic intent and is being executed competently.

You will implement the following processes to monitor and manage the inception and progress of your transformation initiatives:

- **Program and Initiative Design, Funding and Inception**
  Although your digital company should have delegated some autonomy over investment decisions, there do need to be guidelines and limits about what types and sizes of programs and initiatives can be undertaken without executive or board oversight. The company needs policies and processes in place to review and approve initiatives that transcend certain limits, which will create the opportunity to assess and manage risks of all types.
- **Program and Initiative Progress Monitoring, Management and Reporting**
  You must have processes in place to monitor and manage work that is being done to transform the company. However, this does not mean that all work must be formalized and reported on in detail. New features and functions of existing Products or Services can be left to the oversight of the Product Management (PM) teams that are implementing them but initiatives that will produce new Capabilities or Enablers that might be shared and reused, should be evaluated and reviewed. Some level of oversight by architecture SMEs is necessary to prevent avoidable technical debt.
- **Continuous Improvement, Retrospective Performance Assessment**
  Continuous improvement is an important enabler of your ongoing competitiveness and business agility. Every aspect of your company's management processes and initiative execution should be subjected to a reasonable level of retrospective review and scrutiny for opportunities to improve performance. In most cases, this can be as simple as assembling the appropriate team and asking and answering these four questions:
  - What was supposed to have happened?
  - What did happen?
  - What explains the difference if there was any?
  - What should we do differently next time?

    Clearly, evaluating the outcome of a major strategic decision, like entering a new market with new or redesigned products, will require greater analysis than looking at why an initiative overran its parameters. However, this framework is surprisingly robust and can yield valuable insight if it is applied conscientiously, objectively and in a blame-free environment.
- **Change Management**
  As you execute initiatives, you will be transforming and creating changes in your company's enterprise and business architecture

and, possibly, your technology infrastructure, as well. The intention to make such changes must be communicated to appropriate SME groups upfront so that they can be properly vetted and accommodated in your repositories, knowledge bases and taxonomies. When information is added to or modified in your EA repository, it should be treated as a triggering event that initiates governance tasks, such as risk management, when it is appropriate. This triggering and response process is the essence of AERM and will contribute to agility in other governance disciplines, as well.

- **Digital Transformation Program Progress Monitoring and Management** The Chief Digital Transformation Officer (CDTO) should be reporting regularly on the status of the overall digital transformation. It will be valuable to report on the progress of each of the digital company pillars—OI, API, DPSF, BI/A, PDP—and Governance.

Transformation program outcome monitoring and management processes

As your company moves away from monitoring 'projects' to ensure that they are remaining within scope, time and cost parameters, you should implement processes to monitor how well initiatives are delivering on the business outcomes they are expected to enable or produce. This will steer you toward managing the delivery of value as well as document important experience that can inform what you do in the future and how you do it. Continuous improvement is an important goal of all transformational work.

It's important to keep in mind that the objective of your transformation is not to implement a bunch of technology and create new processes and job roles; it's to achieve business outcomes. Examples of these are mentioned in the section ***Analyze transformation portfolio and develop transformation program*** as a predicate to designing your transformation program, specifically with respect to sequencing activities.

There is no dearth of guidance about measuring transformation outcomes on sites across the Internet. There is some thoughtful advice about it in this article from The Digital Transformation People.[1] It's fairly easy to achieve progress in defining and building things and delude yourself into believing you're transforming your company and improving your competitiveness. This parallels the syndrome Eric Ries describes in *The Lean Startup*, which we discussed earlier. Budding entrepreneurs focus on product development, with which they may be comfortable, but never expose the product to a representative sample of their intended market and learn too late that no one is interested in what they have worked so hard on. In much the same

[1] https://www.thedigitaltransformationpeople.com/channels/delivery/measuring-digital-transformation/

way, corporate executives and transformation program managers thrill to the progress of individual initiatives being completed but don't really learn until they have spent years and $Millions whether their investments are actually paying off.

Keep in mind that how you describe and define outcomes invariably incorporates inherent assumptions. For instance, say one of your near-term transformation goals is to improve customer satisfaction. You decide that you will measure this by changes in your Net Promoter Score (NPS)[2] which is determined by polling a number of your customers and subtracting the percentage of those that would not recommend your product from the number of them that would. The assumption inherent in this is that this is an indicator of your customer loyalty and equates with higher sales and profitability, which is, after all, your real goal.

One of the easier ways to engender customer loyalty is to over-deliver on value or services to the point of unprofitability. If you are willing to sell a commodity product at a loss, you will probably develop a following of people happy to buy from you. One of my business school professors once said that he could build a $Billion business in a matter of weeks. "All you have to do," he said, "is sell dollar bills for 99 cents." Profits in the loss-leader scenario, needless to say, are elusive. It is incumbent on you to discern what is outcome and what is cause and ensure that you don't expend your energy and resources on things that don't produce the actual outcomes you're aiming for.

Customer loyalty is a commendable achievement, but it does not make your interest payments or fund your stock buyback or the dividends you would like to pay your shareholders; profits do. Be cognizant of which of your objectives are intermediate goals and which are your ultimate goals. How you choose to measure these things and how and how often you analyze your company's performance and test your assumptions can determine whether you will be able to recognize whether you are making actual progress or spending a lot of time and resources and deluding yourself.

So, what are the ultimate business goals that should inform the hierarchy of monitoring your outcomes? According to Milton Friedman, shareholder value creation is the only thing that should drive a company's business activities.[3] Stakeholder, employee and societal interests are obviously important, but Friedman's view is that these would be best served by companies that focus on creating shareholder value. We will ignore this for the purpose of this discussion—they are another book.

Now, shareholder value creation is the final result of a long chain of causes and effects. We discussed the Market Share Growth Model in the

2 https://en.wikipedia.org/wiki/Net_Promoter

3 https://en.wikipedia.org/wiki/Friedman_doctrine

earlier section ***Invention and Innovation***, which assumed a positive correlation between market share and profitability. So, it's one reasonable business goal for your transformation. It may not be the long-term bedrock foundation of value creation that it once was, but there's still a positive correlation between the two.

I have been touting business agility as *the* goal for your transformed business. Obviously, it's not the only goal but I would make the case that it contributes mightily to all others.

At this point, it seems worthwhile to revisit the subject of business agility. As we've discussed, it does not equate with Agile software development, other than superficially. Agile software methodologies provide for defining or evolving a project deliverable (often referred to as 'the product') as the 'product owner' evolves his or her idea of what it should be. If an Agile software development project is inserted into a traditional project management approach under legacy funding, then the outcome is constrained within the scope, time and cost envelope originally set for it. The result is that the owner and the development team end up handcuffed to each other in a zero-sum game. The owner wants as much functionality as he or she can get and the developers want to remain within the original parameters (unless, of course, they can get the product owner to execute a change order that increases them). This has been referred to as Water-Scrum-Fall,[4] a snide but not-inaccurate reference to an Agile project in a Waterfall wrapper. It's not a path to business agility.

Here are some capabilities that will create business agility:

- The ability to build, modify and release products and services iteratively, evolving them at speed,
- The ability to incorporate and integrate new technologies in your company's operations rapidly and with minimal staff resistance,
- The ability to optimize and adapt to revised business processes rapidly and with minimal staff resistance,
- The ability to acquire and develop staff and skills rapidly,
- The ability to understand customers' motivations and behavior and exploit this knowledge to create or customize products or services for them,
- The ability to detect and act on patterns in the markets in which your company competes and respond to threats and opportunities rapidly and
- The ability to identify and attract potential partners and implement profitable partnerships rapidly.

[4] https://stefanedbrittain.medium.com/the-insidious-institutionalisation-of-water-scrum-fall-4af7de8865b9

Having identified your target business outcomes, then, the transformation program management team, either the CDTO or the Change Management team should report at reasonable intervals on the following framework:

- **Business Outcome Goal**
  What is the goal? e.g., increase product evolution velocity,
- **Measurement Metric**
  How will the company's performance relative to the goal be measured? e.g., interval between releases of updated software functionality, diminishing backlog of features or functions awaiting development and deployment.
- **Current Metric Value**
  What value is currently achieved? e.g., two releases per month.
- **Metric Target**
  What value is targeted? e.g., three releases per day.
- **Targeted Outcome Achievement Timeframe**
  The point in the program plan or the date by which it is expected that this goal will be achieved.
- **Dependencies on Transformation Program Objectives**
  On what does making progress toward the goal depend? e.g., implementing Value Stream PM processes and CI/CD technology and processes.
- **Assumptions**
  What assumptions underlie the goals, targets and dependencies associated with this outcome? e.g., the ability to deliver software rapidly will make the company more competitive in the marketplace or it will enable the company to increase the throughput of the developmental product pipeline.
- **Problems or Issues**
  Is there anything that is adversely impacting the progress toward this outcome? e.g., we do not currently practice DevOps, CI/CD software development.
- **Status**
  What is the status of the progress toward achieving the goal and the various dependencies that will determine whether the outcome will be achieved on time?

Operational management and governance processes

The processes covered, above, relate to your transformation—the first set for monitoring and managing its execution and the second for monitoring whether you are achieving the business goals underlying the whole endeavor. You're committing a lot of time and resources on your transformation, not to mention building a foundation for your company's future success, and there's no cut and dried straight line between what your spending and the results you're hoping to achieve. As this is a long process, you must continually test to ensure that you are on a viable trajectory and be prepared to course correct whenever you find yourself veering off your path.

As you progress, you will need to migrate your operating processes to be consistent with your new digital incarnation. This will take place over time, as you execute more and more of the transformation program. However, many, if not most, of your existing processes will not change substantially. If you manufacture physical goods, processes associated with fabrication may not change even while some associated with managing it, such as scheduling production, may change a lot.

The processes covered below are the management processes that are most closely related to digital business capabilities and AERM.

Product development processes

Value-stream Product Management

Value-Stream PM incorporates processes that are executed within the scope of Aktiasolutions' Lean Product Management Lifecycle[5]:

- **Ideation,** in which you develop prospective business ideas
- **Exploration,** in which you explore them in enough detail to determine their viability
    - **Product-Solution fit** focuses on determining whether a contemplated product will solve a problem that will motivate consumers to buy. Building a solution in search of a problem is a sure-fire way to not succeed. (See this article from Studiozao[6] for more information.)
    - **Product-Market fit** (see this Wikipedia article[7]), in which you validate that your product is in a viable market
- **Execution,** in which you release your product into the marketplace, where it will naturally undergo three phases of life:
    - **Grow,** as it achieves consumer uptake, sales volume and increasing market share
    - **Sustain,** as it maintains steady state sales levels
    - **Retire,** as it loses traction or becomes obsolete

Whereas most processes have concrete and observable results—something physical is created or a case is routed for further processing—Value Stream or Lean PM is a series of iterations through which a product or service concept is materialized, evaluated for feasibility, embedded in a business model

[5] https://aktiasolutions.com/lean-product-management-methodology/

[6] https://studiozao.com/resources/what-is-problem-solution-fit-and-how-to-achieve-it-lean

[7] https://en.wikipedia.org/wiki/Product/market_fit

and eventually brought to market. Your company and your PM teams will have to adopt lifecycles and build stage-gated processes around them to guide the product development process. It may be different for each division or even each product group, but you should have a defined process to ensure that product development concerns are addressed comprehensively.

Rapid product evolution and delivery

For digital products, Agile, CI/CD and SRE are applied to development and evolution. You require standardized approaches and tooling to ensure consistent and predictable results as you develop and deploy new versions of your software. Hopefully, you will have selected tools that are consistent with the way that you would like to work because inconsistencies can bog your development down considerably.

Site Reliability Engineering (SRE)

You adopt SRE to maintain the highest possible service levels for your customers. You will require processes that cut across your development pipeline and your service team to ensure that you achieve the service levels you have targeted.

Developmental product portfolio management

The development product portfolio should be managed in a lean fashion, much the same as your existing product portfolio. However, a management process should be applied to grow, develop and prune the portfolio as prospective products progress through the lifecycle. The process should include such things as regular portfolio reviews and rebalancing to maintain an appropriate overall risk level.

Operational management and governance processes

IT operations management

IT operations management is a broad and diverse set of disciplines, especially when public or hybrid clouds are involved, that requires a suite of processes to ensure consistent and cost-effective operations. Many of these processes are excellent candidates for automation, by the way.

Change management

Change Management, as reflected in the EA and other repositories, is at the heart of agile governance. It is critical that any process that may produce changes to the metadata in them is tied to a companion reporting process that alerts relevant governance teams to a new or changed entity that requires attention. In the case of risk management, this might mean that each new Capability or Enabler or any that become newly attached to other entities be scrutinized and risk managed.

Technology management

This is the purview of the Chief Technology Officer's (CTO) team, who should also be responsible for most of the architecture SME teams. Technology evolution is accelerating rapidly and almost always leads businesses' applications by quite a bit. According to this Deloitte article,[8] Blockchain technology has considerable promise and is said to be poised to become much more widely used but it is still quite early in its integration, even though it has been around in something approximating its current form since 2008 (see the Wikipedia article[9]). This Harvard Business Review article from 2017[10] provides some useful perspective on technology adoption in general and Blockchain, in particular.

To the degree that early adoption of new technology can create inside-out opportunities to beat your competitors to market with new products or services, it is crucial that your company monitor the market for emerging technology and tools that you might exploit for competitive advantage.

Business process management

Updating and automating business processes to increase efficiency and consistent execution is a major goal of your digital transformation. Process re-engineering and automation is a specialized discipline and automation, where it is applied, yields substantial amounts of performance information that can be analyzed to identify opportunities to streamline and consolidate processes. Optimizing processes requires dedicated data collection, compilation and vigilance and, thus, oversight and management processes.

Human resource management: staff availability, utilization, acquisition

Staff with requisite skill sets and experience are and will continue to be a strategic asset, which will need to be managed carefully. You must maintain an inventory of your staff and their skills and experience, the assignments on which they are currently working and their presumed availability for new assignments. You will also need to maintain an inventory of planned initiatives and the staffing requirements for them. Finally, you will need to keep track of where it may be possible to upskill staff to fill upcoming requirements.

As you plan for and approve initiatives and make decisions regarding technology standards and processes, a huge element of your transformation

8 https://www2.deloitte.com/us/en/pages/consulting/articles/blockchain-adoption-by-industry.html

9 https://en.wikipedia.org/wiki/Blockchain

10 https://hbr.org/2017/01/the-truth-about-blockchain

program but also an ongoing operational concern, you will need to update your staffing requirements to reflect them. Change Management processes are the right place to source this information and you must have a process in place to ensure that up-to-date data is available to whoever is managing talent acquisition for your company.

IMPLEMENTING AGILE ERM

Before addressing AERM, it is worth reiterating what makes it agile and what makes ERM as traditionally practiced not agile. Traditional ERM is often practiced on a periodic basis—risk assessments are conducted annually or every quarter and maybe only for a subset of the company at a time. This makes the process retrospective and reactive. Depending on how risks are identified, some may be missed, which makes the whole process less than comprehensive.

AERM is designed to avoid both failings. Because it is tied to a repository of prospective or highly current metadata, risk managers should be aware of potential new or changing risks as they are developing, not after they are already attached to things that have been implemented. Thus, no missed risks and timely opportunity to address them.

Implementing AERM requires, then, several precursors and a set of operational and retrospective processes. It is presumed that you will have already implemented most of these during the digital transformation in which you are probably already engaged. Therefore, implementing AERM need not be a from-scratch proposition.

Precursors

To implement and operate AERM, you will need the following in place:

- The working enterprise and business architecture model,
- A set of operational processes that ensure the EA/BA mode is maintained. This should be overseen by the Change Management team.
- The Taxonomy, which will ensure the data in the EA/BA model and other repositories is consistently tagged and therefore useful and usable,
- Knowledge Management Processes that ensure that data flowing into your company's metadata repositories are categorized and tagged properly.
- Transfer, or linkage and consolidation of risks from the existing risk register to the new repository that will correlate them with Capabilities and Enablers, the basis on which most of them will be monitored going forward.

AERM operational processes

Once the elements on which it depends are in place, AERM requires processes to execute on its responsibilities:

- Processes for monitoring the relevant repositories, recognizing and then acting on triggering events.
- Triage—RM must have a process to prioritize and perform initial evaluation of events to identify their scope and the urgency with which they should be addressed.
- Evaluation and analysis—RM should have a standard approach to risk appraisal and treatment and control formulation.
- Propagation of controls—RM requires a standard process for disseminating and activating the treatments and controls it determines are necessary.
- Compliance monitoring—your company must have a process for monitoring compliance with the policies and controls it defines and enacts.

Retrospective processes

ERM will require a few retrospective processes, some event-driven, some periodic, that it will execute to facilitate continuous improvement:

- Retrospective evaluation will address all actions taken by ERM over a prior period to assess the effectiveness and value of its work. This is intended to surface opportunities to improve along any of the measurable dimensions that your company applies to its ERM efforts. This process can be executed on a schedule or an as-needed basis.
- Risk Audit and Risk Assurance are performed on a regular basis to assess how ERM is performing with respect to several measures, as described earlier in the chapter *Traditional Enterprise Risk Management*. The difference between the two is that Risk Audit may be performed by internal auditors or other staff and Risk Assurance is usually performed by external auditors, who provide an opinion to the company's executive management and board. AERM is entirely consistent with the input requirements of both processes.

MEASURING YOUR PROGRESS

Transformation is a process, which you've partitioned into individual initiatives. You can monitor them to see how they're progressing easily enough, but the return on the investment you've made in them must be evaluated against the assumptions and expectations you started with.

Over the course of your transformation, it is critical that you revisit and reconfirm the validity of your assumptions regularly. You have committed to what is probably one of the largest and most consequential investments you ever have, and you need to know whether you're heading in the right direction. You have likely taken some of the justification for what you're doing on faith. You may have intuitively felt that you needed to do this. A lot of industry pundits have told you that you need to do this. I have told you that you need to do this. A lot of the logic may have seemed a little fuzzy to you and, it was. The fact is, this is the only way that your company is going to be able to keep up with the changes that will occur constantly in the markets in which you compete. Ultimately, a crucial outcome of your transformation is to hone your ability to transform better and faster.

So, you must look at your results in the context of three layers of outcomes, which mirror the three layers of risk that we discussed earlier:

- **Strategic:** If we are achieving the functional results we expected, are they contributing to our business goals? Are savings being generated and are they flowing to the bottom line? If our new collaboration tools are attracting and being used regularly by a majority of our staff, have we reduced turnover?
- **Operational:** Are the Enablers we've implemented producing the functional results that were expected of them? For instance, is the CI/CD pipeline up and running? Are our product managers getting accustomed to value-stream PM? Are they integrating properly with the technical team that has become part of their organization? Are we seeing the accelerated iteration and maturing of our digital products we expected? Has the RPA implementation we did in the customer support area increased our processing throughput and reduced the time and staff required to manage customer cases?
- **Transformational:** How are we progressing on implementing and coordinating the elements of the program we have thus far initiated?

Answering these questions requires both data and perspective. We have discussed the need for you to identify metrics for all your objectives and goals and implement monitoring processes that will allow you to collect and evaluate them.

Here are some resources that can inform how you select what you will monitor and the metrics you will measure to do so:

- This article from McKinsey[11] identifies a number of metrics that focus on the operational and strategic objectives,

[11] https://www.mckinsey.com/business-functions/mckinsey-digital/our-insights/how-do-you-measure-success-in-digital-five-metrics-for-ceos

- This Forbes article[12] identifies a number of them that span the spectrum of the three layers,
- This presentation from Broadcom[13] provides additional perspective and
- This article from Microsoft[14] describes the process they employ to monitor their own digital transformation.

At the operational level, you should also be monitoring and assessing the evolution of your governance processes. How are you progressing with your adoption of AERM? Are you beginning to tie it and other governance processes to the data and metadata repositories maintained by the Change Management team? Have you begun to see acceleration in your risk management responses to changes as they are being made?

In every case you should be assessing what the metrics are telling you and what they may indicate about the validity of your assumptions. As Mark Twain is reputed to have said,

> It ain't what you don't know that gets you into trouble. It's what you know that just ain't so.

CHAPTER SUMMARY

Key concepts addressed in this chapter include:

- What you should have in place as you begin your transformation.
- The *disciplines* and *competences* you will require:
  - Those that enable digital adoption,
  - Those required to enable AERM and
  - Those required to execute and manage the transformation process.
- The management *and governance processes* you will need to monitor and manage:
  - Your transformation program progress,
  - Your transformation program outcomes,
  - Your ongoing operations as you progress from your current to in-transition to to-be states and
  - Your progress viz. your targeted business objectives.
- Considerations for implementing your AERM process.

[12] https://www.forbes.com/sites/forbestechcouncil/2020/06/25/14-important-kpis-to-help-you-track-your-digital-transformation

[13] https://docs.broadcom.com/doc/keeping-score-why-digital-transformation-matters-research-paper

[14] https://www.microsoft.com/en-us/itshowcase/metrics-that-matter-how-we-track-our-digital-transformation

- Monitoring and measuring your progress across three layers of concerns:
    - Strategic—the impact of your operational improvements on your company's financial performance,
    - Operational—the impact of your transformation on your operational metrics and
    - Transformational—the results of your program initiatives.

CASE 3: THE HUMAN-POWERED TRANSPORTATION COMPANY (HPTCO)

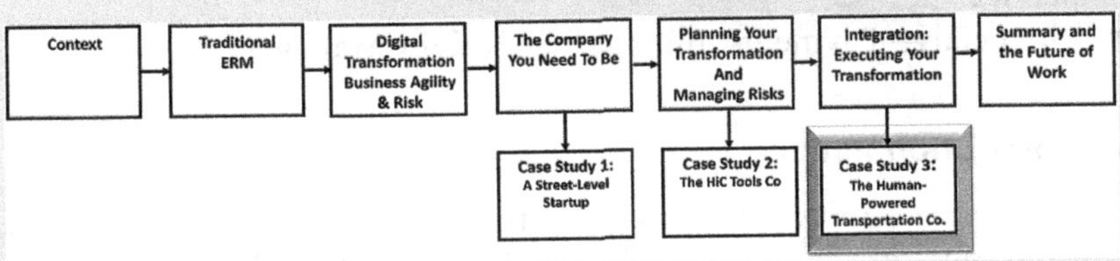

This case describes the Human Powered Transport Company (HPTCo) and some business opportunities it is considering. After reading and assimilating the information presented, we will assess the important decisions the company has to make, identify preliminary preferred alternatives and then apply risk-based thinking to revisit the decisions in light of additional perspective. What HPTCo may choose to do or how they choose to do it could change as a result of the additional review. The differences between the preliminary and revised plans and approaches should be instructive.

Overview

HPTCo makes bicycles. Currently, it has two lines—the Competition line, high-tech, very expensive bicycles which are purchased by professional bicycle racers, and the Standard line, which is purchased by bicycle-riding members of the public who are looking for a ride that is a step above mass market products. HPTCo is considering getting into the market for children's bicycles and must plan for how this could be achieved.

The lifecycle of an HPTCo bicycle

A lot goes into designing, building, selling and servicing bicycles. The tasks and processes, below, must all be performed to be in the markets that HPTCo targets:

- Product Management, Marketing, Advertising, Publicity
- Design
- Detailed Specifications (materials, tolerances, etc.)
- Parts Fabrication or Procurement
- Assembly Process Design (lay out plant and map out workstations and process path)
- Assembly Process Implementation (set up assembly plant)
- Assemble bikes
- Manage pre-assembly and finished goods Inventory and Warehouse
- Sales
- Shipping and Receiving
- Service
- Financials—Payments, Billing, Receivables Management

The competition line

These bikes are almost all customized to some extent. Some of them are completely one-off, i.e., custom designed and built to the exact specifications required for a particular rider. They are built out of exotic materials—graphite, ceramics and titanium. Professional racing versions can weigh as little as 3.5 pounds and cost more than $30,000. HPTCo currently has the capacity to produce no more than 20 of these bikes per month in an access-controlled facility that contains high-end manufacturing equipment normally associated with the aviation industry, such as computer numerical controlled (CNC) milling machines,[15] graphite ovens and extremely sensitive testing tools.

The factory is staffed with employees that are expert in a wide range of advanced, high-tech manufacturing and assembly skills. They are relatively highly paid and would be extremely difficult to replace.

The Competition Division sells all the bikes they make and has a waiting list that can vary between nine months and two years. It might be profitable to increase capacity and sell a few more bikes but HPTCo believes exclusivity and limited availability enhance the cachet of their brand, which projects onto their Standard Line bikes. In any event, the current facility is fully utilizing all available space so increasing capacity would require that they build or acquire a new facility and relocate to it.

An expensive and specialized CAD system running on HPTCo's infrastructure is used by the division's design engineers. It has a high per-seat cost, which is justified by the advanced engineering calculations that it automates, its integration with some of the plant's fabrication equipment and the time savings it enables.

The Competition Division fabricates most, but not all of the parts that go into its competition bikes. It purchases raw materials and some

[15] https://en.wikipedia.org/wiki/Numerical_control

manufactured sub-assemblies from a jealously guarded group of vendors. The Purchasing Department for the Competition division is always on the lookout for new materials, and vendors that can produce component parts from them.

The Competition Division's factory and assembly plant has its own, custom-built work management and tracking system. It's not pretty but with the relatively small volume of work moving through the plant, it's good enough. For the same reason, shipping is managed semi-manually; manufacturing workers enter shipping information into a system that integrates with their shipping vendors', captures acknowledgments throughout the transit process, prints labels and some reports and not much more. Because Competition bikes are manufactured to order and shipped as soon as they're completed, there is minimal need for finished goods warehouse space, though some is needed for pre-assembly parts inventory.

HPTCo markets Competition bikes mostly to the small group of professional bike racers and the people who manage the teams for whom they ride. They advertise only in industry trade magazines and appear at trade shows only a few times a year. Mostly, HPTCo's Competition Division brings in business from existing customers and word of mouth. They have an excellent reputation among the highest-end clients and that suffices for them to sell all the competition bikes they can make. The sales staff supporting the Competition Division are order-takers more than they are sales representatives. Orders come to them more than they have to go out looking for them and are entered by hand into a rudimentary custom system that is little more than a spreadsheet with some macros.

HPTCo employs a SaaS ERP system that automates procurement, purchasing, payment processing, inventory management, billing, receivables and accounting functions. It's not the most sophisticated system available, but it suffices for the division's needs. It is rather expensive, however, but finding a replacement is not particularly high on anyone's list of things to do.

Finally, HPTCo operates a web site that is mostly a brochure site—more for promotional purposes than e-commerce. There are plenty of pictures, stories and posts on the site, but no bikes are sold on it. Accessories and logo goods are, however. Sales of these items are managed through a third party, who operates the web store connected to the site, and takes a hefty cut of the sales it generates.

The standard line

HPTCo's Standard bikes are made of high-quality materials, such as aluminum and lightweight steel tubes, have a number of features that echo those that appear on some Competition bikes and can be configured and customized at the specialty shops where they are sold. HPTCo decided early in its life that it would be better served to sell Standard bikes through specialty retailers rather than over the web, through its own dealer network or through mass-market retailers, such as toy chains or big-box retailers, such as Walmart or Target. Although retail markets are evolving rapidly, this is not a decision that can be easily changed at a moment's notice.

Unlike Competition bikes, Standard bikes face price competition from many other manufacturers. Being the 'little brother' of the famous HPTCo Competition Division allows HPTCo to charge enough to maintain a healthy margin on Standard products but it cannot count on this to be the case forever. The Standard division must maintain a close eye on costs and manage its profitability carefully. After all, more than 80% of the company's profits are generated by Standard products.

The Standard division employs a SaaS CAD system that allows it to share design specifications and work collaboratively with many of its suppliers to support its own design engineers. It works very well for them, overall.

In contrast to Competition bikes, Standard bikes are composed of subassemblies (such as entire frames and gear cartridges) rather than custom-fabricated parts. Most of the frames are constructed of welded aluminum or lightweight steel tubes and provided by vendors who produce them to HPTCo's specifications. Therefore, the plant in which Standard bikes are assembled contains very limited fabrication equipment and few staff with fabrication capabilities—only enough to address some supplier production errors or assembly mishaps.

Standard bikes are produced in a facility separate and remote from the Competition bike facility. HPTCo currently utilizes about 60% of the facility's capacity between manufacturing and warehousing and can produce up to 3,000 standard bikes in various sizes and configurations (stock-keeping units, or SKUs) per month. The division makes every effort to limit finished goods inventory to no more than two month's production and pre-assembly component inventory to no more what is needed for one month's predicted production requirements. If these inventory levels are exceeded, it will push Standard's footprint beyond the 60% of the plant that it is currently using and HPTCo is trying to avoid that to maintain flexibility. Generally, Standard has been successful in meeting these goals, exceeding them only in rare circumstances and then only for very limited periods.

The Standard division operates a purchased and heavily customized work order management system that is tied to its order entry and inventory systems on its own infrastructure. This system is used by the plant controllers to schedule and monitor work in the plant.

The Standard bike division shares the ERP system with the Competition division, which is adequate for its needs, though more expensive than it would like.

As opposed to the Competition division, the Standard division actively monitors its shipping costs, employs several competing shipping suppliers, has a number of staff dedicated to logistics and a home-built shipping management system that integrates with each of the suppliers' and can automate the process of requesting and assessing bids for shipping needs as they arise. Orders usually comprise 20 to 100 units or more at a time and are shipped in either large crates or shipping containers via common carriers.

The HPTCo website also serves the Standard division. It is used by them in the same way that it is by the Competition division—as something of an on-line brochure with no e-commerce capabilities except for accessories and logo gear.

Opportunities and challenges: the children's division and digital transformation

HPTCo has recognized an opportunity to sell children's bikes and is evaluating options in preparation for finalizing the product line and planning how it will prepare to do so. At the same time, HPTCo realizes that it will have to undergo a digital transformation to remain competitive in its existing and prospective markets.

To evaluate the new division opportunity, HPTCo will have to answer both WHAT and HOW questions and take into consideration how the changes it will make to build the new division can be integrated with the changes it will make to execute digital transformation. This can be a complicated and recursive process in which changes needed to meet objectives for the Children's Division impact on those required for digital transformation and vice-versa. This can create a fuzzy vision for the to-be architecture and an impediment to determining a concrete path for going forward. It can be one of the biggest challenges a company can face in contemplating substantial changes to its EA—the need to balance time, costs and risks. Costs can be minimized, and timelines shortened by taking large steps from as-is to what is currently thought to be the long-term to-be. However, it amplifies risks and can ultimately delay realization of a to-be state by introducing issues that are not apparent at the outset of the program, but which reveal themselves as it progresses.

Earlier, we mentioned the validity of a strategy that incorporates intermediate states between as-is and to-be. In programming, infinite loops are often created by recursive processes in which state changes are executed by one process and then undone by another. The way these loops are broken when they are detected is to randomly kill one of the processes. HPTCo will have to pursue similar strategies in some cases by enabling new Capabilities with existing Enablers that don't match the to-be planned architecture, in order to eliminate the risks inherent in building something where the business model is in flux with technology that is, also.[16] When one or the other (or both, preferably) have settled into a stable state, then the situation can be resolved. This may take longer and cost more but it is decidedly lower risk.

[16] This is one of the places in which APIs can play a huge role. An existing system can be hidden behind an API and replaced later with one that meets to-be architectural standards.

HPTCo will employ the four-level EA schematic model to explore issues and options for how to go forward.

Strategic level

HPTCo is pursuing a growth strategy by looking to implement a new division and a sustainability and growth strategy by pursuing a digital transformation. It firmly believes that the market for Children's bikes provides an opportunity that will be profitable in its own right, but which will also serve as a conduit for the Standard line as younger riders grow up. HPTCo is considering a trade-in, trade-up program to encourage Children's customers to make that transition when the time comes.

After performing market research, HPTCo has developed expectations about the prospects for sales in the Standard and Children's markets over the next three years. These figures will have implications on the options available to HPTCo for the divisions' operating models and operational architectures, mainly with regard to whether to share the Standard factory, acquire a separate one for the Children's Division or identify a different solution for Children's bike assembly.

HPTCo has conducted a statistical analysis of how the aggregation of these two divisions in the Standard plant could play out. This is presented in the section on operational risks, below.

Business model level

HPTCo wants to ensure that the Children's line will be profitable from the outset or as close to it as possible. In that regard:

- What Children's bike characteristics will sell best?
- How can costs be constrained?
- Is it worth seeking marketing partnerships with toy or media brands?
- What digital services can it provide? Does it have the abilities required to define, create, validate and deliver these services?
- How can a digital customer interface and services enhance the Children's Division and the HPTCo brand?

In addition, it must understand implications that the new division might have on its place in the market for the bikes sold in the Competition and Standard Divisions:

- Can the digital strategies that will be employed for Children's be employed for the other two divisions?
- Can it reconcile adding an Internet sales channel for Standard bikes? What will this do to its relationships with its existing customers (bike specialty stores) and the terms on which it will be able to sell its bikes to them?

HPTCo has a symbiotic relationship with its Standard bike distributors. In addition to merely stocking and selling the bikes, they perform customizations to order, such as upgrading some of the bikes' components or adding new ones at the time of purchase. They also service the bikes, which doesn't provide revenue to HPTCo but adds to the value proposition of the products, overall. Normally, bikes require a tune up and attention to wear and tear every 12 to 18 months. While some riders can perform routine maintenance themselves, many would rather that it be done by professionals.

HPTCo must navigate these relationships carefully. If it elects to pursue factory direct sales, it must find a way to avoid cutting the current distributors out of the picture. Perhaps taking orders online and delivering locally through the existing network could work for both parties.

Operating model level

Clearly, adding a new division will necessitate changes. While it understands that it is impossible to do much in complete isolation, HPTCo is unwilling to do anything that could create significant risks in its existing operations:

- Nothing can be allowed to impair the business and operating models of the flagship Competition Division.
- The Standard Division provides 80% of HPTCo's profits. Risks associated with anything that the company might do to implement a Children's Division must be assessed with consideration given to this fact.
- Digital transformation will have to be planned and executed carefully so as to minimize disruption and maximize synchronization with the business models of both the existing and prospective divisions.
    - HPTCo must identify an approach to creating Value Streams that embody the core business processes introduced in the chapter *The company you need to be*, in the section *The anatomy of your company:*
- **Concept to Product Process Stream**
  The company must define its Children's products. Will it purchase and relabel other suppliers' products? Will it design its products to be built from available components it can purchase in the marketplace? Will it design its products from scratch and then contract fabrication, and possibly assembly, out? These are strategic and marketing decisions, but they also have impact on how HPTCo will approach the division's operating model and operational architecture.
- **Market to Customer Process Stream**
  This process will certainly influence the success of the division and will have significant influence on its operating model and operational architecture. HPTCo will have to make numerous decisions about product characteristics and how to publicize, advertise, market and sell

Children's bikes, regardless of who actually makes them and where. Ultimately, constructing and operating this value stream's business process successfully will necessitate that HPTCo coordinate its PM and operational processes carefully. It will also have to be cognizant of the financial impact of all the choices it might make in this regard.

- **Order to Cash Process Stream**
  This process is intrinsically tied to the business and operating models HPTCo elects. The company will have to implement the Capabilities required to enable the models if they do not already exist. For example, if HPTCo decides to pursue direct-to-consumer sales via the web, it will need to implement the appropriate applications on its website, a new sales order management process, new work order management processes and new shipping capabilities. Needless to say, there are new risks associated with all these things and implications for existing risks that may result from changes that HPTCo will have to make.
- **Demand to Supply Process Stream**
  This is an important area to consider. HPTCo will have to decide how to accommodate Children's manufacturing, assembly, inventory and servicing from the time the line is introduced through the first few years of operations. If both the Standard and Children's Divisions flourish, HPTCo will outgrow the Standard factory, which will create dislocation and incur expenses. The aggregate unit sales of both divisions together could fall either below or above the capacity of the factory, so risk/reward modeling and risk-based thinking must be applied to making this important decision.

All decisions made to enable the new Children's Division and to undergo a digital transformation that includes the other two divisions will have substantial implications for the Capabilities and Enablers that comprise the operational architecture

Operational architecture level

This level is where the rubber meets the road, so to speak. HPTCo will have many decisions to make, dependencies that it will have to assess and risk implications it will have to manage. It is impractical to identify and address all of them in the scope of this case study, but here are the most salient and meaningful ones:

- **Value Streams**
  - Competition's are largely fixed, even with the potential for the division to participate in digital transformation. To the degree that it shares little but the company name and its reputation with the other divisions, it should be able to continue to operate as it has for some time.

    - Standard's are subject to some change. The order to cash and demand to supply business process streams can change as a result of the implementation of the Children's Division or the digital transformation or both.
    - Children's value streams have yet to be defined and will undoubtedly have an impact on Standard's.
    - HPTCo will have to decide whether the Standard and Children's Divisions will share Value Streams and the Capabilities and Enablers that are embodied in them or operate with separate Value Streams that incorporate separate versions of some or most of their Capabilities and Enablers.
- **Capabilities**
    - To the degree that designing and building bikes isn't going to change much, some of the existing capabilities aren't going to change much, either. However, evolving business models and digital transformation will create the need for some new Capabilities and the evolution of others. For instance, a move to online sales and digital services will necessitate a variety of new Capabilities, such as Business Intelligence and Analytics, Value-Stream PM and CI/CD software development. Essentially, HPTCo will have to address all of the pillars of a digital company eventually if it is to evolve into one.
- **Enablers**
    - Aside from digital business Enablers (People, Processes, Technologies) that we have discussed previously, HPTCo will have to add or evolve Enablers for the Children's Division. Specific Enablers that HPTCo must consider include:
        - Production space for the Children's Division's assembly and inventory requirements,
        - Accommodating change in order management, shipping and collections if it elects to pursue online, direct-to-customer sales,
        - Those required to create, operate and support new digital service offerings and
        - Development of new partnerships and relationships with existing partners to offer new services collaboratively.

Risk considerations and management

In the chapter *Planning the transformation journey and managing its risks*, section *Risk management and the transformational digital enterprise* we discussed three layers of risk:

- Strategic Risk
- Operational Risk
- Transformational Risk

HPTCo will have to manage risks at all three levels as it goes forward.

Strategic risks

HPTCo is pursuing both growth and sustainability strategies by adding the Children's Division and pursuing a digital transformation. Keep in mind that business agility is a key attribute that contributes to sustainability and that digital transformation is a major contributor to that.

A question that has not been explored explicitly to this point is this: what are HPTCo's overall strategic objectives? Growth? Profitability? Business Agility? Sustainability? Other things?

Does HPTCo *have to* start the Children's Division to achieve these goals? Will it survive if it doesn't? Are there other opportunities that HPTCo could pursue that should also be considered, such as building industrial or commercial wheeled carts? Could they be more profitable?

We shall assume that since it is spending the time to evaluate the opportunity in Children's bikes, it is an appropriate and preferred option for HPTCo. However, questions such as these should be explored prior to embarking on major initiatives such as launching a new division, buying another company or undertaking enterprise-wide digital transformation.

In this case study, we will focus more on the risks in the lower layers of the model, but it is worth identifying the major risks that are of concern at this level:

- *The Children's line fails to acquire market share and, therefore, fails to generate profits and establish the on-ramp to the Standard line that HPTCo had hoped.*
- *Children's meets its sales targets but is not profitable.*
  HPTCo must determine its target return on the investment in Children's and the shortfall or losses it is willing to tolerate and for how long to achieve the results it's after.

  Children's product design and marketing will be a primary determinant of its success in the marketplace and, therefore, essential to profitability. HPTCo will adopt a *Lean Startup* approach to define and evolve Children's products incrementally, rapidly and as economically as possible before committing to going live with the division. This is *de-risking* the product line, as Strategyzer refers to it in *The Invincible Company*. Success, in this regard, is dependent on HPTCo's product managers and we will note that but focus more on operational interdependencies in this case study.
- *Implementation of the Children's Division interferes with the operations of the existing Divisions.*
  The company has already dictated the imperative that Competition and Standard Divisions' operations not be impeded or impaired by any changes that the company might make to their operations. This is a statement of risk appetite and tolerance. It is willing to invest effort, time and money to consider a new division and undergo digital

transformation to realize the benefits from it, but it has zero tolerance for disruption of existing operations.

- *Digital transformation is disruptive and fails to create the benefits and business agility that is targeted.*
- HPTCo is not successful in developing digital services that enhance their product's value propositions.

  HTPCo has identified opportunities that would be foregone, and threats associated with it not undergoing digital transformation. The possibility of failing to realize the desired return on the investment in transformation, therefore, is implicitly within its **tolerance for risk.**

With respect to each of the divisions:

- Strategically, the Competition Division is autonomous. It has a stellar brand identity and as long as it continues to invest in R&D, HPTCo assumes that it will not face material threats from competitors.
- Standard is in a more competitive market, in which it is a premium-priced provider. It needs to explore additional sales channels, the potential for digital services and alternative business models that may accompany them. If it elects to pursue direct sales via the Internet, it will have to revise its relationships with its current dealers, who are, in essence, its direct customers, customers with whom it will be placing itself in competition.
- Children's bikes is a blank page at this point but one that the company believes will have a future of its own and the potential to deliver synergy in the form of channeling customers to the Standard Division over time. The unit sales projections HPTCo is starting with are reasonably modest but their variance is wide. HPTCo will have to devise a tactical plan to enter the children's market that allows it to minimize what it has at stake at any point as it refines children's products and its business model. This is, among other things, a chance to pilot the *Lean Startup* and *Invincible Company* developmental business portfolio model that a digital company should have.

To manage *strategic-level risks*, HPTCo will, therefore:

- Continue the strategy with which it operates the Competition Division and maintain the isolation of its operations from that of the other divisions,
- Conduct a careful analysis of as-is and to-be EAs, specifically, Capabilities and Enablers, to identify and mitigate potential risks that could impact the divisions' operations and performance,
- Develop a plan to implement the Children's Division in as lean and incremental a manner as possible to minimize financial risks as it evolves and matures into at least an MVP rollout,

- Apply the best practices that we have identified to plan, execute and manage the digital transformation and
- Explicitly analyze and plan to manage interdependencies between Standard's existing operations, the Children's Division implementation and the digital transformation.

Operational risks

Operational risks will emanate and propagate from additions and changes to HPTCo's Capabilities and Enablers.

The Competition Division has limited integration with and few interdependencies on anything in the Standard Division and a similarly low level of integration with the prospective Children's Division if it is implemented. Thus, potential new or modified risks to its operations are minimal. The only risk that might present itself would result from HPTCo migrating from the ERP system that Competition and Standard currently share to a new one. In view of all the other things that might be going on, this seems like an unnecessary and low-reward project to undertake at this time, therefore.

For the time being, then, we can simplify things by focusing on the Standard and Children's Divisions in our analysis.

With respect to the Standard and Children's Divisions, here is a list of the Capabilities they require:

- Manage Products, Marketing, Advertising, Publicity
- Design Bikes
  - Produce Detailed Specifications (materials, tolerances, etc.)
- Configure factory—Design Assembly Processes (lay out plant and map out work stations and process path), update and reconfigure as required
- Implement Assembly Processes (set up assembly plant)
- Fabricate or Procure Parts
- Manage Inventory and Warehouse Capacity and Operations (where received parts go, where completed bikes go)
- Sell bikes
- Manage Customer Orders
- Manage Work Orders
- Build bikes
- Manage Shipping and Receiving
- Provide Service for bikes
- Manage Financials—Payments, Invoicing, Receivables

Questions relating to Enablers for each of the above Capabilities that are required to be in the business of Children's bikes must be addressed:

Design bikes

Who will design the products and what enabling tools will they require? Can Children's share the CAD software used by Standard? Could they consolidate and get a better deal? Should other options be considered?

Facilities—assembly, inventory, shipping, etc.

Currently, 40% of the Standard Division's plant capacity is available, which would enable Children's to produce about 1,500-2,000 units per month, depending on the exact mix of SKUs required. Will that be enough for Children's to get started? How long will Children's take to grow out of the space if it is successful? Unsuccessful? What happens if Standard suddenly needs space that Children's is using?

Parts fabrication or procurement

Will Children's bikes use industry standard, customized or a mix of parts? Who will make them for HPTCo and how much will it have to pay for them? What is the lead time and minimum purchase quantity for new or restocked parts? What options are available, such as making volume commitments and negotiating relaxed payment terms?

Sales order management, assembly, work order management, inventory

How will Children's manage its production and assembly processes? Can it share Standard's work order and assembly management system? What will happen if Children's has to relocate to a remote location because one or the other of them has run out of room in the facility?

ERP and accounting

Can Children's share the ERP system with the other two divisions? With three sets of users, might it be time to start looking for a shareable upgrade for all of them?

Marketing, sales

Children's division has to decide how it will sell and distribute its bikes. What channels will it employ and what administrative requirements do they have? What of them may be new to HPTCo? Will they sell direct to consumers through their website? How will that impact the relationship with potential retailers and the company that currently sells accessories and logo gear?

Shipping

Are there major differences in requirements for managing shipping between the Standard and Children's divisions? Should HPTCo consider employing a third-party logistics company to handle Children's bikes? Might it make sense to consolidate Standard and Children's logistics with the same company if it makes sense for Children's alone?

The lion's share of operational risks at this point, then, involve anything that might be shared by the Standard and Children's Divisions. Identifying these requires close examination of the operating model that Children's will employ and how it aligns with that of Standard's.

For instance, in the Standard operating model, parts and components are ordered and received at the plant where they are inventoried, bikes are assembled and then shipped out in lots of 20 or more units. It is not a given that this model will be echoed by Children's. One option that Children's is exploring is to have their products assembled by a supplier and shipped directly from them to retailers. Another is direct sales via the Internet.

It should also be noted that Children's could start with one operating model and transition to another as its business gains traction. Some steps HPTCo might need to take to mitigate risks associated with the Standard production facility later, might not be required early on. Depending on the expense associated with potential responses, being flexible about Children's initial business and operating models could provide some time and breathing room for experimentation and development. And, the same can be said about changes relating to the impacts on business and operating models resulting from the digital transformation.

In any case, the largest set of risks center around the Standard factory. Although not explicitly articulated to this point, transcending the factory's capacity is exactly the type of disruption for which HPTCo has no **appetite** or **tolerance**. It is also obvious that the operating models of the two divisions will have a major impact on how easy it will be to manage risks that might contribute to this and what options there might be to minimize the potential for it.

Previously, it was mentioned that HPTCo had made some estimates for three years of future sales (in units/month) for the two divisions.[17] By adding the estimates for each and calculating a *covariance* for the estimates through simulation, we can create estimates for the expected range of the utilization of the plant with both divisions operating in it:

Table CS3.1 Summary of aggregate factory utilization statistics.

	Standard Mean Demand		*Children's Mean Demand*		*Combined Mean Demand*		*Confidence Levels*			
Yr	*(units/ month)*	*Std Dev*	*(units/ month)*	*Std Dev*	*(units/ month)*	*Std Dev*	*95%*	*Range*	*99%*	*Range*
1	2,700	128	1,200	77	3,900	148	3,603	4,197	3,455	4,345
2	3,000	169	1,800	105	4,800	212	4,377	5,223	4,165	5,435
3	3,300	188	2,500	179	5,800	252	5,296	6,304	5,044	6,556

[17] It is assumed that the projected sales are normally distributed with the stated means and standard deviations.

In the table, above, we can see the following:

- For each division the table shows the expected sales in units/month and the standard deviation of the estimate for each of the next three years.
- The **Combined** column contains the sum of the two means and a standard deviation for the sum, calculated from a randomized simulation, which accounts for *covariance* of the estimates. These statistics represent the total expected utilization of the existing plant.
- The **Confidence Levels** columns show the lower and upper limits of the distribution of expected combined unit sales with both divisions sharing the factory. The 95% confidence level is the mean plus or minus two standard deviations and the 99% confidence level is the mean plus or minus three standard deviations. This implies that the expected combined sales of the two divisions are expected to fall between the upper and lower bound either 95% or 99% of the time, respectively.

You will notice that in the second and third years, the upper estimates at both confidence levels exceed the capacity of the plant, which is assumed to be approximately 5,000 units per month. In the third year, the lower end of the estimate range does so, as well.

With the information contained in this table, it is possible to calculate the percent chance that the sales of the two divisions together will exceed the capacity of the plant. These are:

HPTCo can apply this information and consider its **risk appetite** to make some decisions about how to implement the Children's Division. It can pretty safely (< 1% chance of transcending capacity) add Children's to the Standard plant in the first year of its operation. If it is willing to take a 15% risk that it will exceed the plant's capacity, then it will plan to allow Children's to remain in Standard's facility for the second year, but it must plan to relocate it or choose some other intervention by the beginning of the third year of operation. It might also select an alternative implementation from the outset, such as contracting out Children's bike assembly and shipping, which would place almost no additional burden on Standard's use of the plant.

Of course, the urgency with which HPTCo moves to address this and what it is willing to do or spend is completely dependent on the impact associated with exceeding the plant's capacity. In fact, there may be a few different forms of this. Some situations might result in an inability to assemble products and others might only create a problem with storing pre-assembly parts or completed bikes until they can be shipped out. If the impact is merely inconvenience, that is one thing; if there is a substantial business impact or cost, it's another. HPTCo must address this analysis as a risk/reward assessment, based on the event probabilities and their impacts.

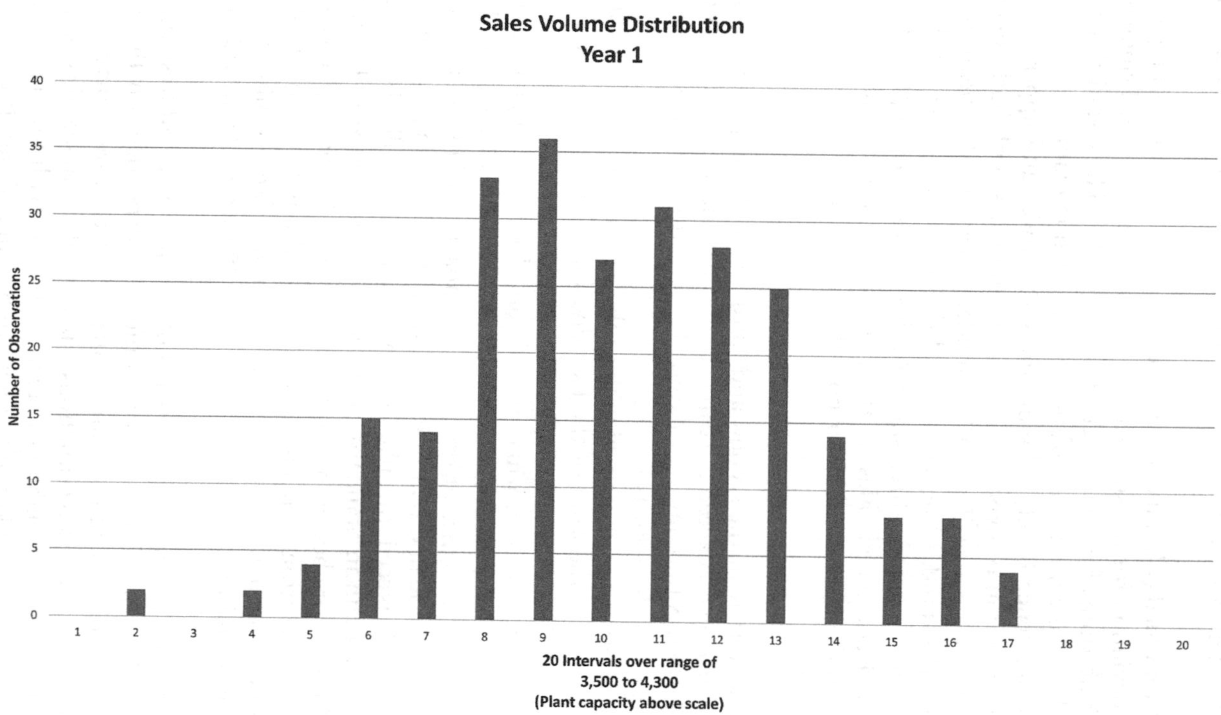

Figure CS3.1 Simulated consolidated sales distribution year 1.

Year 1: < 1% (The upper bound of the 99% confidence range is below 5,000).

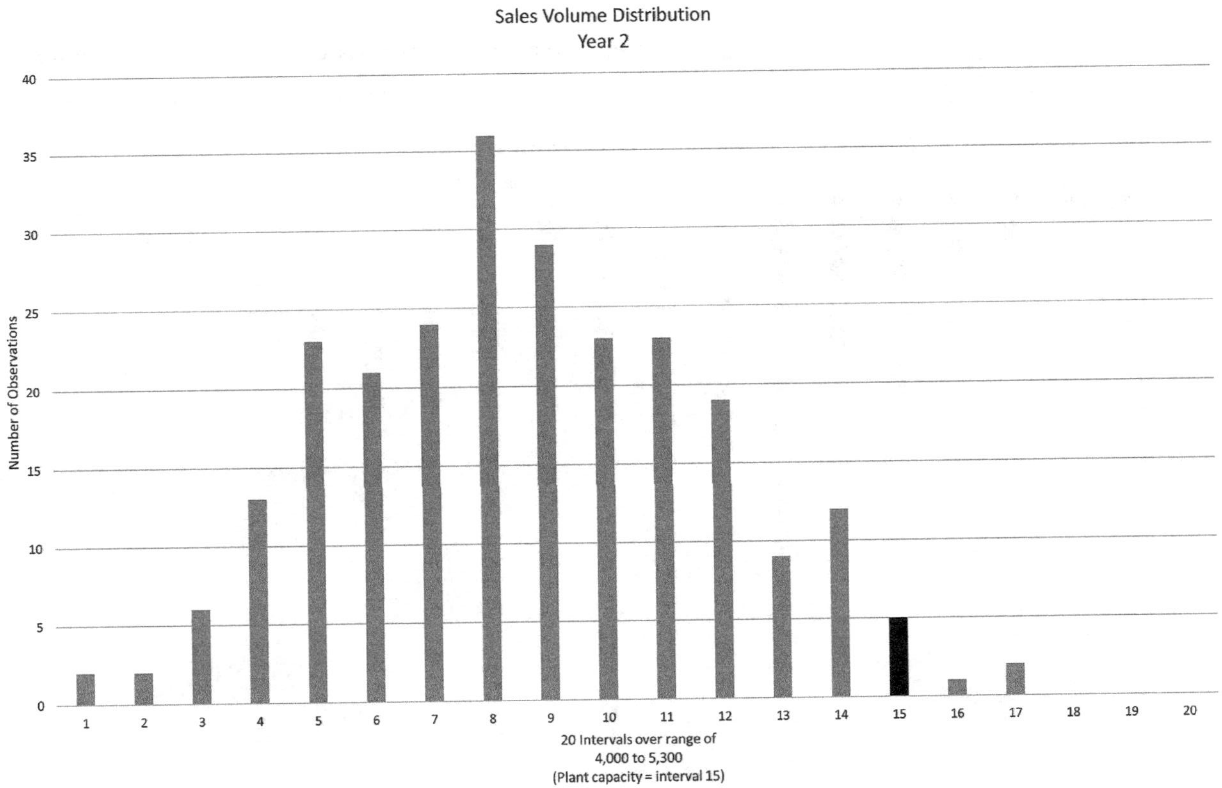

Figure CS3.2 Simulated consolidated sales distribution year 2.

Year 2: ~ 15% (5,000 is 1.03 standard deviations above the mean, which means that 15% of observations are expected to be above it and 85% below it).

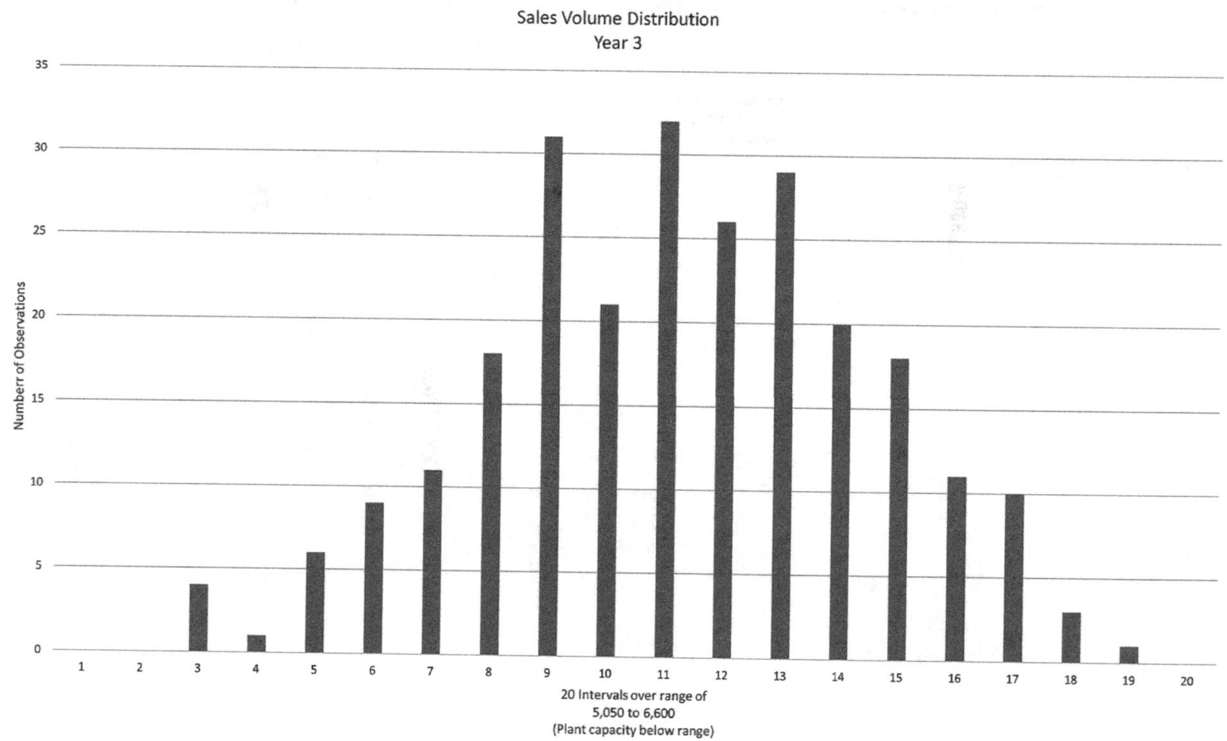

Figure CS3.3 Simulated consolidated sales distribution year 3.

Year 3: > 99% (The lower bound of the distribution is already above 5,000).

In summary, then, shared Enablers include:

- The physical plant, itself,
- The SaaS CAD system,
- The plant's production teams and their skill mix,
- The custom built, in-house sales order management system running on-premise,
- The purchased and customized work order management system that is running on-premise,
- The custom-built, in-house shipping management system running on-premise and
- The processes relating to each of these functions.

All of these should be assessed in the context of the operating model that is under consideration for the Children's Division.

Transformational Risks

HPTCo is, in essence, planning to execute two transformations simultaneously—the digital transformation and the addition of the Children's Division. This will create some significant challenges for it to manage and resolve along the way.

In general, the challenges will take a number of forms:

- **Politics**
  We've discussed the need for transformations such as the two that HPTCo is undertaking to have sufficiently senior sponsorship and be run by hands-on management. The company must appoint an appropriately senior Chief Digital Transformation Officer (CDTO) to run the program and head of the Change Management Team who are empowered to make business decisions, navigate contention problems and adjudicate disputes.
- **Conflicting Time Frames**
  Implementing the Children's Division cannot be successful if it is strung out for too long. The iterative approach that HPTCo will be piloting does not work well if the iterations are too far apart or the roll out is put off beyond a reasonable point. Digital Transformation, on the other hand, can be assumed to be a multi-year and multifaceted process. HPTCo will have to consider the requirements of the Children's rollout to inform the priorities of the digital transformation and vice-versa and the difference in the horizon of the two will complicate this.
- **Lacking Experience and Expertise**
  HPTCo will be piloting the Children's rollout at the same time as it is adopting a plethora of new processes for the digital transformation. As we discussed earlier, shooting at a moving target from a moving

platform represents the highest level of risk. Therefore, the company will have to be careful to avoid initiating program activities without ensuring that they have been planned and will be overseen by people with the appropriate level of expertise.

- **Evolving Definition of End-States or Desired Outcomes**
  The rationale for Agile software development approaches, DevOps and BizDevOps is that things change, and business agility demands that the company enable itself to adapt at speed. Given the duration of both transformations that HPTCo is undertaking, changes that may necessitate revisions to the initial plan are inevitable and HPTCo will have to institute a process within the Change Management Team to review and revise the combined execution plans of the two transformations whenever circumstances dictate.

  HPTCo must keep in mind that a significant part of what it is doing is developing its ability to transform rapidly. While the Children's Division is the only transformation it is planning for in addition to the digital transformation now, new opportunities are likely at any time, especially in view of the fact that it is pushing into digital products and services. Any new business initiative will only add more dependencies and contention issues to the ones that it is striving to manage in the current programs.
- **Sequencing Delivery, Managing Concurrent Initiatives**
  The company will have to incorporate intermediate to-be states in its implementation plans to avoid creating what in programming is known as a race condition.[18] This occurs when two processes share dependencies that can cause unpredictable behavior. For instance, if HPTCo were to begin implementing an Enabler based on assumptions about how an element of one of the digital pillars was going to function and the team implementing the pillar changed its design or implementation in some incompatible way, this could create such a situation.[19]

  In HPTCo's case, it will likely have to make decisions about whether to accelerate or decelerate initiatives to avoid creating such dependencies. Where it's not practical to avoid implementing initiatives concurrently, the company will have to coordinate them carefully.
- **Risk Amplification**
  HPTCo must remain vigilant about how elements of both programs can combine to amplify risks associated with either of them, by creating the potential for a race condition, mentioned above, for instance.

[18] https://en.wikipedia.org/wiki/Race_condition

[19] NB—Designing components for versatility and plasticity is a crucial tactic for dealing with this, as is employing APIs to minimize dependencies between services users and services providers.

AS-IS EA/BA MODEL

In defining the starting point for the transformation plan, HPTCo will have to look at both transformations and identify the relevant Capabilities and Enablers that currently exist.

Existing standard division operations

From the standpoint of the current Standard operations, these include:

Capabilities

- Manage Products,
- Marketing, Advertising, Publicity, Promotion
- Design Bikes
- Produce Detailed Specifications (materials, tolerances, etc.)
- Fabricate or Procure Parts
- Configure factory—Design Assembly Processes (lay out plant and map out work stations and process path), update and reconfigure as required
- Implement Assembly Processes (set up assembly plant)
- Manage Inventory and Warehouse Capacity and Operations (where received parts go, where completed bikes go)
- Sell bikes
- Manage Customer Orders
- Manage Work Orders
- Build bikes
- Manage Inventory of pre-assembly parts and finished bikes
- Manage Shipping and Receiving
- Provide Service for bikes
- Manage Financials—Payments, Invoicing, Receivables

Enablers

- Standard's Plant and the team that works in it
- Standard's Product Management, Sales, Marketing, Manufacturing and Operations Teams
- Parts Suppliers
- Shipping Vendors
- Dealer Network
- Systems Standard employs:
  - CAD
  - Sales Order Management
  - Work Order Management
  - ERP, Procurement, Inventory Management, A/P, Invoicing, A/R
  - Shipping management

Existing HPTCo digital capabilities and enablers

Given that HPTCo is planning to undertake a digital transformation, it will need to define the starting point for that, as well. The digital pillars model is the framework within which to do that. HPTCo's existing digital Capabilities and Enablers are:

Operational infrastructure

Capabilities

- HPTCo operates a traditional IT infrastructure and has the in-house expertise to do that but it has little hands-on experience with managing cloud-based infrastructures, especially hybrid clouds.

Enablers

- It has a corporate data center co-located with its headquarters and utilizes some SaaS applications that are cloud-based.
- It has satellite data centers at each of its assembly plants.
- It maintains and manages a network that spans the geographic locations it operates and a high-speed VPN (Virtual Private Network[20]) between the corporate network and the cloud provider where its SaaS applications are hosted.
- Applications it operates are:
  - CAD System (SaaS)
  - Sales Order Management (purchased, on-premise)
  - Work Order Management (purchased, on-premise)
  - Shipping Management (custom, on-premise)
  - ERP (SaaS, shared with Competition)
  - Website (outsourced)

API management

Capabilities

- HPTCo has minimal experience with implementing and managing APIs as a service.

[20] https://en.wikipedia.org/wiki/Virtual_private_network

Enablers

- none

Digital products and services factory

Capabilities

- None

Enablers

- None

Business intelligence and analytics

Capabilities

- HPTCo is just beginning to experiment with this.

Enablers

- Rudimentary, proof-of-concept level experiments localized to the corporate data center
- Limited staff and expertise

Partner development platform

Capabilities

- None

Enablers

- Some linkages with parts and services providers but these do not meet the definition of elements of a PDP

Distributed governance

Capabilities

- Where distributed authority exists, governance policies are limited and unformalized.

Enablers

- Virtually none.

TO-BE EA/BA MODEL SCENARIOS

Targeted to-be business and operating models

So, what does HPTCo want to look like in the future? What is the target architecture of the company?

HPTCo is a manufacturing company. It designs, fabricates, procures parts, assembles, sells and delivers products, at the moment, bicycles. It has a direct relationship with the dealers that sell and service its bikes, but only an arm's-length relationship with the people who purchase and ride them. It sees a near-term opportunity in adding a line of bikes for a segment of the bike-riding public that it doesn't already serve, but ultimately, it knows that it will need to add more products than that to achieve the sustainability it desires. Growth and profitability are significant objectives that will enable it to realize its goals.

HPTCo knows that people do not purchase new Standard (adult-sized) bikes frequently, so improving the sales experience can only provide so much benefit. Direct sales may also be problematic with respect to its dealer network. Diminishing or eliminating the profit that they make on sales could result in many of them dropping out of the network and could complicate the company's ability to service the bikes it sells.

Partnering has the potential to create opportunities for digital products. For instance, partnering with a company that provides web-enabled fitness tracking services that are mostly geared toward personal mobility (walking, jogging or other aerobic exercise, all which are combined with heart rate monitoring) to incorporate GPS and bike-riding could be a winner for HPTCo.

All of this implies that the digital pillars that it should pursue early-on are the Digital Products and Services Factory, Partner Development Platform and Business Intelligence and Analytics. A strategy it can apply to the Operational Infrastructure and API Management is to define the overall technical and logical architecture for them and then implement components consistent with the design as it builds out the higher-priority pillars. One problem that HPTCo doesn't have is a tremendous inventory of existing systems to migrate to the cloud, which will make the OI and API management pillars easier to realize in the long run.

As we will lay out, below, the Children's Division is a challenge. If the ultimate end state that HPTCo wants to achieve is one in which it is able to define and roll out new products rapidly with hybrid operating models that will enable multiple options for manufacture, assembly, sales and distribution, then the new division is a good prototyping exercise. However, it will require that HPTCo balance risks among making Children's sales goals, protecting Standard's operating stability and executing the enterprise's digital transformation. It may well be that intermediate end-states will be necessary.

The to-be state for which HPTCo must plan is a multidimensional space with the following dimensions:

- Children's product maturity in terms of the states of the Lean Startup model:
  - Experimentation
  - Development
  - Minimum Viable Product
  - Production Release
- Standard's and Children's future operational models with respect to:
  - Product Assembly—in-plant or contracted
  - Sales Model—wholesale through dealer network or direct-to-consumer
  - Servicing Model—required for direct-to-consumer sales
  - Shipping requirements—lots of 20+ or individual shipments
  - Potential partnerships—affinity marketing programs
  - Development of digital or digitally enabled services and products
- The sequencing, state and timing of the implementation of HPTCo's digital transformation
  - Potential opportunities or impacts to Competition Division

Operating Model and Operational Architecture Scenarios

In order to determine the to-be state that it should target with respect to its divisions' operations, HPTCo will define a handful of scenarios and apply risk-based thinking and risk/reward analysis to rank them. These scenarios are:

Minimal change

This scenario represents the least amount of change possible. Essentially, Children's bikes will be treated as new SKUs within the Standard operating model and operational architecture. Adding production of Children's bikes creates a potential risk of exhausting the production capacity in Standard's plant.

- **Procurement and Assembly**
  HPTCo will order component assemblies or even largely assembled Children's bikes, complete assembly in Standard's plant with the existing team (though possibly augmented to accommodate the increased volume), systems and facilities.
- **Sales**
  It will sell Children's bikes through the existing dealer network.
- **Shipping**
  It will ship Children's bikes using the same providers that it is currently using, consolidating shipments with Standard as much as possible.

- **Servicing**
  Servicing will be performed by the dealers who sell the bikes.
- **Partnerships**
  The existing dealer network will remain the only partnership for the time being.
- **Capabilities**
  All of the existing Capabilities will be employed as-is, and no new ones will be required.
- **Enablers**
  All of the existing Enablers will be exercised as-is, and no new ones will be required.

Outsourced assembly

In this scenario, HPTCo will be responsible for Children's product design and specification but the bikes will be fabricated, assembled and shipped by outside vendors. The main advantage this provides is that it minimizes the potential to exhaust the capacity of Standard's plant.

- **Procurement and Assembly**
  HPTCo will contract with suppliers to perform these tasks. Existing shared Enablers, such as systems, may require mod¡ifications.
- **Sales**
  It will sell Children's bikes through the existing dealer network.
- **Shipping**
  It will ship Children's bikes directly from the outsourced contractors who assemble them. The existing group of shipping contractors may or may not be used for this.
- **Servicing**
  Servicing will be performed by the dealers who sell the bikes.
- **Partnerships**
  The existing dealer network will remain the only partnership for the time being.
- **Capabilities**
  All of the existing Capabilities will be employed but new or modified Enablers may be required.
- **Enablers**
  The following Enablers must be evaluated for compatibility with the planned operations:
  - Work order management system
  - Shipping management system

In-house assembly, hybrid sales

In this scenario, HPTCo will be responsible for Children's product design and specification and Children's bikes will be built in Standard's plant.

However, HPTCo will sell Children's bikes direct to consumers through its website and they will be shipped directly to them. Sharing the plant may create potential to exhaust capacity but there may be options to minimize that.

- **Procurement and Assembly**
  HPTCo will order component assemblies or even largely assembled Children's bikes, complete assembly in Standard's plant with the existing team (though possibly augmented to accommodate the increased volume), systems and facilities.
- **Sales**
  It will sell Children's bikes mainly through the website and possibly also through the existing dealer network.
- **Shipping**
  It will ship Children's bikes directly to consumers. The existing group of shipping contractors may or may not be amenable to this.
- **Servicing**
  Servicing will be performed by the dealers who sell the bikes. It is assumed that since they will derive revenue from service even if they have not sold Children's bikes, they will be amenable to it.
- **Partnerships**
  The existing dealer network will be the initial partnership but HPTCo will seek additional value-added partnerships, such as co-branding, co-marketing opportunities.
- **Capabilities**
  Existing Capabilities will be exercised but new or modified Enablers may be required. Some Capabilities will require modification, such as direct sales and managing direct-to-consumer shipping will, also.
- **Enablers**
  The following Enablers must be evaluated for compatibility with the planned operations:
  - CAD system
  - Sales order management
  - Work order management
  - Shipping management
  - ERP

  The following Enablers must be implemented or redefined to support the direct-to-consumer sales model:

  - PM processes, especially with respect to digital services and products
  - Website management

Hybrid assembly, hybrid sales

In this scenario, HPTCo will position itself to assemble Standard and Children's bikes in the existing plant or outsource this to a network of suppliers. It will sell bikes from both lines through the existing dealer network *and* direct to consumers through its website. It will ship in lots to dealers and direct to purchasers. It might also support a buy online, pick up at dealer option. This scenario provides the greatest flexibility but is also the most complex and has the greatest risks. This benefit of transforming to enable the required Capabilities must be scrutinized carefully.

- **Procurement and Assembly**
  HPTCo will order component assemblies or even largely assembled Children's bikes, complete assembly in Standard's plant with the existing team (though possibly augmented to accommodate the increased volume), systems and facilities.
- **Sales**
  It will sell both lines through the website and through the existing dealer network.
- **Shipping**
  It will continue to ship as it has been to the dealer network and directly to consumers.
- **Servicing**
  Servicing will be performed mainly by the dealers who sell the bikes, but alternative models will have to be considered.
- **Partnerships**
  The existing dealer network will become more of a partnership and HPTCo will seek additional value-added partnerships, such as co-branding, co-marketing opportunities.
- **Capabilities**
  A review of Capabilities will be required. In this operating model, much will have to change.
- **Enablers**
  Just as Capabilities are being redefined, Enablers will have to be, also. The following Enablers must be implemented or transformed to support the direct-to-consumer element of the sales model:
  - PM processes, especially with respect to digital services and products
  - Website management

  These Enablers must be evaluated and evolved to be compatible with the planned operations:

  - CAD system
  - Sales order management
  - Work order management
  - Shipping management
  - ERP

Risk-based thinking, risk-based decision-making

The table, below, summarizes the scenarios that HPTCo has developed as potential candidates for its immediate target operating model:

Scenario	*Assembly*	*Sales*	*Delivery*
Minimal Change	In-house	Dealer Network	Shipped in lots to dealers
Outsourced Assembly	Standard: In-house Children's: Outsourced	Dealer Network	Shipped in lots to dealers regardless of where assembled
In-house Assembly, Hybrid Sales	In-house	Standard: Dealer Network Children's: Hybrid	Standard: Shipped in lots to Dealer Network Children's: Hybrid, some to Dealer Network, some direct to purchaser
Hybrid Assembly, Hybrid Sales	Hybrid	Hybrid	Hybrid

Assumptions and concerns

In deciding on what the immediate and subsequent end states should be, HPTCo must take into consideration:

- Standard and Children's can probably co-exist in Standard's plant for two to three years.
- Outsourced assembly of either or both divisions products can preserve Standard's plant capacity and it is probably a strategic Capability in the long run.
- Ultimately, the Capability to manage direct-to-consumer shipping will be required regardless of the path taken.
- Direct sales will create potential conflicts with the dealer network. This will have to be reconciled and resolved no matter what path HPTCo chooses.
- HPTCo will have to intertwine the execution of both its product and digital transformations. Among other things, this will mean selecting intermediate end states and execution approaches carefully.

So, with respect to Business Models, the Capability of web-based, direct-to-consumer sales and service is critical to determining HPTCo's to-be architecture.

With respect to Operating Models, two Capabilities are—the ability to manage outsourced assembly and the ability to manage direct-to-consumer delivery, which will also include shipments from outsourced providers that assemble HPTCo's products.

These Capabilities involve the following Enablers:

- Product Management Team and Processes, especially with respect to digital services and products
- Website Management Team and Processes
- CAD System
- Sales Order Management System and Processes
- Work Order Management System and Processes
- Shipping Management System and Processes
- ERP System

These Capabilities and Enablers are where some of HPTCo's most relevant risks attach to the to-be architectures and its digital transformation. These will be addressed further in the Gap Analysis and Transformation Program design.

GAP ANALYSIS, TRANSFORMATION PORTFOLIO CONSTRUCTION

Earlier, we identified the following Capabilities as necessary for HPTCo to be in the bicycle business:

- Product Management, Marketing, Advertising, Publicity
- Design Bikes
- Produce Detailed Specifications (materials, tolerances, etc.)
- Configure Factory—Design Assembly Processes (lay out plant and map out work stations and process path), update and reconfigure as required
- Implement Assembly Processes (set up assembly plant)
- Fabricate or Procure Parts
- Manage Inventory and Warehouse Capacity and Operations (where received parts go, where completed bikes go)
- Sell Bikes
- Manage Customer Orders
- Manage Work Orders
- Build Bikes
- Manage Shipping and Receiving
- Provide Service for Bikes
- Manage Financials—Payments, Invoicing, Receivables

We've also identified the following new or transformed Capabilities that HPTCo has targeted as part of the two transformations it is undergoing:

- Revised enterprise governance processes
- Value-Stream PM Processes, especially with respect to digital services and products

- Website Management, online prospect and customer engagement and sales
- Product Development and Incubation Processes
- Digital Partnership Enablement
- Business Intelligence and Analytics
- Outsourced Product Assembly
- Direct-to-Customer Delivery

These Enablers must be evaluated and either implemented or evolved:

- PM Enablers:
  - Integrated PM/Technology Teams
  - Value-Stream PM Processes
  - CI/CD software development and delivery Processes and Technology
  - SRE Processes and Infrastructure
- Partner Development Platform
- CAD System integration with outsourced manufacturers or assembly service providers
- Sales Order Management Processes, Team and Systems
- Work Order Management Processes, Team and Systems
- Shipping Management Processes, Team and Systems
- ERP Processes, Team and Systems
- AI/ML Processes, Team and Infrastructure
- Operational Infrastructure and API support

These new or evolved Capabilities and Enablers constitute the preliminary Transformation Portfolio. Its next step is to analyze the portfolio, prioritize outcomes, identify dependencies, assess and mitigate implementation risks and create a program to effectuate HPTCo's transformations.

TRANSFORMATION PORTFOLIO ANALYSIS AND PROGRAM CONSTRUCTION

Its next step is to analyze the portfolio, prioritize outcomes, identify dependencies, assess and mitigate implementation risks and create a program to effectuate HPTCo's transformations.

The outcomes HPTCo is seeking, in priority order, include:

1. Get the Children's Division up and running.
2. Develop the ability to engage prospects and customers and sell online.
3. Adopt value-stream and agile PM practices.
4. Develop the ability to outsource and manage manufacture, fabrication and assembly of products.

5. Develop the ability to manage lot or direct-to-customer shipping from its own plants or those of outsourcers.
6. Implement an internal business development incubator to design and develop new products.
7. Rationalize the company's technical infrastructure, migrating most of it to the cloud.
8. Achieve Business Agility across the enterprise.

Dependencies

Given HPTCo's objectives, here are dependencies for which its implementation program will have to account:

Children's division

- CAD system integration with fabrication and assembly process
- Sales order management processes and system
- Work order management processes, system and integration with potential outsourced suppliers
- Shipping management system and processes
- Website management and online sales capability
- Value-stream, agile PM capability

Digital transformation

- Expertise in various disciplines
  - EA/BA
  - BPM
  - KM and Taxonomy
  - Architecture—technical, data, solution
  - Strategy and Scenario Analysis, Road mapping, Transformation planning
  - Program and Project Management
- Digital Pillars—DPSF, PDP, BI/A, API, OI
- Staffing and skills development
- Revised governance models
- Governance and Management Processes redesigned to be consistent with the digital company model

All factors taken into consideration, HPTCo should pursue a program to reach three intermediate end states and then a final end state that includes the complete architecture of its digital self. The state list, below, focuses on the Capabilities, Enablers and Digital Pillars associated with the Standard and Children's operating models and operational architecture. The task list that follows is more detailed.

The combined transformation program

HPTCo's top-level program consists of the following intermediate and final end states:

- State 1
  - Implement the minimal change or outsourced assembly scenario
  - Begin implementing the DPSF
- State 2
  - Implement the in-house assembly, hybrid sales scenario
  - Continue implementing the DPSF
  - Begin implementing the BI/A
- State 3
  - Implement the hybrid assembly, hybrid sales scenario
  - Complete implementing the DPSF
  - Begin implementing the PDP
  - Continue implementing the BI/A
- State 4
  - Complete implementation of HPTCo's digital pillars

Program task breakdown by stage

Below is a list of the individual tasks that are in and out of scope for each end state:

State 1 Tasks for Minimal Change or Minimal Change or Outsourced Assembly Scenarios

- Initiate the DPSF
  - Create integrated PM/Technology teams
  - Train in Value-Stream PM Processes
  - Instantiate CI/CD software development and delivery processes and technology
  - Select tooling
  - Execute Agile SDLC adoption
  - Train in CI/CD and SER processes
  - SRE processes and infrastructure
- Evaluate and evolve existing Enablers:
  - Update CAD System—check for integration with outsourced assembly providers, if required
  - Update Sales Order Management Processes, Team and Systems—not in scope
  - Update Work Order Management Processes, Team and Systems—in scope only if assembly is outsourced (Outsourced Assembly vs. Minimal Change scenario)
  - Update Shipping Management Processes, Team and Systems—in scope only if assembly is outsourced (Outsourced Assembly vs. Minimal Change scenario)

  - Update ERP Processes, Team and Systems—check for integration with Enablers transitioned in this scope

State 2 Tasks for In-House Assembly, Hybrid Sales Scenario

- Continue implementation of the DPSF
- Initiate implementation of the PDP
- Initiate implementation of the BI/A
- Initiate implementation of API Management
- Initiate implementation of the OI
- Evaluate and evolve existing Enablers:
- Update CAD System—check for integration with outsourced assembly providers, if required
- Update Sales Order Management Processes, Team and Systems—in scope and requires integration with web-based ordering
- Update Work Order Management Processes, Team and Systems—in scope only if assembly is outsourced (Outsourced Assembly vs. Minimal Change scenario)
- Update Shipping Management Processes, Team and Systems—in scope if direct-to-consumer shipping is enabled
- Update ERP Processes, Team and Systems—check for integration with Enablers transitioned in this scope

State 3 Tasks for Hybrid Assembly, Hybrid Sales Scenario

- Complete implementation of the DPSF
- Continue implementation of the PDP
- Continue implementation of the BI/A
- Continue implementing API Management
- Continue implementing the OI
- Initiate implementation of the Business Development Portfolio teams and processes
- Evaluate and evolve existing Enablers:
  - Update CAD System—check for integration with outsourced assembly providers
  - Update Sales Order Management Processes, Team and Systems—requires integration with web-based ordering
  - Update Work Order Management Processes, Team and Systems—requires integration with all assembly teams and processes, whether in-house or outsourced
- Update Shipping Management Processes, Team and Systems—requires integration with all assembly teams and processes, whether in-house or outsourced
- Update ERP Processes, Team and Systems—check for integration with Enablers transitioned in this scope

State 4 Complete Implementation of Digital Pillars

- Complete implementation of the DPSF
- Complete implementation of the PDP
- Complete implementation of BI/A
- Complete implementation of API Management

- Complete implementation of the OI
- Complete implementation of the Business Development Portfolio teams and processes

RISK MANAGEMENT AS REFLECTED IN THE PROGRAM DESIGN

The very bottom-line goals and constraints for HPTCo's dual transformation are:

- Get the Children's Division going and make it profitable,
- Make progress on becoming a digital company and achieving Business Agility and
- Don't impair or impede anything that's currently running.

Here's how the program plan it developed addresses these goals and concerns:

- Tasks from the two transformations are planned to execute in parallel with dependencies accommodated, mainly by avoiding cases in which one requires capabilities that would be under construction in the other. For instance, the Children's Division development and rollout will not be dependent on the DPSF implementation. Rather, it will be managed with existing PM practices and migrated to value-stream, agile processes when they can be supported properly.
- The Competition Division is completely isolated from either of the transformations as they are occurring. Because Competition shares little with Standard and Children's, this is not particularly onerous.
- HPTCo has elected to execute the experimentation, development and maturation of Children's products in the existing Standard plant, with its manufacturing team and using all existing systems and processes. There is a slight risk that as Children's grows, it will cause the combined output of the two divisions to exceed the plant's capacity, but this risk has been assessed and determined to be unlikely enough for long enough to be within HPTCo's risk appetite and tolerance.
- Options for managing the Standard plant's capacity are built into the program plan. These include outsourced assembly and direct-to-consumer sales and shipping models, both of which obviate or minimize Children's utilization of the plant
- There are three operating model changes to be accomplished, each of these represents a transformation risk—direct-to-consumer sales, outsourced assembly, multi-location lot and direct shipping. HPTCo is mitigating these risks by staging them separately to the degree it is possible to.

- Because a lot depends on factors not completely within HPTCo's control, the program can be adjusted and re-sequenced. For instance, direct-to-consumer sales requires either shipping to a dealer for customer pickup or shipping directly to the consumer. Dependencies such as this are documented and can be accommodated as the program progresses.
- Because dependencies between the digital and Children's transformation have been avoided, tasks associated with each can be executed independently. For instance, BI/A Capabilities can be undertaken at any point without impacting the Children's development. Thus, the combined programs are designed to work iteratively and incrementally.

These approaches address the Capabilities and Enablers that were identified in the section *To-be EA/BA model scenarios*, subsection *Assumptions and concerns*. This is entirely consistent with the AERM approach.

CASE 3 SUMMARY

This case incorporates many of the techniques that are seminal components of AERM in the context of a company that it is undergoing two transformations at once—implementation of a new business unit and product line and digital transformation. This is a common occurrence these days.

Opportunities, challenges and risks were explored across the four layers of the EA model: strategy, business model, operating model and operational architecture. HPTCo performed some statistical analysis at the operating level to gain insight into the probability of exhausting resources associated with installing the Children's Division in the Standard plant.

Identified risks were classified and analyzed over three levels: Strategic, Operational, Transformational. The first two were applied mainly to the Children's opportunity and the last was applied mainly to issues relating to the digital transformation.

Application of the recommended transformation process:

- As-is EA/BA model creation
- To-be EA/BA model creation
- Gap Analysis and Transformation Portfolio Creation
- Transformation Portfolio Analysis and Program Construction

Finally, HPTCo documented how the transformation program that it constructed accounts for outcomes and priorities, dependencies and risks.

Overall, the analysis and execution design of the transformation programs was articulated in terms of the elements of the EA model at the heart of AERM—Markets, Strategy, Products and Services, Value Streams, Capabilities and Enablers.

Chapter 7

Book summary and the future of work

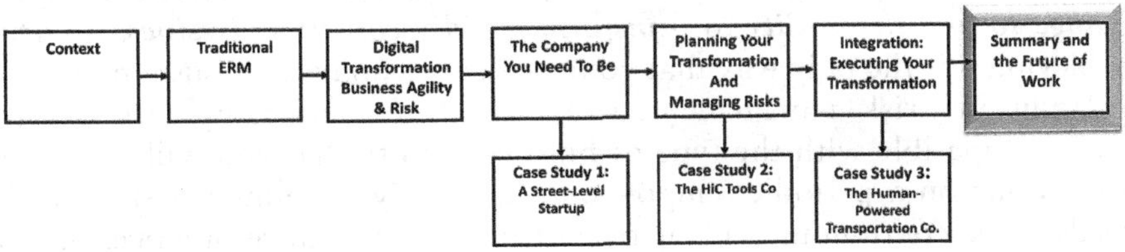

COVERED IN THIS CHAPTER

- A summary of the book
    - Context
    - ERM today
    - Digital transformation: what, why and what do i get from it?
    - The company you need to be
    - Planning the journey
    - Navigating the journey and adopting AERM
- What does future of work mean?
    - To enterprises?
    - To individuals?
- Conclusion

SUMMARY

We've covered a lot of ground in this book, from the context in which companies will be operating going forward, to how risk management has been executed up to now and how it should change, to what your company should look like to meet the requirements of the future to how to plan for and transform it to prepare for what's to come. I've incorporated frameworks from several disciplines that you should employ to manage your

DOI: 10.1201/9781003188605-8

company to enhance your understanding of how the pieces of your business interconnect, how to model them and how to identify and treat risks. These include architectural, statistical, design and process-oriented disciplines. I've provided three case studies to illustrate the use of them.

This section summarizes what is contained in the book.

Context

VUCA is Volatility, Uncertainty, Complexity and Ambiguity. We're living with it now and more is ahead. To the degree that you can't know exactly what's coming, the need for business agility is urgent. ***Your ability to recognize a need to change, the knowledge and wisdom to determine what to change to and the ability to transform rapidly constitute business agility.*** Achieving it is the only way that your company can become sustainable.

Traditional risk management, as practiced by many companies, is simply incompatible with the type of business agility that you will need. It's often done on a periodic tempo—on a quarterly or annual basis—but it needs to be continuous. This is true of many governance practices and, I believe, they also need to be converted to operate continuously, as well (but that is another book). ERM is also frequently practiced more qualitatively than quantitatively, which can lead to omissions and sub-optimal decision-making.

Digital Transformation is a necessity. You can't achieve a competitive level of business agility without undergoing one. However, any transformation has its risks and one as all-encompassing as a digital transformation has many. A complicating factor is that your digital transformation will take place while you are executing other transformations of your business—implementing new products or services, re-engineering parts of your infrastructure, executing acquisitions or divestitures. All the transformations you are executing will be intertwined and have dependencies on one another. You will have to be careful in planning and executing them to avoid traveling down dead ends or cul-de-sacs.

Enterprise Architecture (EA) and Business Architecture (BA) are disciplines employed to model and understand your company. They are often implemented in an overblown and unnecessarily granular fashion, which results in massive and unusable work products—walls full of arcane diagrams and encyclopedic volumes of shelfware. Under these circumstances, they fall out of use because they are too laborious and expensive to maintain at the level of detail at which they were established. I've avoided that by adopting a minimal entity palette that can be maintained with a reasonable level of effort. I also recommend that you implement a Pattern Library, which is an archive of diverse, reusable knowledge you generate from your own business activities and other selected sources, from technology component designs to business plans to market research. You'll need a Knowledge Management (KM) capability that provides a managed taxonomy, which will make your Pattern Library and the rest of your KM repository searchable by and accessible to the people who should benefit from it.

Your EA/BA models, KM repository and Taxonomy will be the anchor of your governance and risk management efforts and are a critical piece of your Agile Enterprise Risk Management (AERM) program. They are required to do AERM.

Traditional ERM

Establishing and executing ERM governance is a multi-step process:

- **Articulate the context in which ERM in your company operates.** It should address:
  - The markets and environment in which it operates, its strategic goals and how it is constituted to enable it to achieve them,
  - The organizational culture in which ERM will function,
  - The enterprise's *risk appetite* and *tolerance* and
  - An inventory of where currently known risks exist.
- **Determine your risk appetite and tolerance**
  Risk is the probability that things will not turn out as you expect them to or as you hope they will and that you will incur some type of loss or experience some other sub-optimal outcome. Risk is tightly related to variance. Your company must establish what types and levels of negative outcomes it is willing to accept to pursue opportunities for positive ones. Risk appetite is the inherent level of risk you are willing to bear in your day-to-day or business-as-usual operations, and risk tolerance is the level of risk that you are willing to accept on a short-term or case-by-case basis to reach for specific opportunities.
- **Identify potential sources of risk**
  To address risks, you must first identify them. This step involves determining where to look so that you can plan your discovery efforts. Risks, once they are identified, are ordinarily documented in a risk register, from which they are drawn for analysis and treatment. The discovery process is intended to populate the risk register. There are many approaches to this and many of them miss risks for a variety of reasons.
- **Perform a risk assessment and risk appraisal**
  Once risks are identified then they must be analyzed and treatments for them formulated. Many traditional ERM practices employ heat maps to guide this process. There are problems with this. Heat maps generally represent some sort of scaled plot of probability of occurrence vs. impact of an event and the scaling employed leaves the quantitative validity of this is open to question, to say the least. There's little doubt that a very likely event that has huge potential impact is one that merits attention but beyond establishing some simple priorities, this doesn't

tell you much about whether you are spending your ERM resources in an optimal manner and it certainly doesn't tell you whether you have identified your risks comprehensively.

There's no question that mitigation, reducing the potential for an event or reducing a negative impact from it, is a good thing. However, a company's aggregate risk arises from the portfolio of individual risks, each of which contributes to it. Yes, having the plant burn down would be a catastrophe worth avoiding, but avoiding a thousand small day-to-day risks is also worth pursuing. It's just not clear that a risk inventory of everything a group of people could think of plotted on a heat map is the best way to identify and manage your company's portfolio of risks.

- **Establish risk controls, policies and processes**
  Once the inventory of risks is established and analyzed, treatments are established. Generally, there are four options for any given risk:
  - Accept the risk (do nothing),
  - Avoid the risk (reorganize the business so that the risk doesn't apply any more),
  - Mitigate the risk (take steps to reduce the probability of an event or its impact) or
  - Transfer the risk (buy insurance or enter into a business relationship in which another party takes the risk on, say through issuing a performance guarantee).

    Treatment options are enacted in the form of business transactions (e.g., insurance purchases), controls (e.g., lending limits at a bank), or processes (e.g., escalating certain decisions to senior management).
- **Implement, execute and monitor ERM performance**
  Clearly, executing ERM practices and implementing the treatments they prescribe costs your company, often, quite a bit. It is incumbent on you to monitor the effectiveness and efficiency of the processes and the cost/benefit ratio and effectiveness of the treatments. Given that you define treatments for perils that don't occur, it can be tricky to determine whether they were cost-effective or not. Yet, it is important to do so. I will reiterate what I said in the chapter:

  ...it is important not to attribute, ex ante, the absence of a negative event that did not occur with the efficacy of your efforts to prevent or mitigate it.
- **Conduct risk audit and risk assurance**
  Risk Audit and Risk Assurance are governance processes exercised by your company's executive management and board to oversee your ERM efforts. Risk Audit is the process of reviewing ERM and reporting on its comprehensiveness, efficiency and efficacy. Risk Assurance is a process usually executed by an outside party and results in an opinion letter on which a board relies to document that the company is meeting its risk management responsibilities.

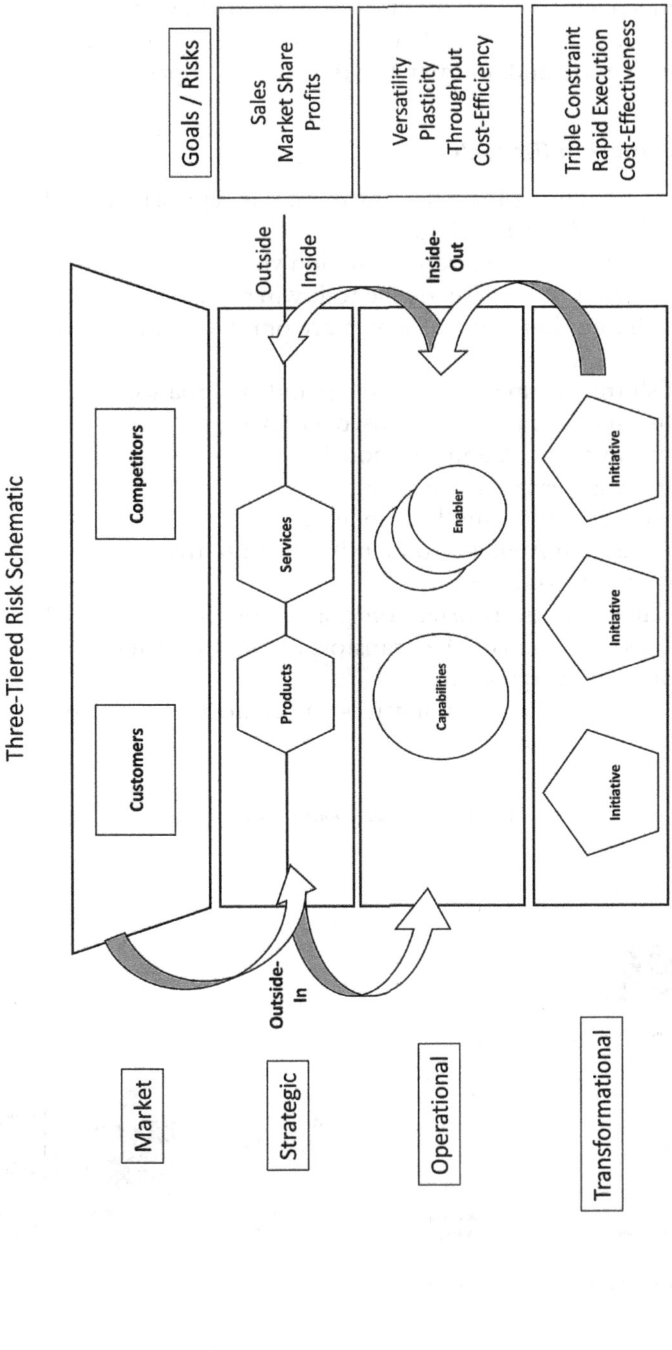

Figure 7.3 Three-tier risk schematic.

- **Transformational Risks**
  The goal of transformation is to deliver change, mostly in the form of new or evolved Capabilities or Enablers, and do it reliably, rapidly and cost-effectively. Transformation is delivered via initiatives and risks of not meeting initiative goals flow upward in the form of sub-optimal business agility and, ultimately, attenuated competitiveness.

The transformation lifecycle

The lifecycle of planning for a transformation is represented in the diagram below, reproduced from the chapter.

Regardless of whether the transformation you're planning for is digital or something different, it consists of the following steps, which are covered in detail in the chapter but some of which are omitted in this recap:

- Establish transformation leadership and governance,
- Establish scope and create a Discovery plan,
- Compile an as-is EA and BA model,
- Instantiate governance processes,
- Compile a to-be EA and BA model,
- Conduct a Gap Analysis to identify the initiatives you will require to effectuate your transformation,
- Articulate your transformation goals, your priorities and your risk preferences to inform the transformation strategies that will guide your planning process and
- Analyze the portfolio of initiatives and create the master program plan for your transformation.

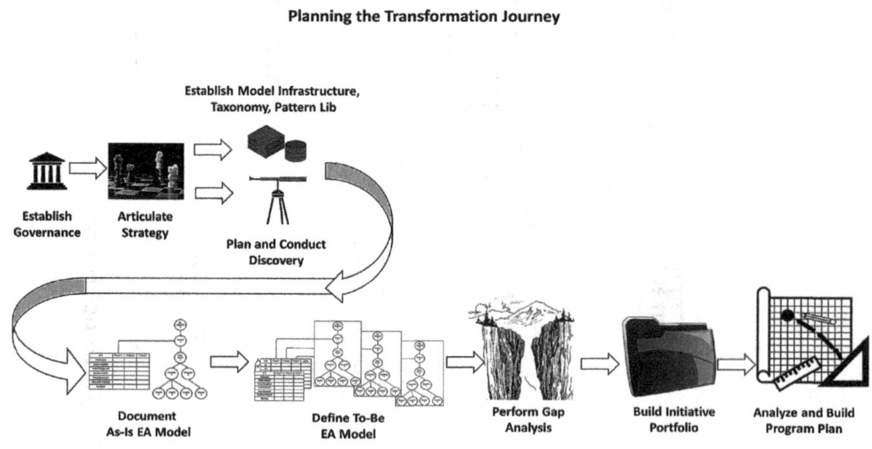

Figure 7.4 Transformation journey.

Establish governance for the transformation and ongoing operations, thereafter

Ensuring proper leadership is a crucial element of any transformation. Without buy-in at the highest levels and sufficiently empowered senior leadership, your transformation has little chance of succeeding.

Your Digital Transformation governance team must include:

- A Chief Digital Transformation Officer, an executive-level officer and
- A Change Management Team, a PMO for the transformation initiative and, downstream, a permanent element of your company's management structure.

Compile the as-is EA/BA model

Consistent with the definition of transformation we are using, you must establish a current as-is EA/BA model for your company as the starting point for your program. The steps in this process are:

- Articulate your company's strategy,
- Establish your model's infrastructure,
- Scope and plan your Discovery effort,
- Establish your initial taxonomy and KM repository,
- Prioritize your Discovery tasks,
- Conduct Discovery and
- Populate your models.

Focus on business processes

It is very important for you to identify and analyze your company's business processes during your Discovery and many of them may not be formalized or documented. Business Process Mining software may help you find implicit processes that are less obvious.

Business process discovery and management decision mapping

Business and decision processes occur at each of the three layers of risk we discussed earlier. They must be identified and assessed because they are potent sources of risk.

Strategic decisions, such as acquisitions or new business line introductions occur irregularly. Operational decisions occur every day. Both are likely to be formalized, possibly even automated, to one degree or another, and both have the potential to create negative outcomes. Strategic decisions may inherently incorporate larger risks, but operational ones can result in death by a thousand cuts.

This diagram, reproduced from the chapter, depicts a business process with embedded decision processes:

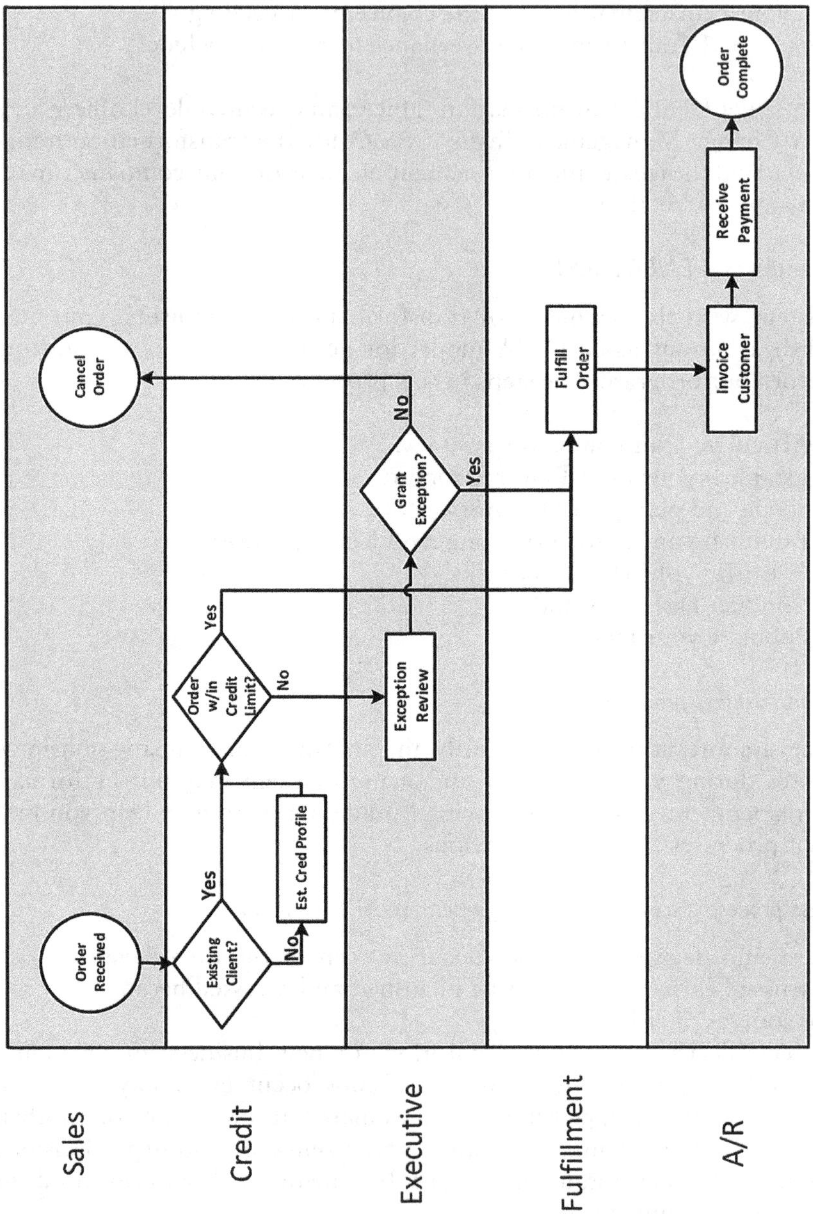

Figure 7.5 Business process flow.

This is an operational process, one that may be partially automated. If it is, the implicit or explicit decision mechanisms embedded in the automation need to be scrutinized for compliance with risk and other standards.

Identify and document management and governance processes

Governance is one of your six Digital Pillars and one to which you will likely be making changes. You should employ an ***inputs, processing, outputs*** framework to document them.

Conduct discovery, populate your as-is model

Data comprehensiveness and consistency are extremely important. There are several recommendations relevant to this in the chapter.

You will need to map existing operational enabling elements to the EA model framework we employ for AERM, which is depicted in the following diagram, reproduced from the chapter:

Map known risks from your risk register onto the as-is model

This may not be straightforward, but it is crucial that you develop some intuition about it now. Ultimately AERM demands that risks be traced to Capabilities and Enablers that are the real source of most of them. Starting with those you already know about will give you a leg up. It's not uncommon for risks to be tied to outcomes: 'If we have a production bottleneck, we could lose sales.' rather than causes: 'Intercontinental shipping is suffering a

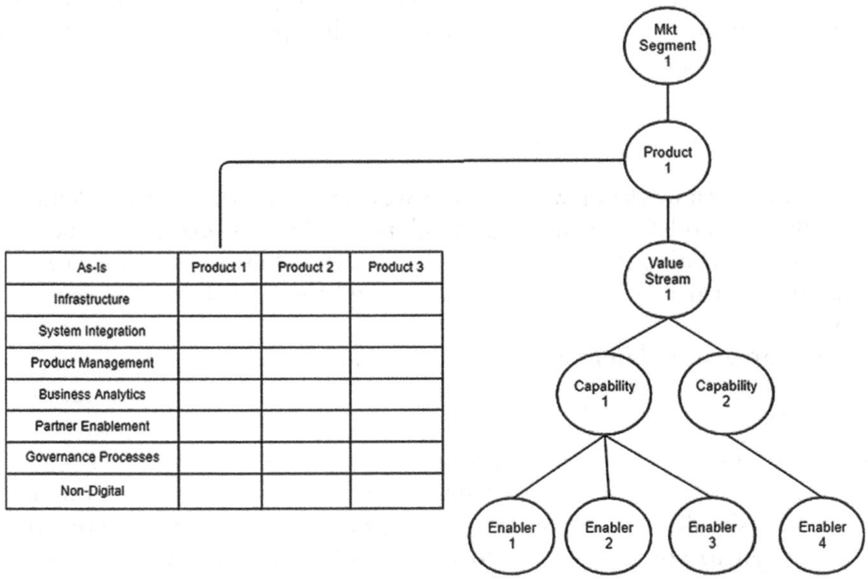

Figure 7.6 As-is mapping.

capacity crisis and our deliveries could run late.' To the degree that it is possible, such situations should be restated to identify the cause or source of risks.

Initiate and monitor your governance and management processes

You are in the process of collecting a host of important information that will drive the remainder of your planning process and establish the working repositories that will enable your ongoing AERM efforts. Initiating your governance and management teams and processes will preserve the value of your work and the assets you're creating.

Establish your preliminary to-be model

You should have an EA/BA model repository set up to house the data you've collected at this point. Defining your path forward to implementing your transformation will require mapping the as-is to the to-be models. Your taxonomy will play a role in enabling you to do this consistently.

Earlier, we discussed the goals of your transformation:

- Strategy enablement,
- Efficiency,
- Being or becoming data-driven,
- Effective collaboration and process execution,
- Product experimentation and development and
- Business agility.

These goals should inform the to-be architecture you will define for your digital business, down to the lowest levels of the operational architecture in your EA/BA model.

The to-be model framework

The model framework you will use is one we discussed earlier. It maps elements from the EA model onto the Digital Pillars: the Operational Infrastructure, API Services, Digital Product and Services Factory, Business Intelligence and Analytics, Partner Development Platform and the Distributed Governance Model.

These are covered in more detail in the chapter.

Define to-be governance and management processes

You will need a detailed specification for the to-be governance and management processes that you will implement and exercise on an ongoing basis. You should employ the same ***input, process, output*** framework that you applied to your as-is state to define and document your to-be state. Subsequently, you will conduct a gap analysis on the two to identify where you will need to implement new processes or modify old ones.

Map as-is to to-be and conduct gap analysis

Now you will need to map your as-is to your to-be models—your EA models, your process models and your governance models—to determine where there are gaps that your program must address.

This diagram, reproduced from the chapter, represents a visual conceptual model that can work for this:

Note that the elements in the vertical dimension of the as-is model are organized into generic buckets (and you may need more or different ones) and in the to-be model, they are organized into the Digital Pillars.

The idea here is that you identify existing Capabilities and Enablers and trace them from as-is to to-be so that you can identify what doesn't currently exist or what doesn't exist in the form that it will need to. You will almost certainly identify redundant or overlapping entities that you will want to resolve. It's all grist for the planning mill.

The AERM EA-driven approach to managing the risks of transformation

Most program and project management disciplines focus on meeting the 'triple constraint'—scope (functionality), cost and schedule. The presumption is that whoever commissioned the work knew what they wanted and will bear responsibility for the value of whatever comes out of the project. We know that that is often not the case, but I will refer you back to the chapter for further discussion.

What is important is that you begin to understand and apply to process of identifying sources of risk and where they attach to your EA entities and understand how they conspire to impact your goals or plans. You will need to understand how the elements of your program and what you are implementing lead to higher-level strategic results.

The BI/A, DPSF, PDP and Governance pillars relate more to *strategic* goals and the OI and API pillars relate more to *operational* goals. The Capabilities and Enablers, whose risks you should be able to identify, map into those and will become the beginning of something that you can trace from cause to effect. To be sure, though, none of the pillars are totally divorced from any of the others. Failing at any will have implications for all of them.

At the *transformational* level, the priorities and dependencies you glean from your analysis will influence your program's staging.

Distill transformation initiatives and populate transformation portfolio

With all the above in place, you can now identify individual initiatives—build this, change that, rationalize three entities into one shared one. Your

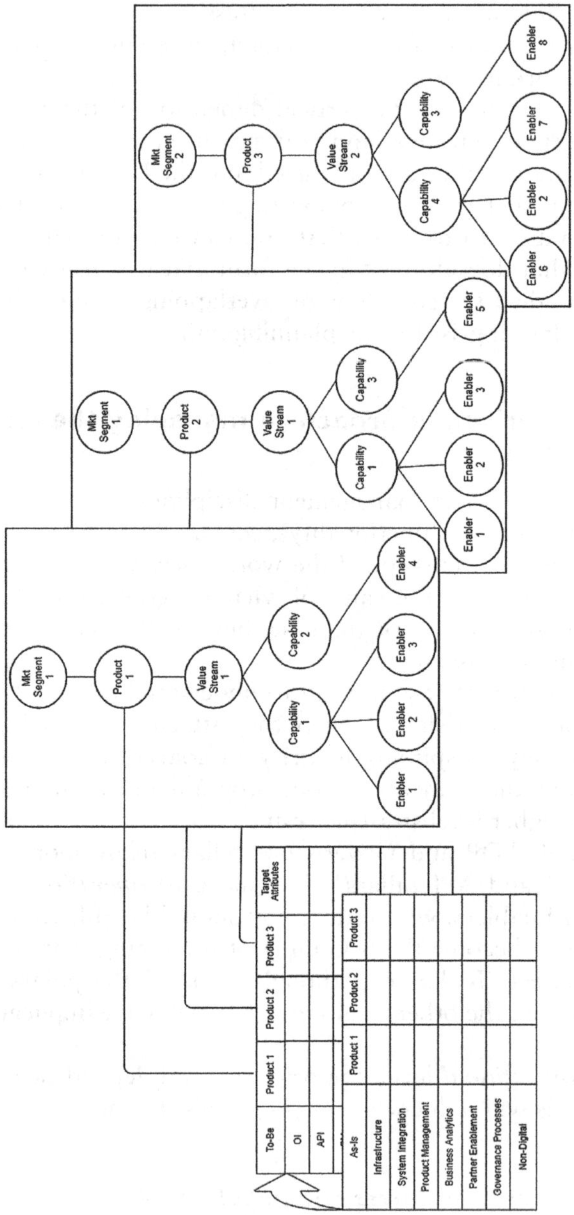

Figure 7.7 To-be mapping.

initial portfolio should contain all the initiatives, which will become the building blocks of your transformation program.

The chapter describes an approach to doing this.

Analyze transformation portfolio and develop transformation program

It's now time to construct a program from the portfolio you created. The chapter presents an approach for that. The main steps are:

- Establish business goals,
- Establish priorities to inform your sequencing, which should incorporate a variety of concerns, the most important being strategic and tactical business priorities and technological and organizational priorities and
- Build your program, which is almost as much art as science.

There is more detailed information on this in the chapter.

Executing your transformation

Having created a program plan, you should now be positioned to begin execution. This chapter addresses what you will need to do that.

What you should have in place at this point

You should have the following artifacts in place at the outset of your execution:

- An elaborated strategy document,
- A WIP inventory of existing in-process or planned projects that pre-date your transformation program,
- A transformation master program plan and schedule,
- A CDTO,
- A Change Management Team,
- Program leads for each of the digital pillars,
- Governance and management process definitions,
- An organization transformation plan,
- Architectural and SME teams:
  - Cloud migration and operations management,
  - Technical solutions (especially for cloud-native applications),
  - Agile development, CI/CD. DevOps, SRE,
  - Business Intelligence and Analytics,
  - Enterprise and Business Architecture,
  - Knowledge Management, Taxonomy,
  - Business Process Management Team,
  - Organizational Design and Development, Change Management and
  - Education and Training.

- As-is and to-be EA models
- The Taxonomy, the Pattern Library and the KM Repositories.

Transformation and operational disciplines

Let's assume that you have prioritized the OI, API DSPF and some of the Governance pillars for your Digital Transformation. Let's also assume that you will be initiating the process of adopting AERM. Then, you will need the following disciplines:

- For the current phase of the Digital Transformation:
  - Cloud migration,
  - Operations, infrastructure management,
  - API Management,
  - Value Stream Product Management,
  - Agile, DevOps, CI/CD, SRE,
  - Technical and solution architecture,
  - Business Process Management and
  - Distributed Governance.
- For the subsequent phase of the Digital Transformation:
  - Artificial Intelligence, Machine Learning,
  - Digital Partner Services Creation and
  - Developmental Business Incubators.
- For AERM adoption:
  - Strategy formulation and scenario analysis,
  - Road mapping,
  - Enterprise and Business Architecture,
  - Knowledge Management and
  - Governance.
- For managing your transformations:
  - Transformation Management and Governance,
  - Program and Project Management and
  - Monitoring transformation program outcomes.

Management and governance processes: transformation, ongoing operations

With elements of your organization and the capability to execute the list of disciplines required in place, you will need to have the capability to monitor and manage your transformation and the operational environment you create in the course of executing your program. You will require these processes:

- Program and initiative design, funding and inception,
- Program and initiative progress monitoring, management and reporting,
- Continuous improvement, retrospective performance assessment,

- Change management and
- Digital Transformation program progress monitoring and management.

Monitoring and management processes: transformation program outcomes

You are transitioning from managing a lot of the development you will be doing from project-based to product- or initiative-based. That is, you will be moving away from managing your initiatives with respect to the triple constraint and focusing more on the business value that they create.

There is no one set of indicators that you can use to measure your progress toward becoming a digital company and realizing the business agility that should produce. Here are some capabilities that will create business agility and which you can use as the basis for establishing Outcomes and Key Results (OKRs) that you will monitor:

- The ability to build, modify and release products and services iteratively, evolving them at speed,
- The ability to incorporate and integrate new technologies in your company's operations rapidly and with minimal staff resistance,
- The ability to optimize and adapt to revised business processes rapidly and with minimal staff resistance,
- The ability to acquire and develop staff and skills rapidly,
- The ability to understand customers' motivations and behavior and exploit this knowledge to create or customize products or services for them,
- The ability to detect and act on patterns in the markets in which your company competes and respond to threats and opportunities rapidly and
- The ability to identify and attract potential partners and implement profitable partnerships rapidly.

The chapter contains a basic framework that can inform the approach you will employ to measure your progress.

Management and governance processes: operations

As your program is implemented and elements of your to-be company are rolled out, you will require the following processes to monitor and manage your operations:

- Product Development Processes
    - Value-Stream Product Management
    - Rapid Product Evolution and Delivery
    - Site Reliability Engineering (SRE)
    - Developmental Product Portfolio Management

- Operational Management and Governance Processes
  - IT Operations Management
  - Change Management
  - Technology Management
  - Business Process Management
  - Human Resource Management: Staff Availability, Utilization, Acquisition

Implementing AERM

Once you have built the information artifacts, such as your EA/BA models, you should begin to implement AERM. You will require the following precursors in place before you begin:

- The working Enterprise and Business Architecture Model,
- A set of operational processes that ensure the EA/BA model is maintained, which should be overseen by the Change Management team,
- The Taxonomy, which will ensure the data in the EA/BA model and other repositories is consistently tagged and therefore useful and accessible,
- KM processes that ensure that data flowing into your company's metadata repositories are categorized and tagged properly and
- Transfer, or linkage and consolidation of risks from the existing risk register to the new repository that will correlate them with Capabilities and Enablers, the basis on which most of them will be monitored going forward.

AERM operational processes

You will need the following process to operate AERM:

- Processes for monitoring the relevant repositories, recognizing and then acting on triggering events,
  - Triage—RM must have a process to prioritize and perform initial evaluation of events to identify their scope and the urgency with which they should be addressed,
  - Evaluation and analysis—RM should have a standard approach to risk appraisal and treatment and control formulation,
  - Propagation of controls—RM requires a standard process for disseminating and activating the treatments and controls it determines are necessary and
  - Compliance monitoring—your company must have a process for monitoring compliance with the policies and controls it defines and enacts.

Retrospective processes

You will need the following processes to evolve and improve your AERM execution capabilities:

- Retrospective evaluation,
- Risk Audit and
- Risk Assurance.

Measuring your progress

Clearly, you must monitor and evaluate your progress to ensure that you are not going off course or heading toward a cliff. This should be focused on each of the three layers—strategic, operational and transformational.

The chapter contains references to some resources that may provide useful guidance on this subject.

CASE STUDY 1: A STREET-LEVEL STARTUP

This case study involves a prospective street-level business and is predicated on and introduces a few concepts:

- Businesses will have to adopt management practices of both startups or early-stage ventures and established enterprises. The disciplines surrounding product or service development and evolution may well be appropriate for a Lean Startup approach.
- Maturing a startup business from an idea to an MVP should proceed in two phases—experimentation and development. This is a risk-based approach. Experimentation is intended to surface anything intractable that will prevent any chance of a venture's success and will set the stage for the work that will take place in the development phase.
- An Enterprise and Business Architecture model of your prospective venture will provide several invaluable benefits, especially to ERM. The scaled-down, yet still comprehensive version that AERM employs is designed to be workable, especially when its maintenance is embedded in the evolutionary and transformative processes in your business.

CASE STUDY 2: HICTOOLS—PLANNING FOR A TRANSFORMATION

This case study focuses on how to plan for a transformation. The case presents an abbreviated version of what an end-to-end digital transformation looks like when it is predicated on EA- and BA-driven disciplines in conjunction with AERM.

HiC's prospective transformation begins with an as-is EA model in which its important Capabilities and Enablers are identified and linked to the Products and Services they support. This essentially allows HiC to identify what it does and how it does it.

Then, a to-be EA is defined. This is informed by HiC's strategy and mapped onto the six pillars of the digital company.

Subsequently, HiC performs a gap analysis between the as-is and to-be architectures to identify the initiatives required to become the company depicted in the to-be model. These initiatives are incorporated into the transformation portfolio repository for analysis.

Ultimately, HiC creates a three-phase program plan for its transformation.

CASE STUDY 3: THE HUMAN-POWERED TRANSPORTATION COMPANY—EXECUTING A TRANSFORMATION

This case study presents the Human-Powered Transportation Company (HPTCo), which makes bicycles, currently in two divisions in two separate plants. It is considering entering a new market and evaluating options for how and where it will assemble and deliver the products from its third division to customers.

In this case, we explore opportunities, challenges and risks in the context of the four-level EA model, the three-layer risk model and core business processes.

We perform a rudimentary statistical analysis to evaluate the risk of adding the new division to one of its existing plants. Then, we examine the company's risk appetite and apply what we know to the decision it is facing.

Subsequently, we follow the transformation process we've defined to evaluate alternative implementation scenarios and apply risk-based thinking and decision-making to determine the approach to follow in executing the transformation.

Ultimately, HiC defines a transformation process through which they will migrate from its current state, through three intermediate states to its to-be state.

At the conclusion of the case, we review the risk-based decision processes and the risk management that informed its planning processes and demonstrate how they are reflected in its go-forward plans.

THE FUTURE OF WORK

The Future of Work (FoW) is a term thrown around a lot these days. It has become the most widely covered (and overexposed) subject in the business press. As we discussed in the preface to this book:

> **The subjects of the moment are Digital Transformation and the Future of Work. Prestigious consultancies and Universities, the business and technology press and pretty much anyone else with a voice are shouting non-stop about the need for you to undergo the former in order to survive the latter.**

Part of what's been written about the future of business relates to how markets and technology will conspire to compress business cycles and create the need to become more agile to survive. Much of the rest focuses on how companies and the workerforce will relate to one-another as we go forward. FoW, in common usage, seems to focus more on the latter, but these are both important and interrelated subjects.

Business Agility will be ever more crucial to navigating the business environment going forward and managing talent resources will be a huge part of that. So, talent management is and will continue to be a major risk that will have to be managed. This McKinsey article[1] speaks to some of the Human Resource risks with which companies will have to wrestle in the evolving environment.

The episode of History Channel's *Modern Marvels* entitled *The Evolution of the Assembly Line*[2] presents a few historical precursors that may provide some insight into what we're experiencing now. The episode recounts the story of Henry Ford's invention and evolution of a new way of producing cars and achieving astounding success—reducing the man-hours required to build a vehicle by a factor of ten and ultimately increasing overall output of his assembly plant thousands-fold. It also reveals the price workers paid for this success—monotony, boredom, repetitive stress injuries and a dehumanizing working environment that resulted in more than a 300% annual staff turnover rate. Ford was able to operate profitably while reducing the cost of a car by some 80% and making it affordable by most middle-class workers, including his own, to whom he gave raises so that they could afford one. Irrespective of anything else, that's quite an achievement.

However, his production scheme, while incredibly effective at producing one product, lacked flexibility and *agility*. Eventually, General Motors overtook Ford in market share when it adopted a new approach—multiple assembly lines producing smaller quantities of differentiated products—that

1 https://www.mckinsey.com/business-functions/organization/our-insights/the-organization-blog/the-future-of-work-managing-three-risks-of-the-hybrid-workplace
2 https://www.youtube.com/watch?v=f5vjJyrlDTw&ab_channel=HISTORY

allowed it to offer consumers a variety of models and options, like colors, which Ford could not match. GM's environment was more worker-friendly and it out-competed Ford for assembly-line workers. Eventually, Ford adopted a similar approach to GM's and got back in the game.

A new approach developed by Toyota after the second world war and still applied in numerous places, including Hyundai's US assembly plant in Alabama (considered the most modern and efficient auto manufacturing plant in the world), demonstrates the importance of getting the balance of worker input to mechanical consistency right. The Toyota and Hyundai Kaizen[3] work models demonstrate this balance. In Kaizen, lean manufacturing techniques, which rely on workers to identify small improvements that add up to large efficiencies over time, are employed. If the workers are not given incentives to suggest improvements, a non-judgmental atmosphere into which to offer them and the ability to enact steps to evolve processes, then the company will not realize the benefit of their experience and knowledge.

Kaizen, as it's practiced today, doesn't just promote worker participation, it demands it. Once a production or assembly process is working consistently, resources are eliminated, and the workers are challenged to devise approaches to meet the original production targets. This process is iterated until the management and the workers agree that there is nothing left to wring out of the system. As efficiency increases, the workers are rewarded, and thus not made to feel as if they have been exploited. Now, certainly automation plays a large role in reducing the need for workers and increasing production efficiency and output, which can be to their detriment, in aggregate. However, this is not unique to Kaizen.

One other difference between Ford's Tayloristic[4] approach and Kaizen is that in lean manufacturing, workers are taught as many jobs as possible to provide diversification and flexibility, as well as to give as many people as possible the opportunity to view problems and come up with solutions for them. Given the diversity of skills required and the complexity of executing a digital transformation concurrent with the need to evolve business models rapidly, you will need all the brainpower you can get your hands on. Ford's employees complained of being made to feel like parts of a machine in addition to suffering repetitive stress injuries. You cannot afford to have the people you will be relying on for your transformation feeling similarly.

The lesson to be taken from this is that workers, whether employees or contractors, must be integrated into the process of transformation and evolution for it to be successful. This should not, at this point in the book, be news to you. However, many companies are still mired in command-and-control management structures and not inclined to accompany their

[3] https://en.wikipedia.org/wiki/Kaizen
[4] https://en.wikipedia.org/wiki/Scientific_management

workers through a collaborative process of designing and executing a transformation. They focus on defining it first and then attempting to re-slot their workforce into new jobs and roles as the process unfolds. Changing the game and expecting talented participants to stay and play it is a risk. Enlisting workers to participate and collaborate is crucial. Earlier, we discussed the concept of giving people an idea and making it seem as if it were theirs. It may sound coercive but, this is something that companies will have to learn to succeed at transformation.

AERM, the future of work and your company

So, how and where does this fit with AERM? Well, you should be preparing for or executing parts of a digital transformation, working toward a to-be EA model that you defined as part of your program plan. That plan should identify the Capabilities and Enablers that you are targeting to create or evolve. Enablers include people and their roles, the processes they will execute and the systems that they will employ in doing so. You've sequenced the plan to account for dependencies, such as the need to define, instrument and adopt CI/CD processes prior to trying to employ them, and then to implement a value-stream-driven product management approach that relies on them.

Taking overly long to get such processes working has both transformational risks—delays and cost overruns—and operational risks—not having your to-be Product Management function working properly. Ultimately, not getting these resolved could result in negative strategic-level impact—failing to achieve the business performance that you were aiming for. A necessary, but not sufficient, mitigation applicable to all these risks is to have the right people with the right skills and experience in place when you need them to be.

A hybrid organization that incorporates employees and contractors, co-located and remote is what the future looks like for many, if not most, businesses. Research from Gartner,[5] Metis Strategy[6] and Accenture[7] all address some of the challenges you will face in creating an effective hybrid organization. Your ability to foster and support digital collaboration is the inward-facing side of your digital transformation and unless you can manage a hybrid, dispersed workforce, you will not get the benefit of this side of it. In fact, attempting to employ traditional command-and-control management practices in a digitized environment may well have the potential to net you worse performance than you might achieve with everyone co-located.

[5] https://www.gartner.com/en/human-resources/trends/how-organizations-are-supporting-a-hybrid-workforce

[6] https://www.metisstrategy.com/enabling-a-hybrid-workforce-for-the-long-term/

[7] https://www.accenture.com/us-en/insights/consulting/future-work

Articles from Forbes,[8] Gartner[9] and Digitalhrtech[10] all present useful information about talent management; however, most of it is focused on attracting, hiring, managing and retaining employees. This is all well and good, but to be successful, you will have to learn to attract full-time, part-time and contract workers with the skills and experience you need when you need them. In this regard, your collaboration tools will have to be well-integrated and present the type of user experience that new users can pick up quickly and enjoy (or at least not hate) using.

If you are working from the EA model that we have discussed, people as Enablers should be identified, their roles defined and the risks associated with them elaborated. I'm not suggesting that people can be reduced to elements of a model so much as I am that who you will need, when and what knowledge, skills and capabilities they will require will be much easier to understand and plan for if you tie it to the planned state-to-state transformation of your company.

This is exactly what AERM and the artifacts you will produce to enable it will provide for your company.

CONCLUSION

We began this book looking at how complicated the world is becoming, how fast it's changing and how much more difficult it will be to run a business as things begin to change even faster. In the world of rapid technological evolution, COVID and the pressures companies are under to allow remote work and everything else that is going on these days, making the case that you need to transform isn't hard to do. I tried very hard to chart a logical path to follow to transform from your current state to a future state while trying to make sense of a complex organism—your company—by looking at it through the lenses of several management disciplines.

I believe, most of it should have been understandable if you backed away from it a little and focused on a limited domain at any one time. You know that if a supplier doesn't deliver that it will cause a problem or that if you can figure out how to increase your plant's output, you can probably sell all the product you can make. These things are not new; perhaps, though, looking at them and seeing all the interconnections and dependencies as reflected in the work products of different disciplines may be.

The whole concept of risk management should be reasonably intuitive for you, even if some of the statistics isn't, but there are a lot of nuances that

[8] https://www.forbes.com/sites/louiscolumbus/2021/02/14/how-to-digitally-transform-talent-management-for-the-better

[9] https://www.gartner.com/smarterwithgartner/use-a-digital-talent-management-framework-to-future-proof-the-it-workforce/

[10] https://www.digitalhrtech.com/talent-management-strategy/

result from subtle dependencies. Often, what we don't know conspires to leave us unprepared when we encounter an event that didn't look quite the way we thought it would or when we suddenly discover that enacting the plan we had in mind for such an occasion would create an unforeseen side effect. It is at such moments when we need to act swiftly, that we first must spend time perseverating at the beginning of the OODA loop rather than acting. My feeling is that traditional ERM, as I have described it, is not optimally designed to help you avoid that sort of situation.

Systems thinking is a school of thought about how pieces of complex entities, like companies, interact to perform the functions required of them. This article about the subject[11] is a good place to start exploring it if you have no previous exposure. Your company is a *system of systems*[12] and you need to manage and govern it recognition of that fact.

You need one source of truth to do that, and I think that source should be an EA model of *what is* and *what is planned*. It won't help you if you don't keep it current and accurate, but if you do, it can be the basis for making the best, most reasoned decisions you probably can. It can be your port in the storm in which we're living right now.

Here's wishing you success with your transformation.

Glossary

The glossary may be found on the book's website.[13]

[11] https://learningforsustainability.net/systems-thinking/
[12] https://en.wikipedia.org/wiki/System_of_systems
[13] https://agileerm.com/aerm-glossary/

9781032037035